DIMENSIONS OF HAZARDOUS WASTE POLITICS AND POLICY

Dimensions of Hazardous Waste Politics and Policy

Edited by CHARLES E. DAVIS and JAMES P. LESTER

Prepared under the Auspices
of the Policy Studies Organization

Contributions in Political Science,
Number 200

GREENWOOD PRESS

New York • Westport, Connecticut • London

Library of Congress Cataloging-in-Publication Data

Dimensions of hazardous waste politics and policy.

(Contributions in political science, ISSN 0147-1066 ;
no. 200)
Bibliography: p.
Includes index.
1. Hazardous wastes—Government policy—United
States. 2. Hazardous waste sites—United States.
3. Environmental policy—United States. I. Davis,
Charles E., 1947-   . II. Lester, James P.,
1944-   . III. Series.
HC110.E5D56 1988   363.7'28   87-17792
ISBN 0-313-25989-5 (lib. bdg. : alk. paper)

British Library Cataloguing in Publication Data is available.

Library of Congress Catalog Card Number: 87-17792
ISBN: 0-313-25989-5
ISSN: 0147-1066

First published in 1988

Greenwood Press, Inc.
88 Post Road West, Westport, Connecticut 06881

Printed in the United States of America

Copyright Acknowledgments

The editors and publisher gratefully acknowledge permission to use the following:

From "An Introduction to Catastrophe Theory and Its Applications." Reprinted with the
permission of the Society for Industrial and Applied Mathematics from *SIAM Review*,
Volume 20, Number 2, April 1978. All rights reserved. Copyright 1978 by the Society for
Industrial and Applied Mathematics.

From *Implementation and Public Policy* by Daniel A. Mazmanian and Paul A. Sabatier.
Copyright 1983 by Scott, Foresman and Company. Reprinted by permission.

To Elizabeth, Kevin, Marguerite, and Sandy

Contents

Tables

Figures

Preface and Acknowledgments

The formulation and implementation of hazardous waste management policies in the 1980s has been complicated by numerous factors, including problem complexity; an unwillingness on the part of many political decision makers to consider policy options that are politically or economically risky; variations in states' political, administrative, and financial abilities to deal with the disposal of toxic chemical wastes; and disputes concerning the appropriate jurisdictional locus of decision-making authority, among others. Coming to grips with these and related issues raises questions of interest to students of public policy as well as policymakers. Thus, we chose to organize the following symposium using level of government as a convenient means of highlighting these concerns.

The siting of hazardous waste facilities has clearly emerged as a key issue for local government officials. Some of the relevant questions explored here include the nature and extent of citizen participation in site selection and the decision-making criteria used in making such choices. A common concern in these and related studies is overcoming the emotion-laden bases of citizen opposition to housing a prospective facility. Several approaches have been suggested, including direct public involvement in project planning, the provision of information to community residents before decisions are made, and the use of incentives to compensate host communities for the risks associated with facility operations. The need for better information is addressed by Albert Matheny and Bruce Williams in their analysis of hazardous waste siting strategies in Florida. A statewide education program aimed at promoting public acceptance of the state government's handling of hazardous waste problems was mandated by the Water Quality Assurance Act of 1983, and the authors indicate that its subsequent implementation may have the laudable effect of increasing citizen respect for the integrity of the decision-making process.

Kent Portney approaches this question from a somewhat different perspective: he focuses on the use of incentives to ameliorate the fears of community residents. A survey of public attitudes in five Massachusetts communities reveals a greater inclination on the part of the citizenry to change their subjective calculations of risk toward the construction of hazardous waste facilities as the result of proposals designed to improve safety precautions than of those offering financial compensation in various guises. In their case study of Clermont County, Ohio, Michael Kraft and Ruth Kraut trace the development of citizen participation in siting decisions. Over time, citizens grew frustrated with existing barriers to public participation and gradually became more knowledgeable about coalition building as a means of expanding their influence. For their part, state and industry officials increasingly recognized the importance of educating the public about the risks associated with the adoption of a particular decision. A kind of "institutional learning" evidently took place for all parties to the controversy as events unfolded.

Whether citizens chose to become involved in controversial environmental decisions at the local level is often associated with a particular set of community characteristics. In an analysis of several New England towns, John D. Powell resurrects the concepts of localism and cosmopolitanism to explain differential community response to the development of groundwater protection policies. Communities identified as "cosmopolitan" were more receptive to environmental protection issues than "localist" towns, a finding which is attributed to a relatively greater emphasis on economic growth within the latter group. The author also indicates that the conservative tenor of localist decision making is at least partially explained by demographic factors; i.e., these towns had proportionately fewer professionals and college-educated citizens and a higher percentage of long-term residents.

C. K. Rowland, S. C. Lee, and D. B. Goetze focus on a different barrier to the implementation of hazardous waste programs by the states—the belief that enforcement of regulatory legislation heightens the operating costs of waste-generating firms and thereby places within-state companies at a competitive economic disadvantage with firms in nearby states with less stringent pollution control laws. A possible consequence, likened to Gresham's law by the authors, is a downward regulatory spiral among states worried more about the prospects of economic decline than the more uncertain risks to public health and the environment posed by the relaxation of environmental standards. The probability that governmental regulators in a given state will succumb to the perception of economic blackmail is affected by the relative political influence of groups favoring industrial development versus environmental protection and by the level of public awareness of hazardous waste problems within the state.

State environmental officials must increasingly walk a political tightrope, encountering local resistance to state siting initiatives on one side while accepting a larger share of hazardous waste management responsibility from the federal government on the other. Several state governments have chosen to address the problem of local opposition to siting decisions by providing themselves with the authority to preempt or override community preferences. In a national survey of state legislative initiatives, Richard Andrews found that a majority of states remain committed to policies allowing a local veto over proposed hazardous waste facility sites while approximately one-third have adopted a more authoritative stance (i.e., preemption or override of local decisions). The author concludes that siting policy differences do not significantly affect the likelihood of approving the construction of a new facility. Accordingly, a policy approach combining local control with state restraints is recommended.

The implementation of federal hazardous waste programs by state environmental officials is often jeopardized by a formidable combination of political, economic, and organizational obstacles. Ann Bowman examines the complex interaction between the federal Environmental Protection Agency (EPA), state environmental regulators, waste generators, waste transporters, facility operators, and (on occasion) the federal Department of Justice and state attorneys general in administering the Superfund program in the Southeast. Her analysis of actions taken against polluting firms by governmental regulators illustrates the difficulty of seeking cooperation between parties with adversarial interests in a diverse and fragmented federal system.

Consideration of hazardous waste management problems at the local and state level referred to thus far represent one of the chief concerns of federal administrators involved in the design of new program areas or the modification of existing ones. According to Richard Barke, an encouraging feature of congressional behavior in the 1984 reauthorization of the Resource Conservation and Recovery Act (RCRA) is that it demonstrated receptivity to the need for policy change stemming from an improved understanding of the seriousness of hazardous waste problems in the United States and the relationships between past regulatory strategies and policy failure. The simultaneous display of policy learning and legislative approval was attributable, in part, to the decision to focus on issues identified by more "neutral" organizations such as the U.S. Office of Technology Assessment (OTA) and the National Academy of Sciences (NAS) rather than the EPA, which was busily attempting to rebuild its credibility from the depths of the 1983 toxic waste scandals.

Another issue within the federal policy arena lies in the interpretation of complex regulatory statutes by the courts. A tendency on the part of federal judges to decide cases on the basis of narrow, technical issues, thereby avoiding larger questions of congressional intent, could easily be used by opponents of environmental protection policies to delay compliance with these laws. This, according to Werner Grunbaum, hasn't happened with regard to the Comprehensive Environmental Response, Compensation, and Liability Act of 1980 (better known as Superfund). In attempting to enforce Superfund, federal judges have held that the doctrine of "joint and several liability" is in effect. The responsibility of deciding which waste generator is responsible for a given leakage is effectively shifted from the government to defendant firms. In addition, the courts have interpreted Superfund as a strict liability statute in accordance with Section 311 of the Federal Water Pollution Control Act. In short, federal regulatory officials attempting to implement Superfund programs now have a much improved negotiating position as a result of expanding judicial policymaking. Finally, Rae Zimmerman discusses the interaction between the federal and state governments as they implement hazardous waste policy in the face of risk uncertainties.

Hazardous waste policy problems are clearly not confined within U.S. borders. A focus on the international policy arena offers the prospect of research on comparative policy approaches and the usefulness of bilateral or multilateral arrangements for the handling, disposal, or even trade of hazardous chemical substances. A comparative approach is utilized by William Mangun in his analysis of hazardous waste policies in Western Europe. His chief concern lies with the cross-national validity of aggregate indicators for governmental units used in the United States to explain variations in state policy responses. In other words, is the presence or absence of hazardous waste management legislation in European countries associated with technological pressures in member states, the availability of financial resources, or administrative characteristics? The data analyses tend to support the importance of all three factors, singly or in combination. Nations ranking low on these indicators were less likely to have a formal hazardous waste management policy in place.

The final contribution to this collection, by Stephen Mumme, describes efforts by the U.S. government and Mexico to achieve cooperation in the management of hazardous waste problems along the border. He argues that dependency theory is commonly and erroneously used to examine issues of concern to both countries. A more accurate framework for analyzing transboundary negotiations, according to the author, is based upon the recognition of interdependence. While the United States clearly possesses greater financial resources than Mexico, it is in no position to impose a unilateral solution to binational pollution problems. Progress will depend upon continuing diplomatic efforts in the short term but may ultimately depend upon the growth of the Mexican economy before the decisions of their own regulatory officials will begin to carry greater weight.

The articles in this collection serve to illustrate that problems of hazardous waste disposal are amenable to analysis from a variety of theoretical perspectives. Understanding the interplay between high-risk policy problems, changing political and economic circumstances, and actions taken by political actors with a stake in decisional outcomes should yield information of substantial value to public administrators as well as students of the public policy process. We wish to extend our sincere gratitude to the contributors for their efforts in the research which follows in the book.

We would also like to express our appreciation for financial support received from Colorado State University and from the Milward Simpson Fund and the Institute for Policy Research at the University of Wyoming.

Finally, we wish to thank Professor Stuart S. Nagel and the Policy Studies Organization for their support, and James Sabin and Mildred Vasan at Greenwood Press for their help in the editorial process.

DIMENSIONS OF HAZARDOUS WASTE POLITICS AND POLICY

1

Hazardous Waste Politics and the Policy Process

Charles E. Davis and James P. Lester

INTRODUCTION

Deciding what to do with the growing accumulation of hazardous wastes has become one of the most serious environmental policy problems of the 1980s in the United States and other countries. The formulation and implementation of corrective management policies has been complicated by numerous factors, including problem complexity; an unwillingness on the part of many political decision makers to consider policy options that are politically or economically risky; variations in states' political, administrative, and financial abilities to deal with the disposal of toxic chemical wastes; and disputes concerning the appropriate jurisdictional locus of decision-making authority, among others. Coming to grips with these and related issues raises questions of interest to students of public policy as well as to policymakers.

Our objective in this chapter is to sort out what is known about hazardous waste policymaking within different stages of the policy process and differing levels of government and to identify critical issues for subsequent research efforts. We begin by discussing toxic waste legislation in terms of substantive policy objectives. Attention is then directed toward the identification of key factors found to be associated with the formulation, adoption, and implementation of these programs. For example, can we attribute the passage of hazardous waste statutes to demographic characteristics of a given jurisdiction, political factors, or situational concerns such as the severity of chemical contamination problems? In a similar vein, what are the major variables that serve to advance or impede the implementation of programs designed to pretreat, recycle, or dispose of toxic pollutants? To what extent is the explanatory power of various indicators a function of jurisdictional level? Finally, we consider the inevitability of policy change. As decision makers grapple with the challenge of translating program objectives into management activities within a policy area characterized by technological uncertainty, they gain experience in the identification of problems and react by offering recommendations for administrative changes or the closing of statutory loopholes.

POLICY FORMULATION AND ADOPTION

Federal Hazardous Waste Statutes

Within the past two decades, efforts by federal policymakers in the United States to enact toxic waste management laws received considerable impetus from a series of events associated with the environmental movement. The increasing saliency of environmental protection issues to the general public in the late 1960s was accompanied by a rise in the political influence of ecological organizations, the passage of tough regulatory policies to deal with air and water pollution, the emergence of the Environmental Protection Agency (EPA) in 1970 as a central clearinghouse for policy development and implementation, and, most importantly, a consensus among political leaders in both parties that pollution problems were of sufficient magnitude to require immediate and forceful action (Mitchell, 1984; Rosenbaum, 1985).

Although the apex of the environmental policy movement was probably achieved in 1972 with the passage of the Water Pollution Control Act, there remained sufficient public and congressional support by 1976 to secure approval of a key hazardous waste statute, the Resource Conservation and Recovery Act (RCRA). Subtitle C of RCRA provided a management framework for the regulation of toxic substances currently generated by chemical manufacturers, refineries, and other firms. Hazardous wastes were defined both in generic terms (as ignitable, corrosive, reactive, or toxic) and by listing specific wastes and industrial waste streams. An elaborate tracking system designed to track the whereabouts of toxic substances from "cradle to grave" was established, and any facility involved in the generation, storage, treatment, disposal, or transport of these wastes was required to prepare a manifest for record-keeping and reporting purposes. Firms performing any or all of these functions were also required to obtain an operating permit from the EPA or an authorized state agency.

The EPA was designated as the lead federal agency in the implementation of RCRA; however, it was assumed that most regulatory responsibilities would eventually be shouldered by state environmental officials. Under an approach termed "partial preemption" by the Advisory Commission on Intergovernmental Relations (1981), states could receive authorization to manage their own programs after passing legislation that was "equivalent to" and "consistent with" RCRA and adopting guidelines, standards, and regulations that were at least as stringent as those promulgated by the EPA. The federal government retained the statutory authority to step in and assume control over the hazardous waste program if the states were unable or disinclined to do the job.

A second area of concern was the removal or decontamination of toxic chemicals from abandoned dump sites. Widespread media attention to the Love Canal tragedy in 1978 and 1979 (Levine, 1982; Landy, 1985) provided a considerable boost to the political fortunes of existing legislative proposals, and in December 1980, Congress passed the Comprehensive Environmental Response, Compensation, and Liability Act (better known as Superfund). A $1.6 billion fund derived, in large part, from a tax on the industrial generators of hazardous waste (87.5%) and, to a lesser extent, from federal revenues (12.5%) was authorized for cleanup operations over a five-year period. These monies could also be spent on epidemiological studies, chromosomal screening, and a registry of persons exposed to toxic substances.

While the EPA bore the primary responsibility for designating the list of sites posing the greatest immediate danger to public health, the states were not totally absolved of financial responsibilities in meeting the costs of soil decontamination or removal. States were required to kick in 10% of the cleanup costs for sites located on private property and 50% for those on public land. The passage of this statute, in combination with RCRA, the Toxic Substances Control Act (TSCA) of 1976,[1] and a number of less publicized environmental policies and interdepartmental agreements dealing with air and water pollution, pesticide use, and ocean dumping of toxic substances has thus provided a legal framework for the control of hazardous wastes.

State Hazardous Waste Policies

The states thus share considerable responsibility in the design of policy approaches to the management of hazardous waste problems. However, it is important to indicate that both the incidence and the direction of state policy actions are affected by a variety of external and internal factors. State autonomy in formulating RCRA-style legislation is achieved at the expense of conformity to minimum federal standards. For a sizable minority of jurisdictions, the minimum degree of activity needed to obtain policy control is exerted. Fifteen states have adopted hazardous waste programs that largely parrot federal statutory language (Bowman, 1985). Another incentive for state policymakers to closely follow federal guidelines is based on the realization that program management activities are subject to oversight and inspection by the EPA. Evaluation of this sort requires performance of detailed administrative tasks such as program audits, reporting requirements, grant reviews and awards, and enforcement actions and is more easily completed with identical or similar policy structures (Anderson, 1978; Schnapf, 1982).

Within-state characteristics are also associated with hazardous waste policy formation in the states. One of the earlier research efforts focused on the relative impact of technological pressures in the environment, economic resources, political demands, and state organizational autonomy on the development of stronger antipollution legislation (Lester, Franke, Bowman, and Kramer, 1983). The best predictors across all states were found to be technological pressures (i.e., the severity of pollution problems within a state), legislative professionalism, and the presence of a single agency to coordinate toxic waste programs; that is, states generating more waste tend to develop more stringent statutes, as do states with a consolidated environmental bureaucracy.

The authors also indicated that varied circumstances lead to shifts in the explanatory importance of certain independent variables. One is the attainment of a severity threshold for hazardous waste problems found within a jurisdiction. States with a higher concentration of toxic pollutants tend to assign a larger share of policymaking responsibilities to the legislature than to the bureaucracy. In addition, regional differences beget differences in the determinants of policy. When southern states are excluded from the analysis, there is a rise in the amount of variance explained by economic wealth. Thus, situational and organizational characteristics of states assume a primary role in facilitating hazardous waste policymaking across all states, while political and economic factors come into play as policy predictors under certain conditions.

A somewhat contrary set of results is found in the research of C. K. Rowland and associates (1981; 1983; 1985). Policy adoption and regulatory commitment on the part of state policymakers is less a function of problem severity or extant organizational arrangements than of the economic importance of hazardous waste generators to the state. Hence, the relevant question for public officials is how economic developmental objectives can be reconciled with public health and environmental quality considerations. Unfortunately, the latter objectives frequently are deemphasized. Because states compete for these industries, policymakers are reluctant to impose strict regulatory standards which would place within jurisdiction waste generators at a competitive economic disadvantage with similar companies in neighboring states. A consequence is the passage of state laws designed to meet *minimum* federal standards in ways that are less costly to industry, that is, a uniformly lax set of hazardous waste programs (Rowland and Walton, 1983).

How can we account for these differences? The answer, according to

Bowman (1984), is largely methodological. In the Lester et al. research, problem severity, or the need for hazardous waste regulation, is measured by indicators which rank the states on the production of toxic chemical substances. State response to pollution problems is represented by the adoption of a hazardous waste program. Rowland and Walton operationalized "need" in a different way. Problem severity was expressed through a combination of factors, including the number of EPA priority sites, the seriousness of the threat posed by the sites, and an EPA ranking of the estimated hazardous waste problem within a state. The policy adoption measure was also altered to incorporate a problem severity component; that is, state hazardous waste program rankings (as measured by a 1979 survey by the National Wildlife Federation) were subtracted from the EPA severity estimate rankings. In short, disparate conclusions were at least partially attributable to the mix of indicators employed in the respective analyses and the differing operationalization of the dependent variable.

Case analyses of specific states also reveal a number of factors found to be contextually relevant. Interest groups have been successful in pushing for environmental legislation in some states, especially where outdoor recreation or scenic values are important (Matheny and Williams, 1983; Williams and Matheny, 1984). Gubernatorial leadership may also be a key factor in shaping the context and direction of hazardous waste policies. Governor Jerry Brown (D-CA) was an early and forceful proponent of legislation designed to encourage alternatives to the land-based containment of toxic chemical substances (Morell, 1983). On occasion, political activity in state legislatures is prompted by media attention to pollution problems, which serves to propel environmental issues to agenda status (Brown, 1980; Epstein, Brown, and Pope, 1982; Levine, 1982). Higher visibility of hazardous waste problems may also work to the advantage of environmental groups whose policymaking efforts have been thwarted by the political influence of subsystems operating within state borders (Kramer, 1983). Moreover, citizens and community officials may be sufficiently frightened by reports of contamination to become an effective part of a larger political coalition seeking a strong policy response (Wurth-Hough, 1982; Rosenbaum, 1983).

Hazardous Waste Facility Siting

Finally, state policymakers respond to numerous factors in deciding how to deal with more specialized policy issues such as the siting of hazardous waste treatment, storage, and disposal (tsd) facilities or the preferred mix of strict regulatory requirements and economic incentives to be included within the abatement program. Under RCRA, decisions on the most desirable location of tsd facilities, the criteria to be used in reaching such decisions, and the appropriate individuals, group, or agency to make such choices were left up to the states. Programs could be more easily tailored to meet local needs as a result. An equally important consideration was the inability of the EPA under RCRA to either build and operate tsd facilities or acquire land which could subsequently be leased to firms specializing in the destruction or containment of hazardous wastes. States had the power of eminent domain and other land-use powers necessary for the operation of siting programs (Hadden, Veillette, and Brandt, 1983).

The formulation of state siting policies is understandably controversial. Over half the states have adopted siting legislation (especially states generating more waste), whose content tends to vary in terms of the relative weight given to state authority versus local control or public participation. Some opt for policies which would effectively preempt local governmental veto powers; for example, Georgia and Arizona have enacted a policy response which effectively excludes local or citizen participation in the decision-making process (Hadden, Veillette, and Brandt, 1983; Wells, 1982). Often states within this category will assume responsibility for the identification of sites for hazardous waste tsd facilities through the creation of an agency or board. Since the chief arguments for this approach are based on the assumptions that there is a compelling statewide public interest in facility development and that state governments are the best judge of appropriate locations, little effort is made to incorporate citizen representation (Andrews and Pierson, 1985).

Other states have adopted a multimember commission or board to offer siting recommendations but have included ad hoc representation from the affected community. This approach does not call for state-mandated selection of a preferred location for tsd facilities but does permit intervention to override local governmental powers that might be used to halt facility construction. A third group of states allows communities to approve or disapprove a decision to site facilities nearby, a position which is sensitive to the notion that local acceptance is a prerequisite for effective program implementation (Morell and Magorian, 1982). Finally, a few states have left primary decision-making authority in the hands of local officials but have included state restrictions on how control is exercised, for example, circumscribing the criteria and procedures under which decisions are made (Andrews and Pierson, 1985).

To date, there is little evidence to suggest that any of these policy approaches is more or less effective in actually obtaining a tsd facility in or near a community (Andrews and Pierson, 1985). However, a number of studies have focused on the amelioration of citizen fear concerning health and environmental risks as the key factor in the attainment of site approval and the identification of community characteristics or policy approaches that would contribute to the attenuation of perceived risks. These risks are more easily accepted by the public if they are voluntary, controllable, known, familiar, and immediate (Dickson, 1983).

A growing body of research focuses upon the manipulation of incentives within policy designs to reduce citizen opposition to siting decisions. Approaches include financial compensation schemes, the provision of more information to the public about the safety of prospective tsd facilities prior to reaching a decision, and the formal representation of citizens in the decision-making process (National Conference of State Legislatures, 1982; Susskind, 1985; O'Hare, Bacow, and Sanderson, 1983; Mitchell and Carson, 1986).

What do analyses of the comparative usefulness of incentive-based siting options tell us? O'Hare (1977) has presented a theoretical argument for the increased utilization of financial compensation to mitigate the social, economic, and psychological impacts of a siting decision on the host community. These include monetary payments such as grants, the in-kind replacement of resources, or a contingency fund. Each is designed to redress the imbalance between the benefits received by citizens dispersed throughout the state and region from safer waste disposal practices and the concentrated costs imposed upon a local jurisdiction as the result of facility operations. Thus far, studies by Portney (1984) and Davis (1986) suggest that financial arrangements do not appreciably alter attitudes of community residents toward housing a toxic waste facility. Or, to quote John Pitney (1984), "bile barrel burdens do not readily translate into dollars and cents."

Public education and an effort to integrate public participation into facility siting processes early on represent major noneconomic approaches to the prospective reduction of citizen discontent (Minnesota Waste Management Board, 1981; Morell and Magorian, 1982). Surveys measuring residential attitudes toward siting issues and various compensation measures in Massachusetts and Wyoming revealed a preference for policies requiring more dissemination of information to citizens prior to the decisional stage or risk-mitigation proposals such as regular safety inspections of hazardous waste facilities and increased state and local efforts to prevent groundwater contamination (Portney, 1985; Davis, 1986). The importance of risk-mitigation procedures to community residents was also affirmed in a series of gaming simulations undertaken by Elliot (1984) in Massachusetts.

In addition to the identification of programmatic incentives considered to be important by the residents of an affected community, the presence or absence of selected political and demographic characteristics can influence the likelihood of facility site approval. Morell and Magorian (1982) analyzed a number of key factors associated with local governmental decisions to accept or reject tsd facilities in New Jersey. Of considerable importance was the economic impact of a prospective facility on the community, its compatibility with existing land-use patterns, and residents' perceptions of costs and benefits. One community gave site approval largely because the need for land-based disposal capacity was demonstrated by a chemical industry already operating within city limits. In addition, the proposed facility was to be located on the premises of the company, somewhat isolated from the rest of the town. Finally, the failure to grant a permit would have adversely affected the local economy. Need, in other words, was tempered by assurances of safe disposal practices.

The attitudes and actions of public officials represent yet another factor in assessing the feasibility of facility siting locations. The importance of information and education in advance of decision making is underscored by the tension between the desire to incorporate technological and administrative expertise in the site selection process and the potentially unsettling effects of public comments and participation. A survey of state hazardous waste administrators and chemical industry officials revealed considerable reluctance among both groups to encourage citizen participation beyond administrative testimony or representation on siting councils. Respondents were strongly opposed to more active forms of involvement such as the use of referenda for the approval of siting proposals or efforts to encourage the debate of these issues in local political campaigns (Davis, 1984-1985). To overcome the problem of mutual suspicion, informational strategies can be designed to place siting issues within the realm of policies requiring shared understanding and concern; hence, consensus becomes the basis for decision making. This, according to Matheny and Williams (1985), is preferable to reliance upon the adversarial model of democracy, which assumes that legitimate decision making is the product of the equal representation of conflicting interests.

The adoption of state hazardous waste policies is accompanied by regulatory approaches designed to induce industry compliance. In general, these approaches can be classified as *directive* or *nondirective*. The directive or "command-and-control" model calls for centralized decision making by political authorities. Rules or standards specifying how program objectives should be achieved are promulgated—an example is the requirement that hazardous waste disposal facilities use clay liners to prevent the seepage of leachate into underground water supplies rather than a process giving facility operators greater latitude in choosing less costly alternatives for waste containment purposes. Proponents of stricter control take the position that noncompliance with pollution abatement programs is a likely consequence of efforts to expand regulatory due process and increased flexibility in the attainment of programmatic objectives. In their view, it is desirable to reduce the likelihood of evasion by establishing performance criteria, timetables, and an enforcement strategy sufficiently strong to deter willful violation of the law (Marcus, 1980). Such an approach might well serve to clarify expectations on the part of regulators and regulatees alike but would also impose substantial informational, administrative, and financial costs on both parties.

Regulatory options termed nondirective by Mitnick (1980) bring greater sensitivity on the part of agency administrators to questions of flexibility and scale in the development of rules or guidelines for industry compliance. Both economic and political strategies are included. Market-based techniques such as taxes, waste exchange systems, or subsidies, singly or in combination with directive approaches, have been advocated by environmental economists (Kneese and Schultze, 1975). Political strategies used or considered by public officials include the partial deregulation of agency decisions, public education, an effort to place relatively greater emphasis on cooperative actions (such as prior consultation) than confrontation, and the selection of regional organizations rather than the federal government as the appropriate forum for developing solutions for policy problems (Derthick, 1974; Bowman, 1985b).

Whether a given approach to the management of hazardous waste is adopted for a particular governmental jurisdiction is often less a function of technological or economic rationality than of political circumstance. A number of factors are likely to affect choices made by state officials, including administrative resistance to change, the degree of scientific uncertainty, existing deficiencies in policy design, media attention to health and environmental risks posed by exposure to toxic chemicals, and the presence or absence of selected policy and institutional characteristics at the state level.

The most plausible reason for maintaining a directive approach lies in the nature of bureaucratic inertia. Organizational routines or standard operating procedures are developed to carry out hazardous waste program responsibilities, and public officials become increasingly resistant to change over time, especially if there is little turnover within the initial cadre of administrators. Nor is innovation likely to occur in a climate of fiscal austerity. Funding has declined for both EPA operations and RCRA planning grants to the states over the past five years (Bartlett, 1984; Lester, 1986), and prospects for an increase in the foreseeable future are not good.

Skeptical attitudes among agency personnel toward new methods of pollution control may also be reinforced by scientific uncertainty, for example, differences in the degree of risk one is willing to assume in setting standards for exposure to toxic substances. Disputes over factual interpretation or even the assumptions used in study designs are more apt to result in efforts by program administrators to defend professional reputation through a series of organizational maneuvers than in a candid admission of limited knowledge (Holden, 1966). A useful example of this process is found in a recent discussion of actions taken by public health administrators during the environmental crisis at Love Canal (Levine, 1982).

Third, inefficient organizational arrangements between related program areas result in an emphasis on correcting existing deficiencies prior to the consideration of less conventional regulatory strategies. Policies and programs leading to inconsistent regulations as well as gaps in regulatory coverage are analyzed in a report issued by the congressional Office of Technology Assessment (1983):

There are programs [in EPA] and several other executive agencies related to hazardous waste that do not appear to be highly integrated. . . . Ocean disposal falls under the Marine Protection, Research, and Sanctuaries Act. Some injection wells used for waste disposal fall under the Safe Drinking Water Act and some under RCRA. Hazardous waste streams destined for municipal water treatment plants fall under the Clean Water Act. A number of aspects of regulating releases into the air or water from management facilities fall under the Clean Air and Clean Water Act. (pp. 91-92)

Similar problems are found in efforts to coordinate activities required under the three federal hazardous waste statutes—TSCA, RCRA, and Superfund. Differing requirements for the disposal of polychlorinated biphenyls (PCBs) under TSCA and RCRA create administrative difficulties for state regulatory officials, while a related lack of concern for programmatic consistency is illustrated by the wide variation in liability insurance rules between RCRA and Superfund (Office of Technology Assessment, 1983).

A fourth factor contributing to the relative feasibility of directive versus nondirective approaches is the visibility of hazardous waste problems within a given jurisdiction. Media attention to the discovery of pollutants will typically lead to public pressure for strong governmental action. Recent examples include the federal response to ground contamination at Times Beach, Missouri, and the rise of citizen opposition to proposed hazardous waste facility sites in Connecticut and Ohio (Kraft and Kraut, 1985; Dickson, 1983). In other words, the benefits of regulation for the general population within the affected area are clearly perceived to outweigh the costs imposed upon a relatively small group of firms. Attempts to formulate a more cooperative set of relationships under these circumstances would likely be perceived as governmental capitulation to corporate polluters or an unwarranted effort to measure the worth of human lives in economic terms.

Receptivity to nondirective regulatory approaches at the state level varies according to both policy and institutional characteristics. A recent study by Bowman and Lester (1985) found that states ranking high on policy leadership and fiscal health indices tend to be more favorably predisposed toward the utilization of economic incentives in regulatory decision making. Perhaps the most notable example is the state of California, which in 1981 embarked on an ambitious effort to phase out the land disposal of highly toxic wastes. Acting on the premise that preventive steps are more effective and less expensive than remedial measures in the long run, policymakers have recommended a series of policy actions which combine the utilization of nondirective regulatory strategies with an eventual ban on the land-based disposal of hazardous wastes (Commission for Economic Development, 1985). Further analysis of interstate policy differences might indicate whether creativity on the state regulatory front is also associated with such factors as the severity of existing waste disposal problems or the existence of a "critical mass" of scientists and administrators specializing in the control or recovery of toxic chemical substances.

Institutional factors which may contribute to the adoption of more flexible administrative arrangements include the continuing emphases on deregulation and decentralization as desirable features of governance. To the extent that more cooperative state-federal and public-private relationships lead to an increase in compliance with current policies or the development of economic incentives for technological alternatives to land-based disposal, a corresponding rise in support for nondirective regulatory strategies may occur (Davis, 1985b). Only time will tell whether the pace of change in the management of hazardous waste programs is slowed by shifting policy priorities or publicity surrounding the discovery of toxic wastes in or near a community.

Transnational Hazardous Waste Policy Formation

In this section, we consider the treatment, transport, storage, and disposal of hazardous wastes in North America and Western Europe. A variety of private-sector and governmental arrangements are also examined, including the international marketplace, policy initiatives within specific countries, bilateral agreements between nations, and efforts by supranational organizations to develop a policymaking apparatus calling for some regulation of toxic chemical substances by signatories. A focus on American and European countries is partially justified by the fact that an overwhelming preponderance of the world's hazardous wastes are generated and consumed within their borders. In addition, data from other areas (particularly Third World countries) were incomplete or nonexistent. Policymakers focus on more pressing issues such as developmental needs; hence, little or no governmental attention is directed toward pollution abatement.

For some waste-generating firms within the United States wishing to cut the costs of compliance with environmental regulations, the export of hazardous wastes to less developed nations represents a possible course of action. A study by Shuman (1983) indicated that American chemical companies spend 44% less on pollution abatement abroad than in the United States. Such actions may originate in the private sector but clearly raise important ethical and foreign policy questions for the government. The reputation of the United States within the international community would suffer if it were perceived as a nation willing to tolerate the dumping of domestically produced hazardous waste in Third World countries (Sefero-vich, 1981; Shue, 1981; Weir and Schapiro, 1981).

A recent analysis of U.S. export policies within the context of bureaucratic politics provides little hope that such problems will be easily resolved. The involvement of numerous administrative actors (e.g., the Departments of State, Commerce, Treasury, and Agriculture and the EPA) on a low-visibility policy issue greatly inhibits the development of a coherent and comprehensive policy for the export of hazardous wastes (Davis and Hagan, 1986). The authors suggest that a practical effect of maintaining a decentralized and internally fragmented policy of this sort is the inability of governmental officials to act quickly and effectively in coping with future crises.

A second means of dealing with transnational pollution problems is the development of bilateral agreements or treaties between countries. The United States and Mexico have attempted to negotiate an agreement to resolve problems associated with the ad hoc dumping of industrial wastes into Mexican municipal sewage systems (which occasionally overflow), pesticide contamination of transboundary rivers and streams, and the handling of air pollution within metropolitan areas spanning the border. To date, negotiations have been difficult, owing in part to the tremendous disparity in economic resources between the two countries that can be committed to environmental protection or cleanup efforts. According to Applegate and Bath (1983), dealing with hazardous waste problems is a secondary concern for Mexican officials, who are placing greater emphasis upon economic development.

This is not to say that bilateral negotiations lack promise. The key lies in recognition by both parties that contributions to a workable solution need not be equal. Moreover, a precedent within the realm of natural resource policy has already been established. According to Mumme (1985):

Under the 1944 Water Treaty, the two countries have agreed to apportion the costs of ameliorative works relative to the perceived national benefits, leaving the question of benefits in any given case to bilateral negotiation. . . . Given the difference in national priorities, it is inevitable that the U.S. absorb a proportionally larger share of the financial burden for hazards abatement than Mexico. While specific responsibility in each case is subject to bargaining and compromise, the United States is able to use its financial resources as a positive incentive when binational projects offer substantial benefits to Mexico. (p. 167)

Other nations, particularly in Western Europe, have developed innovative hazardous waste policies. These policies vary in terms of reliance upon national authority versus subnational regulation and the preferred options to be selected for treating or disposing of toxic chemical by-products (Piasecki, 1984; Lehman, 1983). Program diversity can be illustrated here by briefly describing the policies adopted in three countries—the United Kingdom, Denmark, and West Germany.

Hazardous waste management in the U.K. is decentralized to a considerable degree. This is, in part, attributable to a philosophical approach to environmental regulation which places greater emphasis on public-private cooperation and local solutions than the promulgation of national standards which uniformly apply to all waste generators (Vogel, 1986). In addition, hazardous waste management in Britain is less an issue of public health than an effort to reclaim derelict land. Wastes have been used to fill unsightly holes created through mining operations (Livezey, 1980).[2] As a consequence, the administration of toxic substances can be viewed as an important component of land-use planning, a public function typically reserved for local government.

The formal assignment of intergovernmental responsibilities for hazardous waste management is spelled out under Part I of the 1974 Control of Pollution Act. Central governmental agencies have relatively little authority; they are responsible for the provision of technical assistance and the development of guideline documents.[3] Local government is assigned the primary role of regulating wastes. Towns and cities are required to maintain sufficient staff and technical expertise to handle waste disposal problems. Overall, this approach leads to considerable duplication of effort and expense. On the other hand, public input on hazardous waste management decisions is taken more seriously than in countries with centrally developed programs (Arnott, 1985).

Denmark has attempted to deal with hazardous waste problems through a more centralized approach. It is a relatively small country (approximately 44,000 square kilometers, or twice the size of Massachusetts), and policy-makers called for the construction of a centrally located tsd facility in Nyborg. All wastes are brought to the Kommunekemi facility (a government corporation owned by Danish municipalities) for disposal or recycling. The complex includes two incinerators, oil recovery and inorganic waste treatment systems, and a large landfill with a limestone alkaline layer designed to prevent the leaching of heavy metal hydroxides (Arnott, 1985).

Under the Law on Disposal of Oil and Chemical Waste passed by the Danish Parliament in 1972, hazardous waste generators are required to inform municipalities of the types, amount, and disposition of wastes they produce. Industries may handle wastes on-site after obtaining a permit (a rarely used option), sell their wastes directly to another industry or indirectly through a waste exchange system, or send wastes to an approved regional or national facility. Municipal officials are responsible for the collection of these wastes and have fulfilled this mandate by developing a network of 21 collection stations for industrial and agricultural wastes and more than 250 stations for household wastes. Wastes are not pretreated at these collection points but are separated and stored until full loads can be accumulated for shipment to the Kommunekemi facility (Paparian, Wells, and Fearey,

1984). In short, the Danes possess a national system for toxic waste collection, disposal, and recovery which is perhaps the most integrated in the world (see also Toffner-Clausen, 1983).

Public involvement in hazardous waste management decisions has not been a source of tension for Danish authorities. Facility construction preceded the emergence of toxic waste as a political issue in the United States and elsewhere. In addition, Kommunekemi officials have worked closely with members of the Nyborg municipal council, the police department, and other local administrators to ensure that community health and safety concerns are being met (Paparian, Wells, and Fearey, 1984).

West Germany, like the United States, has a system of federalism which divides political authority between the central and state (*Länder*) governments. Hazardous waste disposal legislation was enacted by the federal legislature in 1972 and was amended in 1977. It establishes a regulatory framework for the collection, transport, treatment, storage, and disposal of most toxic wastes and leaves implementation-related responsibilities in the hands of *Länder* officials. These jurisdictions must fulfill a variety of reporting and handling regulations (much like the RCRA manifest system) but generally enjoy considerable leeway in the design and administration of programs tailored to meet regional concerns (Livezey, 1980).

The *Länder* vary in their ability and willingness to meet program management responsibilities. Some German states have serious waste control problems, while others such as Hesse and Bavaria have established a reputation for innovation and professionalism (Arnott, 1985). These states have created public/private corporations with elaborate waste disposal facilities which utilize incineration and other techniques designed to minimize reliance upon land-based containment as a waste disposal option. The latter objective is also a concern of the central government, which subsidizes and sponsors research on recycling (Arnott, 1985).

Citizen opposition to hazardous waste management issues, particularly facility siting, is more evident in West Germany than in Denmark. Ad hoc community groups tend to focus on the uncertainty of risk to health or agricultural crops posed by nearby facility operations. However, local government officials have not chosen the politically expedient path of vetoing plans for the construction or expansion of tsd facilities but have instead approached the issue by requiring mitigation measures. Public education is also utilized extensively in the early phases of decision making to increase the knowledge and acquiescence of community residents (Paparian, Wells, Fearey, 1984).

Japan, Canada, New Zealand, Australia, and other Western European nations have adopted variations on these policy/management themes and have contributed a variety of policy ideas as well (e.g., Japan's policy of requiring waste-generating firms to assume full liability and cleanup costs for problems associated with the inadequate storage, transport, or disposal of toxic chemical wastes). In addition, supranational approaches to hazardous waste management problems have been recommended and, in some cases, implemented. The NATO/CCMS (Committee on the Challenges of Modern Society) Symposium on Hazardous Waste Disposal was convened in 1981 to promote the dissemination of results from an eight-year research project dealing with technical, organizational, and regulatory approaches to the management of toxic wastes within and between nations (Wolbeck, 1983). The conference represented an effort not only to share information about a pressing environmental policy issue but to serve as a catalyst for institutional responses, such as a clearinghouse for research and development and the development of waste exchange systems.

Similar attempts to find a multinational collaborative solution to the disposal of hazardous wastes have been undertaken by the Organization for Economic Cooperation and Development (OECD), an international body whose members include most countries in Western Europe, Turkey, the United States, Australia, Japan, and New Zealand, and the Commission of European Communities (CEC). The latter organization has attempted to standardize hazardous waste management practices through the development of programs and directives. For example, the Directive of March 20, 1978, on toxic and hazardous waste requires EEC countries to dispose of toxic chemical by-products without endangering human health or the environment, while the Directive of December 6, 1984, calls for the surveillance and control of cross-frontier hazardous waste transfers (Mangun, 1985).

Despite the rather laudable policy intentions of the EEC, the degree of follow-through on the legislative front has varied considerably. Some of the rules have been implemented within a majority of member countries, but a study by Crawford (1981) indicated that West Germany and the Netherlands were the only representatives found to be in substantial compliance with EEC directives. In a cross-national study of policy responses in Western Europe, Mangun (1985) concluded that the nations most likely to have a strong hazardous waste management program were those with severe pollution problems, greater economic wealth (GNP per capita), and the administrative apparatus to implement such policies.

In short, policy formulation patterns vary according to the magnitude of hazardous waste problems, jurisdictional level, the political and economic characteristics of states or countries, and the type of issue under examination. However, a few generalizations can be gleaned from our literature review. The adoption of hazardous waste policies at either the state (within the United States) or the national level is often associated with fiscal resources and the presence of administrative staff with the requisite expertise to carry out these programs. Policymakers also tend to be more responsive in jurisdictions plagued with serious pollution problems. Finally, an examination of studies dealing with the relationship between the public and facility siting questions in the United States and West Germany revealed the importance of noneconomic incentives as a means of gaining acquiescence from community residents affected by such decisions. We now turn to a review of the literature on hazardous waste policy implementation.

THE IMPLEMENTATION OF HAZARDOUS
WASTE POLICIES

In the view of Mazmanian and Sabatier, the "crucial role of implementation analysis is the identification of the variables which affect the achievement of legal objectives throughout their entire process" (1983: 21). These variables may be divided into three broad categories: (1) the tractability of the problem being addressed, (2) the ability of the statute to structure favorably the implementation process, and (3) the net effect of a variety of political variables on the balance of support for statutory objectives. In this final section, we examine each of these component variables and their effects on the implementation of hazardous waste policy in the United States.

Tractability Variables

The tractability of the problem, according to Mazmanian and Sabatier, concerns the inherent nature of the problem involved. *Tractability* refers to difficulties in measuring changes in the seriousness of the problem, in relating such changes back to modification in the behavior of target groups, and in developing the technology to enable target groups to institute such changes (Sabatier and Mazmanian, 1980: 541). The control of toxic substances is a good example of at least some of these conditions (Mann, 1982: 14). For example, it is presently agreed among most scientists and policymakers that the problem of hazardous waste is a very serious one. Indeed, in its report on hazardous waste disposal, the Subcommittee on Oversight and Investigations of the House Interstate and Foreign Commerce Committee summarized this particular problem:

The hazardous waste disposal problem cannot be overstated. The Environmental Protection Agency (EPA) has estimated that over 77,140,000,000 pounds of hazardous waste are generated each year, but only 10 percent of that amount is disposed of in an environmentally sound manner. Today, there are some 30,000 hazardous waste disposal sites in the United States. Because of years of inadequate disposal practices and the absence of regulation, hundreds and perhaps thousands of these sites now pose an imminent hazard to man and the environment. Our country presently lacks an adequate program to determine where these sites are; to clean up unsafe active and inactive sites; and to provide sufficient facilities for the safe disposal of hazardous wastes in the future. (House Committee on Interstate and Foreign Commerce, 1979, p. 1)

However serious the problem, the EPA has experienced great difficulty in obtaining accurate measurements of the magnitude of the problem. For example, there is substantial uncertainty about how many firms are actually involved in hazardous waste management, the total volume of chemical wastes that are generated in the United States each year, and the total number of sites used for hazardous waste disposal (Conservation Foundation, 1982).

Although estimates vary widely as more data are collected and made available to the public, a somewhat conservative view is that over 400,000 firms are involved in handling hazardous wastes. However, the data base for this figure is incomplete, and the EPA therefore has no reliable estimate of the total number of firms involved. Precise figures on waste generation of disposal sites are also uncertain. The EPA estimates that anywhere from 41 million to 57 million metric tons of industrial hazardous wastes are generated each year. Similarly, the estimated number of hazardous waste sites in the United States ranges from 32,000 to 50,000 (U.S. General Accounting Office, 1981).

In October 1981, the EPA identified 115 sites with the potential to pose imminent threats to health and the environment; however, the methodology used to identify these priority sites for remedial action under the Superfund program was soundly criticized by the Congressional Office of Technology Assessment (OTA). Other estimates suggest that the number of waste sites posing a significant threat to public health or the environment is anywhere from 1,200 to 34,000 depending on the estimation technique used (Hart, 1979).

In any case, EPA Administrator Anne Gorsuch, in October 1981, identified 24 of these 115 sites as posing a "greater potential danger" to public health than New York's Love Canal because they threatened to pollute drinking water supplies in densely populated areas (*Inside EPA*, 1981). On July 23, 1982, the EPA added 45 more hazardous waste dumps to its list of the 115 worst sites in the country, making them eligible for cleanup under the $1.6 billion Superfund program (*Washington Post*, 1982). On December 20, 1982, the EPA released a list of the 418 worst toxic sites that are eligible for cleanup under the Superfund program (*Houston Post*, 1982). On September 1, 1983, the EPA added 133 more sites to the Superfund list. In 1984, the EPA released a new Superfund list of 786 sites. In 1987, there were 964 Superfund sites. All of these estimates at the national level illustrate the difficulties encountered in assessing problem tractability. Essentially, the EPA still does not know the dimensions of the hazardous waste problem (Mosher, 1983).

State efforts to assess the magnitude of the problem have also confronted difficulties. Florida, for example, attempted to identify its most serious hazardous waste sites. However, the EPA's ranking of Florida's sites showed almost no correspondence to the ranking by Florida's Department of Environmental Regulation (DER). Moreover, both rankings were criticized for ignoring potentially more serious sites simply because adequate information was available for only twenty-seven sites (Williams and Matheny, 1983: 93).

A second tractability problem is concerned with the availability (and accuracy) of scientific and health information on which to base public policy. For example, "little is known about health hazards associated with exposure over a long period of time to small amounts and combinations of chemicals in ground water or elsewhere" (Conservation Foundation, 1982: 145). Moreover, as noted by Professor Beverly Paigen in her testimony before the House Subcommittee on Oversight and Investigation, "epidemiological studies can never prove cause and effect; these studies only show an association of disease with geographical location" (U.S. House Subcommittee on Oversight and Investigation, 1979). Thus, a dilemma exists in the sense that we simply do not have enough solid scientific information to identify with certainty the "right" level of regulation (Senkan and Stauffer, 1981).

A third problem is concerned with the scope of those affected by implementing RCRA regulations. As Mazmanian and Sabatier indicate, the smaller and more definable (isolatable) the target groups whose behavior needs to be changed, the more likely the mobilization of political support in favor of the program and thus the more probable the achievement of statutory objectives (Sabatier and Mazmanian, 1980). However, an effective solution to the hazardous waste problem will require substantial cooperation that extends well beyond the federal government to include state and local officials, the private sector, and individual citizens. In fact, the effective control of hazardous waste is an issue that transcends all levels of government, the private sector, and all lines of socioeconomic status, age, race, and lifestyles (Lester, 1983: 7). Thus, subnational implementation is being impeded by the sheer number of affected groups.

Finally, another tractability problem is concerned with the effectiveness of existing technologies in controlling hazardous waste. Effective implementation is contingent upon finding reliable and relatively inexpensive technology. The EPA, in its landfill regulations issued on July 26, 1982, stipulated that synthetic liners (versus clay liners) were to be used in new landfills (*Federal Register*, 1982). However, recent research continues to suggest that both clay and plastic liners are inadequate in containing hazardous waste (Montague, 1981). Even the EPA, in its new landfill regulations, recognized that there is no such thing as a "secure landfill," because liners will eventually leak, and that landfills may only be viewed as temporary collection facilities or "controlled releases" into the environment (*Federal Register*, 1982: 32284-32285). Thus, there is substantial uncertainty over the most appropriate technology to be used in controlling hazardous waste. This uncertainty, in turn, affects the timely implementation of RCRA guidelines at the state level.

In short, the effective implementation of hazardous waste regulation presents a number of highly intractable problems. However, as Mazmanian and Sabatier suggest, "even relatively difficult problems can be ameliorated through a more adequate understanding of the manner in which statutory and political variables affect the mobilization of support necessary to bring about rather substantial behavior change" (Mazmanian and Sabatier, 1983: 24-25). It is to an examination of these variables that we now turn.

Statutory Variables

The second set of variables that affect policy implementation are those that concern the extent to which the statute coherently structures the implementation process. These variables include the validity of the causal theory on which the policy is based; the precision and clarity with which objectives are ranked, the financial resources available to the implementing agency, the extent of hierarchical integration within and among implementing institutions, the extent to which decision rules of implementing agencies are suportive of statutory objectives, the assignment of responsibility to officials and agencies committed to the statutory objectives, and the extent to which opportunities for participation by actors external to the implementing agencies are biased toward supporters of statutory objectives (Mazmanian and Sabatier, 1983: 29). Once again, the implementation of hazardous waste policy illustrates many of these factors.

For example, RCRA contains very broad, encompassing goals which demand extensive cooperation among the EPA, the private sector, state governments, local governments, and the public. For this to occur, some consensus must be reached on the severity of the problem, how best to resolve that problem, and what constitutes successful performance. However, these matters have frequently been left to the EPA and target groups, and the result has been delay (Riley, 1983: 41). The complexity of this situation stems from the fact that "each set of actors responds to different incentives. It is still an open question whether their divergent and incompatible interests can be meshed through a series of continuous mutual adjustments into an effective regulatory scheme" (Getz and Walter, 1980: 405).

Second, developments in the implementation of RCRA guidelines from the early spring of 1982 until the 1984 presidential election indicated ambivalence within the Reagan administration on which goals are more important—reducing the burden and cost of enforcing environmental regulations or maintaining faith with past legislative mandates to protect public health and safety (Riley, 1983; Barke, 1985). For example, the administration's FY 1982 budget cut the preliminary hazardous waste investigation and cleanup capability from 1,300 to 900 waste sites (*Audubon Leader*, 1981).

Furthermore, after announcing that it intended to make major concessions to industry, the Reagan administration, in February 1982, proposed a reversal of rules that banned (under RCRA) the buying of hazardous waste at landfills (Shabecoff, 1982a). Then, in March 1982, the EPA also suspended its previous requirement that manufacturers of hazardous wastes report each year on what happened to those wastes. Instead, it was proposed that the EPA take an annual survey of 10% of the companies involved (Shabecoff, 1982b). Shortly thereafter, the EPA announced its "national contingency plan" for dealing with hazardous waste sites. Essentially, this plan proposed to replace the Carter administration's stringent blanket licensing procedures for all disposal sites with controls based on the "degree of hazard" posed by chemicals stored or disposed of at the sites. In effect, these actions represented important concessions to the chemical industry. Moreover, a refusal by EPA Administrator Anne Gorsuch to turn over documents in compliance with a subpoena led to an unprecedented contempt of Congress charge against her in December 1982. Apparently, her refusal fueled suspicions in Congress that the EPA was allowing hazardous waste polluters to "buy out" of potential damage suits too cheaply (Shabecoff, 1982b; Russakoff, 1982).

Earlier, in late March 1982, it appeared that the EPA was taking a more conciliatory approach to hazardous waste management by making several major concessions to the environmentalists. For example, the EPA reversed its three-week-old decision to permit burial of drums of toxic wastes in landfills and issued interim rules to prohibit burial of toxics (Shabecoff, 1982c). Second, the EPA reversed a preliminary decision made in October 1981 and required an estimated 10,000 hazardous waste facilities to obtain liability insurance to protect citizens against possible contamination (*Washington Post*, 1982). Finally, it retained the cleanup standards originally proposed by the Carter administration for all incinerators that burn hazardous wastes and imposed more stringent standards for new hazardous waste landfills which became effective on January 26, 1983 (*Wall Street Journal*, 1982). Thus, these earlier policy shifts by the EPA, as well as delays in finalizing RCRA regulations and delays in undertaking cleanup action under the Superfund program, have added to the extreme uncertainty associated with the current administration goals in this area of public policy (Cohen, 1984; Cohen and Tipermas, 1983).

Third, the availability of financial resources to implementing agencies has been a very significant factor in the implementation of RCRA. For example, at the federal level, money is obviously necessary to hire the staff and to conduct the technical analyses involved in the development of regulations, the administration of permit programs, and the monitoring of compliance (Sabatier and Mazmanian, 1980: 545). However, the current cutback in federal environmental expenditures clearly has negative implications for hazardous waste management grants and assistance (Lester, 1986: 165). While the FY 1983 administration budget proposed increases for Superfund activities, it also sought to reduce Subtitle C grants to the states by more than 10% at the same time that federal funding and technical assistance for solid waste management planning had been completely eliminated (Lieber, 1983: 69). These proposed hazardous waste grant reductions led at least ten states to consider withdrawing their interim authorization and returning these programs to the EPA (*Inside EPA*, 1982: 8). Indeed, the inadequacy of states' fiscal resources has been repeatedly cited as a major factor in delaying implementation of RCRA (Williams and Matheny, 1983; Worthley and Torkelson, 1983; Kramer, 1983; Rosenbaum, 1983; Lester et al., 1983).

A fourth statutory factor affecting implementation of RCRA is the extent of hierarchical integration within and among implementing institutions. Numerous studies of the implementation of regulatory programs have demonstrated that one of the principal obstacles is the difficulty of achieving coordinated action within any given agency and among the numerous semiautonomous agencies involved in most implementation efforts (Kamieniecki et al., 1986; Sabatier and Mazmanian, 1980: 546). In Texas, for example, the administrative responsibility for the implementation of hazardous waste policy was highly fragmented until 1985, inasmuch as four agencies (the Texas Department of Water Resources, the Texas Department of Health, the Texas Railroad Commission, and the Texas Air Control Board) shared that responsibility. This administrative fragmentation "led to agency jurisdictional questions which some groups and officials characterized as negatively affecting the efforts to deal effectively with state hazardous waste problems" (Kramer, 1983: 117). Conversely, it has been found that consolidation of environmental (especially hazardous waste) responsibility into a single agency is associated with greater responsiveness to the hazardous waste problem (Kramer, 1983: 119; Lester et al., 1983; Lester and Bowman, 1986). Other studies also point to implementation delays brought about by fragmented administrative responsibilities for hazardous waste management (Worthley and Torkelson, 1981; Bowman, 1985a: 100-110),

A fifth statutory variable affecting implementation is the receptivity of the agency charged with implementation. Any new program requires implementers who are not merely neutral but sufficiently persistent to develop new regulations and standard operating procedures, and to enforce them in the face of resistance from target groups (i.e., the private sector) and from public officials reluctant to make the mandated changes (Sabatier and Mazmanian, 1980). In the case of hazardous waste implementation, Matheny and Williams argue that the tensions between those government actors responsible for the implementation of RCRA (i.e., the state bureaucracy) and those actors that are affected by implementation (i.e., the private sector) help explain why RCRA has not been successfully implemented in Florida (1981: 10). Similarly, Bowman (1985a) notes that the decision rules of implementing agencies have adversely affected the implementation of hazardous waste programs in the southeastern United States.

In addition, Davis (1985b) examines the degree of consensus found among relevant political actors in the control of hazardous wastes. He finds considerable agreement between federal and state administrators on the one hand but concludes that considerable dissension exists between governmental and industry officials. This dissension is "sufficiently pronounced to greatly complicate efforts to find a common ground on policy/regulatory concerns" (Davis, 1985). Thus, the present political climate existing between these public and private actors precludes the large-scale adoption of several recommended hazardous waste regulatory reforms. Similarly, Kramer finds that a "technical-engineering" orientation among state-level bureaucrats responsible for hazardous waste policy implementation in Texas has had a major impact upon the nature of state policy developed there (1983: 131-132). Clearly, the receptivity of the agencies involved has influenced the timely implementation of RCRA.

Finally, another factor affecting implementation is the extent to which opportunities for participation by actors outside the implementing agencies are biased toward supporters of legal objectives. RCRA allows for formal access by outsiders through Section 7004, which requires the EPA and the states to encourage, provide, and assist public participation in the development, revision, implementation, and enforcement of any regulation, guideline, or program. However, local citizens express strong dissatisfaction with siting hazardous waste disposal facilities in their jurisdictions (EPA, 1979). Indeed, it is suggested that public participation vis-à-vis the hazardous waste siting issue leads to extensive polarization among citizens and heightened political conflict (Carnes, 1982: 30; O'Brien et al., 1984; Morell and Magorian, 1982; O'Hare et al., 1983). Moreover, this citizen activism has been shown to have a decisive influence in the siting of hazardous waste facilities (Rosenbaum, 1983; Kraft and Kraut, 1985: 52-61; Matheny and Williams, 1985). The directionality of that influence, however, is unclear. That is, increased citizen opposition to new hazardous waste disposal facilities may encourage waste generators to use other, often safer forms of disposal or to reduce the amount of waste generated. On the other hand, local opposition to new hazardous waste sites may ultimately encourage implementation delays or even encourage more illicit disposal of hazardous wastes (Hadden, Veillette, and Brandt, 1983: 211).

All of these statutory variables have influenced the implementation of RCRA. We now turn to an examination of the influence of nonstatutory variables upon hazardous waste policy implementation.

Nonstatutory Variables

According to Sabatier and Mazmanian (1980):

Implementation also has an inherent dynamism driven by at least two important processes: (1) the need for any program which seeks to change behavior to receive constant and/or periodic infusions of political support if it is to overcome the inertia and delay inherent in seeking cooperation and acquiescence among large numbers of people, many of whom perceive their interest to be adversely affected by successful implementation of statutory objectives; and (2) the effect of continuous changes in socio-economic and technological conditions on the reservoir of support for those objectives among the general public, interest groups, and sovereigns.

First, variation in the severity of the problem or in socioeconomic conditions can affect perceptions of the relative importance of the problem addressed by a statute. Thus, the more serious the problem, the more diverse an economy, and the more prosperous the target groups, the more probable the implementation (Sabatier and Mazmanian, 1980: 549). In the case of hazardous waste, the severity of the problem (i.e., the amount of waste generated) has been found to be related to the implementation of hazardous waste policy in the states (Bowman and Lester, 1985). The diversity of the state's economy has also been linked to regulatory behavior (Rowland and Walton, 1983; Lester and Bowman, 1986).

Second, the amount and continuity of media attention to the problem addressed by a statute are believed to be related to policy implementation (Sabatier and Mazmanian, 1980: 550). Two recent studies have found that media attention given to the hazardous waste problem is a crucial determinant of policy activity (Levine, 1982: 189-193; Kramer, 1983: 135-137). Specifically, it is suggested that media attention played a critical role at Love Canal by pressuring key decision makers to formulate courses of action more rapidly than they would have without such pressure (Levine, 1982: 191). Conversely, the absence of sustained extensive media attention has been cited as a primary reason why state regulatory agencies and industrial groups in Texas operate in a political subsystem that works to prevent the enactment of more stringent hazardous waste policies (Kramer, 1983: 135).

Third, variation in public opinion is likely to result in pressures for ambiguous regulation and considerable discretion to local officials—both of which probably make behavioral change more difficult to achieve (Sabatier and Mazmanian, 1980: 550). With the passage of RCRA, together with the extensive media attention to Love Canal, public opinion in general seems to be quite concerned about risks to health and safety from exposure to toxic chemicals (Council on Environmental Quality, 1981: 415). However, in some jurisdictions, the absence of more extensive statewide media coverage on the hazardous waste problem has "meant that major state policy decisions about hazardous waste (as opposed to decisions about permitting a particular waste site) have taken place without intensive public scrutiny." In such instances, these policy decisions have, as we noted above, taken place within a political subsystem composed of state agency bureaucrats, petrochemical interest groups, and, to some extent, state legislative committees (Kramer, 1983: 135-137).

Fourth, constituency groups (both proponents and opponents) influence the policy outputs of implementing institutions (e.g., the EPA) and target groups (e.g., the state bureaucracy and legislature). The basic dilemma confronting proponents of any regulatory program seeking a change in the behavior of one or more target groups is that public support for their position will almost invariably decline over time. On the other hand, the opponents of the mandated change generally have the resources and incentives to intervene more actively in the implementation process (Sabatier and Mazmanian, 1980: 551).

In addition, public perception of hazardous waste severity fluctuates over time and determines the adequacy of state regulatory effort (Goetze and Rowland, 1985). This situation certainly applies to the politics of hazardous waste management. Environmental interest groups have been quite active in this area, and their support has increased among the public over the past few years (Rosenbaum, 1983: 191-195). However, this recent interest and activity by environmental interest groups over the hazardous waste issue has been matched by the involvement of industrial interest groups (i.e., hazardous waste producers, transporters, and disposers). These private interest groups with greater political skills and financial resources at their disposal, have, in many instances, been able to exert more influence upon policy implementation than their environmental counterparts (Kramer, 1983: 132-135; Williams and Matheny, 1983: 99-101; Walter and Getz, 1986; Morell, 1983: 175).

A fifth factor influencing policy implementation is the support provided by sovereigns (i.e., the legislature, the chief executive, the courts) for statutory objectives (Sabatier and Mazmanian, 1980: 551-552). For example, we often find a "fixer" who provides invaluable support for policy implementation (i.e., an important legislator or executive official who controls resources important to crucial actors and who has the desire and the staff resources to closely monitor the implementation process and to intervene on an almost continuous basis (Sabatier and Mazmanian, 1980: 552). Governor Edmund G. Brown, Jr., played such a role in the implementation of California's hazardous waste policy. Indeed, without the governor's personal support—together with the creation of an unusual government agency, the Office of Appropriate Technology, or OAT—it seems unlikely that California would have pursued an innovative response to hazardous waste problems by barring landfills as a disposal option (Morell, 1983: 145-147).

A final variable influencing policy implementation is the commitment and leadership skill of implementing officials. This variable comprises at least two components. First, the direction and ranking of statutory objectives by agency officials should be spelled out, and second, their skill in carrying out those objectives, that is, their ability to go beyond what could reasonably be expected in using the available resources, should be exhibited

(Sabatier and Mazmanian, 1980: 553). A number of authors suggest that the commitment found among public and private actors affects the development and implementation of hazardous waste policy (Davis, 1985b; Kramer, 1983; Morell, 1983; Powell, 1985; Bowman, 1985a). Kramer, for example, argues that hazardous waste management policy in Texas has tended to be based on the dominant cognitive perspective found among the bureaucrats responsible for policy implementation, that is, an "engineering perspective" (Kramer, 1983: 131). This has meant that certain stringent policy solutions to the hazardous waste disposal problem (e.g., nonlandfill options such as resource recovery) are not considered technically optional solutions. Rather, "proper" management, from their perspective, dictates that landfills (with clay or plastic liners) be utilized as the most technically efficient response to the disposal problem (Kramer, 1983: 132).

In summary, we have utilized the framework suggested by Mazmanian and Sabatier (1983) to analyze factors contributing to an explanation of hazardous waste policy implementation at national and state levels. In the final part of this chapter, we suggest some areas for future research on hazardous waste policy in the American and other contexts.

FUTURE RESEARCH ON HAZARDOUS WASTE POLICY

Several questions guide our discussion in this final section. First, how might research on this topic be conducted in the future? What improvements might be made in this research from either a conceptual or a methodological pespective? Finally, what new research is underway in this area?

A summary of published research on hazardous waste policymaking is displayed in Table 1.1. It is evident that a serious imbalance is found in comparing the amount of scholarly work focusing on the United States with the literature on cross-national and international policy processes. Much remains to be done. For example, very little attention has been directed toward an examination of factors affecting policy formulation outside the American and West European contexts. Recent work by Stephen Mumme and Richard Bath serves to enhance our understanding of hazardous waste policymaking within Mexico but little is known about comparable efforts in other Third World countries. Moreover, research on international policies (i.e., bilateral and multilateral agreements on the regulation of hazardous wastes) is virtually nonexistent at this time.

Similarly, while there is some work on the determinants of American state hazardous waste policy formulation (Lester et al., 1983; Williams and Matheny, 1984; Rowland and Walton, 1983; Bowman, 1984b; Bowman and Lester, 1985; Goetze and Rowland, 1985), there is (as of 1987) no longitudinal analysis of policy formulation and its determinants. Moreover, from a conceptual standpoint, more work needs to be done in deriving or testing an acceptable body of theory to explain state hazardous waste policy

Table 1.1
Status of Research on Hazardous Waste Politics and Policy

Stages in the Policy Process	Levels of Analysis:				
	International	Cross-National	National	State	Local
Policy Formation	Mumme (1985) Davis & Hagan (1986) Weir & Shapiro (1981)	Mangun (1985) Arnott (1985) Ristoratore (1985) Piasecki (1984) Toffner-Clausen (1983)	Epstein, et al. (1982) Grunbaum (1985) Landy (1985) Sheehan (1985) Worthley & Torkelson (1981)	Lester, et al. (1983) Bowman (1984) Bowman & Lester (1985) Rowland & Marz (1981) Rowland & Walton (1984) Rowland & Feiock (1984) Hadden, et al. (1983) Kramer (1983) Williams & Matheny (1983) Williams & Matheny (1984) Wells (1982) Morell (1983) Wurth-Hough (1982) Matheny & Williams (1985)	Davis (1984-85) Davis (1986) Elliot (1984) Levine (1982) Mitchell & Carson (1986) Morell & Magorian (1982) O'Brien, et al. (1984) O'Hare (1977) O'Hare, et al.(1983) Portney (1984) Portney (1985) Powell (1985) Rosenbaum (1983) Susskind (1985)
Policy Implementation			Carnes (1982) Riley (1983) Cohen (1984) Cohen & Tipermas (1983) Getz & Walter (1980)	Lester (1985) Lester & Bowman (1986) Bowman (1984) Davis (1985) Worthley & Torkelson (1983)	Kraft & Kraut (1985)
Policy Change			Barke (1985) Lester & Hamilton (1986)	Goetze & Rowland (1985)	

Source: Compiled by the authors.

formulation. That is, much of the work in this area is based on bivariate hypotheses rather than an extant body of theory, although studies by Williams and Matheny (1984) and Goetze and Rowland (1985) show considerable promise for subsequent research efforts.

In the area of hazardous waste policy implementation, we know a good deal more about the factors that promote (or inhibit) this behavior. Still, most of what we know is limited to the U.S. subnational context. Little is known about hazardous waste policy implementation in non-U.S. contexts. The conceptual frameworks on policy implementation developed by Edwards (1980), Sabatier and Mazmanian (1980) and Van Horn and Van Meter (1976) may be useful as guides for research in other countries in this regard. All of the work in this area, however, is cross-sectional in design, and thus we have no satisfactory explanations of hazardous waste policy implementation over time.

Finally, aside from recent work by Barke (1985) and Lester and Hamilton (1986), very little is known about the politics of hazardous waste policy change. It would be useful to understand what factors influence a basic shift in the direction and content of hazardous waste policy, either within the United States or in other contexts. Sabatier's (1985) recent model of policy change is a potentially useful guide toward understanding this important type of policy behavior.

In the following chapters, we present some new research on hazardous waste policy formulation, implementation, and change. Together with the previous literature on hazardous waste politics and policy, these studies add a great deal to our knowledge in this important area of public policy.

NOTES

1. The Toxic Substances Control Act (TSCA) of 1976 represented an effort to emulate Western European policies in the development of an adequate data base designed to assess the health and environmental effects of chemicals before their entry into the marketplace. The law, designed to hold chemical manufacturers responsible for the provision of needed information directed the EPA to oversee the premarket testing of potentially dangerous chemicals. If it determined that the sale and distribution of these substances posed an "imminent hazard" to either public health or the environment, the EPA was authorized to hold up marketing pending further tests. Thus far its usefulness as a preventive policy has been severely restricted owing to controversies involving testing procedures and governmental handling of information considered to be proprietary by affected industries.

2. The potential for groundwater contamination through the use of hazardous wastes as filler material is less serious in the U.K. than in the United States, since there are no private wells. The entire population relies on a system of public water which is both well protected and distant from chemical pollutants. A survey cited by Livezey indicated that fewer than 2% of the hazardous waste sites in Britain posed even a potential risk for groundwater pollution.

3. Guideline documents within the British government are meant to be advisory. This is in sharp contrast to the meaning of policy guidelines within the American system of intergovernmental relations. Noncompliance with the letter as well as the spirit of federal guidelines by state or local governments typically results in the failure to obtain grants or the authority to manage federal programs.

REFERENCES

Advisory Commission on Intergovernmental Relations, *Protecting the Environment: Politics, Pollution, and Federal Policy* (Washington, DC: Government Printing Office, 1981).

Alsop, Ronald, "Local Citizen Groups Take a Growing Role Fighting Toxic Dumps," *Wall Street Journal* (April 18, 1983).

Anderson, Roger, "The Resource Conservation and Recovery Act of 1976: Closing the Gap," *Wisconsin Law Review* (1978).

Andrews, Richard N. L., and Terrence K. Pierson, "Local Control or State Override: Experiences and Lessons to Date," *Policy Studies Journal* (September 1985).

Applegate, Howard, and Richard Bath, "Hazardous and Toxic Substances in U.S.-Mexico Relations," *Texas Business Review* (September–October 1983).

Arnott, Robert, "Waste Management in Northern Europe," *Waste Management and Research*, no. 4 (1985).

Barke, Richard, "Policy Learning and the Evolution of Federal Hazardous Waste Policy," *Policy Studies Journal* (September 1985).

Bartlett, Robert, "The Budgetary Process and Environmental Policy," in Norman Vig and Michael Kraft, eds., *Environmental Policy in the 1980s: Reagan's New Agenda* (Washington, DC: CQ Press, 1984).

Bowman, Ann O'M., "Intergovernmental and Intersectoral Tensions in Environmental Policy Implementation: The Case of Hazardous Waste," *Policy Studies Review* (November 1984a).

_____, "Explaining State Response to the Hazardous Waste Problem," *Hazardous Waste* (Fall 1984b).

_____. "Hazardous Wate Cleanup and Superfund Implementation in the Southeast," *Policy Studies Journal* (September 1985a).

_____, "Hazardous Waste Management: An Emerging Policy Area within an Emerging Policy Area within an Emerging Federalism," *Publius* (Winter 1985b)

_____, and James Lester, "Hazardous Waste Management: State Government Activity or Passivity?" *State and Local Government Review* (Winter 1985c).

Brown, Michael, *Laying Waste* (New York: Washington Square Press, 1980).

Carnes, Sam A., "Confronting Complexity and Uncertainty: Implementation of Hazardous Waste Management Policy," in Dean E. Mann, ed., *Environmental Policy Implementation* (Lexington, MA: Lexington Books, 1982).

Cohen, Steven, "Defusing the Toxic Time Bomb: Federal Hazardous Waste Programs," in Norman Vig and Michael Kraft, eds., *Environmental Policy in the 1980s: Reagan's New Agenda* (Washington, DC: CQ Press, 1984).

_____, and Marc Tipermas, "Superfund: Preimplementation Planning and Bureaucratic Politics," in James Lester and Ann Bowman, eds., *The Politics of*

Hazardous Waste Management (Durham, NC: Duke Univesity Press, 1983).

Commission for Economic Development, State of California, *Poisoning Prosperity: The Impact of Toxics on California's Economy* (Sacramento, CA: Commission for Economic Development, 1985).

Conservation Foundation, *State of the Environment: 1982* (Washington, DC: Conservation Foundation, 1982).

Council on Environmental Quality, *Environmental Quality: 1980* (Washington, D.C.: Government Printing Office, 1981).

Crawford, P. J., "The OECD Approach to Chemicals Control," in European Environmental Bureau, *Report of an International Workshop on Toxic Substances, Bonn, September 6-8, 1981* (Brussels: European Environmental Bureau, 1981).

Davis, Charles E., "Substance and Procedure in Hazardous Waste Facility Siting," *Journal of Environmental Systems*, no. 1 (1984-1985).

———, "Implementing the Resource Conservation and Recovery Act of 1976," *Public Administration Quarterly* (Summer 1985a).

———, "Perceptions of Hazardous Waste Policy Issues among Public and Private Sector Administrators," *Western Political Quarterly* (September 1985b).

———, "Public Involvement in Hazardous Waste Facility Siting Decisions," *Polity* (Winter 1986).

———, and Joe Hagan, "Exporting Hazardous Waste: Issues and Policy Implications," *International Journal of Public Administration*, no. 4 (1986).

Derthick, Martha, *Between State and Nation* (Washington, DC: Brookings, 1974).

Dickson, Paul, "Citizen Risk Perception and Participation Strategies: Siting Centralized Hazardous Waste Management Facilities in the Northeast," Paper delivered at the 1983 Annual Meeting of the American Society for Public Administration, New York, NY.

Eckhardt, R. C., "The Unfinished Business of Hazardous Waste Control," *Baylor Law Review*, vol. 33 (1981).

Edwards, George, *Implementing Public Policy* (Washington, DC: CQ Press, 1980).

Elliot, Michael, "Improving Community Acceptance of Hazardous Waste Facilities through Alternative Systems for Mitigating and Managing Risk." *Hazardous Waste* (Fall 1984).

Environmental Protection Agency, *National Priorities List* (September 1984).

"EPA Adds 45 Waste Dumps to List of Sites for Superfund Cleanup," *Washington Post* (July 24, 1982), p. A8.

"EPA Shifts on Liability Insurance," *Washington Post* (April 13, 1982), p. A-17.

"EPA Unveils List of 418 Toxic Waste Sites for 'Superfund' Cleanup Program," *Houston Post* (December 21, 1982), p. A27.

Epstein, Samuel S., Lester O. Brown, and Carl Pope, *Hazardous Waste in America* (San Francisco: Sierra Club Books, 1982).

Federal Register, 97, no. 143 (July 26, 1982), p. 32284-32285.

Getz, Malcolm, and Benjamin Walter, "Environmental Policy and Competitive Structure: Implications of the Hazardous Waste Management Program," *Policy Studies Journal*, vol. 9 (Winter 1980).

Goetze, David B., and C. K. Rowland, "Explaining Hazardous Waste Regulation at the State Level," *Policy Studies Journal* 14 (September 1985): 111-122.

Goldfarb, William, "The Hazards of Our Hazardous Waste Policy," *Natural Resources Journal*, vol. 19 (1979).

Grunbaum, Werner, "Developing a Uniform Federal Common Law for Hazardous Waste Liability," *Policy Studies Journal* (September 1985).

Hadden, Susan G., Joan Veillette, and Thomas Brandt, "State Roles in Siting Hazardous Waste Disposal Facilities: From State Preemption to Local Veto," in James P. Lester and Ann O'M. Bowman, eds., *The Politics of Hazardous Waste Management* (Durham, NC: Duke University Press, 1983).

Hart, Fred C., *Preliminary Assessment of Cleanup Costs for National Hazardous Waste Problems*, prepared for the U.S. Environmental Protection Agency (Washington, DC: EPA, 1979).

"Hazardous Waste Rules on Burning Kept Tough," *Wall Street Journal* (June 23, 1982), p. 19.

Holden, Matthew, Jr. "Imperialism in Bureaucracy," *American Political Science Review*, vol. 60 (December 1966).

Inside EPA (October 30, 1981).

———— (April 23, 1982), p. 8.

Jorling, T. C., "Hazardous Substances in the Environment," *Ecology Law Quarterly*, vol. 9 (1981).

Kamieniecki, Sheldon, Robert O'Brien, and Michael Clarke, "Environmental Policy and Aspects of Intergovernmental Relations," in David Morgan and Edwin Benton, eds., *Intergovernmental Relations and Public Policy* (Westport, CT: Greenwood Press, 1986).

Kamlet, Kenneth S., *Toxic Substances Programs in U.S. States and Territories: How Well Do They Work?* (Washington, D.C.: National Wildlife Federation, 1979).

Kneese, Allen, and Charles Schultze, *Politics, Pollution, and Prices* (Washington, DC: Brookings, 1975).

Kraft, Michael, and Ruth Kraut, "The Impact of Citizen Participation on Hazardous Waste Policy Implementation: The Case of Clermont County, Ohio," *Policy Studies Journal* (September 1985).

Kramer, Kenneth W., "Institutional Fragmentation and Hazardous Waste Policy: The Case of Texas," in James P. Lester and Ann O'M. Bowman, eds., *The Politics of Hazardous Waste Management* (Durham, NC: Duke University Press, 1983).

Landy, Marc, "Ticking Time Bombs!!! EPA and the Formulation of Superfund," in Helen Ingram and Kenneth Godwin, eds., *Public Policy and the National Environment* (Greenwich, CT: JAI Press, 1985).

Lehman, John, ed., *Hazardous Waste Disposal* (New York: Plenum Press, 1983).

Lester, James P., "Hazardous Waste and Policy Implementation: The Subnational Role," *Hazardous Waste* (Fall 1985).

————, "New Federalism and Environmental Policy," *Publius* (Winter 1986).

————, and Ann O'M. Bowman, eds., *The Politics of Hazardous Waste Management* (Durham, NC: Duke University Press, 1983).

————, James Franke, Ann O'M. Bowman, and Kenneth Kramer, "Hazardous Wastes, Politics, and Public Policy: A Comparative State Analysis," *Western Political Quarterly* (June 1983).

————, and Ann O'M. Bowman, "Subnational Hazardous Waste Policy Implementation: A Test of the Sabatier-Mazmanian Model," Paper delivered at the 1986 Annual Meeting of the American Political Science Association, Washington, DC.

_____, and Michael S. Hamilton, "Intergovernmental Relations and Ocean Policy in the 1980s: The Politics of Policy Change," in Maynard Silva, ed., *National Ocean Policy in the 1980s* (Boulder, CO: Westview Press, 1986).

Levine, Adeline G., *Love Canal: Science, Politics, and People* (Lexington, MA: Lexington Books, 1982).

Lieber, Harvey, "Federalism and Hazardous Waste Policy," in James P. Lester and Ann O'M. Bowman, eds., *The Politics of Hazardous Waste Management* (Durham, NC: Duke University Press, 1983).

Livezey, Emilie Tavel, "Hazardous Waste: A Worldwide Search for Solutions," *Christian Science Monitor* (December 28, 1980).

Mangun, William, "A Comparative Analysis of Hazardous Waste Policy Formulation Efforts among West European Countries," *Policy Studies Journal* (September 1985).

Mann, Dean E., *Environmental Policy Implementation* (Lexington, MA: Lexington Books, 1982).

Marcus, Alfred, *Promise and Performance: Choosing and Implementing an Environmental Policy* (Westport, CT: Greenwood Press, 1980).

Matheny, Albert R. and Bruce A. Williams, "Hazardous Waste Policy in Florida: Is Regulation Possible," in James P. Lester and Ann O'M. Bowman, eds., *The Politics of Hazardous Waste Management* (Durham, NC: Duke University Press, 1983).

_____, "Knowledge vs. NIMBY: Assessing Florida's Strategy for Siting Hazardous Waste Disposal Facilities," *Policy Studies Journal* (September 1985).

Mazmanian, Daniel, and Paul Sabatier, "The Implementation of Public Policy: A Framework for Analysis," *Policy Studies Journal*, vol. 8, Special Issue #2 (1980), p. 548.

_____, *Implementation and Public Policy* (Glenview, IL: Scott, Foresman and Company, 1983).

Minnesota Waste Management Board, *Charting a Course: Public Participation in the Siting of Hazardous Waste Facilities* (Crystal, MN: Waste Management Board, 1981).

Mitchell, Robert, "Public Opinion and Environmental Politics in the 1970s and 1980s," in Norman Vig and Michael Kraft, eds., *Environmental Policy in the 1980s: Reagan's New Agenda* (Washington, DC: CQ Press, 1984).

_____, and Richard Carson, "Property Rights, Protest, and the Siting of Hazardous Waste Facilities," *American Economic Review* (May 1986).

Mitnick, Barry, *The Political Economy of Regulation* (New York: Columbia University Press, 1980).

Montague, Peter, *Four Secure Landfills in New Jersey: A Study of the State of the Art in Shallow Burial Waste Disposal Technology* (Princeton, NJ: Department of Chemical Engineering, Princeton University, 1981.

Morell, David L., and Christopher Magorian, *Siting Hazardous Waste Facilities* (Cambridge, MA: Ballinger, 1982).

Morell, David L., "Technological Policies and Hazardous Waste Politics in California," in James P. Lester and Ann O'M. Bowman, eds., *The Politics of Hazardous Waste Management* (Durham, NC: Duke University Press, 1983).

Mosher, Lawrence, "EPA Still Doesn't Know the Dimensions of the Nation's Hazardous Waste Problem," *National Journal* (April 16, 1983).

Mumme, Stephen, "Dependency and Interdependence in Hazardous Waste Management along the U.S.-Mexico Border," *Policy Studies Journal* (September 1985).

National Conference of State Legislatures, *Hazardous Waste Management: A Survey of State Legislation, 1982* (Denver: NCSL, 1982).

O'Brien, Robert, Michael Clarke, and Sheldon Kamieniecki, "Open and Closed Systems of Decision-Making: The Case of Toxic Waste Management," *Public Administration Review* (July–August 1984).

Office of Technology Assessment, *Technologies and Management Strategies for Hazardous Waste Control* (Washington, DC: OTA, 1983).

O'Hare, Michael, "Not on My Block You Don't: Facility Siting and the Importance of Compensation," *Public Policy* (Fall 1977).

_____, Lawrence Bacow, and Debra Sanderson, *Facility Siting* (New York: Van Nostrand, 1983).

Organization for Economic Cooperation and Development, *Economic Aspects of International Chemicals Control* (Paris: OECD, 1983).

Paparian, Michael, Patricia Wells, and Peter Fearey, *Integrated Hazardous Waste Systems in the Federal Republic of Germany and Denmark* (Sacramento: California Foundation on the Environment and the Economy, 1984).

Piasecki, Bruce, ed., *Beyond Dumping* (Westport, CT: Greenwood Press, 1984).

Pitney, John J., Jr., "Bile Barrel Politics: Siting Unwanted Facilities," *Journal of Policy Analysis and Management*, vol. 3 (Spring 1984), p. 447.

Portney, Kent, "Allaying the NIMBY Syndrome: The Potential for Compensation in Hazardous Waste Treatment Facility Siting," *Hazardous Waste* (Fall 1984).

_____, "The Potential of the Theory of Compensation for Mitigating Public Opposition to Hazardous Waste Treatment Facility Siting: Some Evidence from Five Massachusetts Communities," *Policy Studies Journal* (September 1985).

Powell, John Duncan, "Assault on a Precious Commodity: The Local Struggle to Protect Groundwater," *Policy Studies Journal* (September 1985).

Riley, Richard, "Toxic Substances, Hazardous Wastes, and Public Policy: Problems in Implementation," in James P. Lester and Ann O'M. Bowman, eds., *The Politics of Hazardous Waste Management* (Durham, NC: Duke University Press, 1983).

Ristoratore, Mario, "Siting Toxic Waste Disposal Facilities in Canada and the United States: Problems and Prospects," *Policy Studies Journal* (September 1985).

Rosenbaum, Walter, *Environmental Politics and Policy* (Washington, DC: CQ Press, 1985).

_____, "The Politics of Public Participation in Hazardous Waste Management," in James P. Lester and Ann O'M. Bowman, eds., *The Politics of Hazardous Waste Management* (Durham, NC: Duke University Press, 1983).

Rowland, C. K., and Roger Marz, "Gresham's Law: The Regulatory Analogy," *Policy Studies Review* (November 1981).

_____, and Linda Walton, "Producer Concentration and Hazardous Waste Regulation: An Interstate Comparison," Paper delivered at the 1983 Annual Meeting of the American Political Science Association, Chicago.

_____, and Richard Feiock, "Political and Economic Correlates of Regulatory Commitment: Interstate Variance in Hazardous Waste Regulation," Paper delivered at the 1983 Annual Meeting of the Southern Political Science Association, Birmingham, Alabama.

Russakoff, Dale, "Hill Has Some Withheld EPA Data," *Washington Post* (December 27, 1982), p. A1.

Sabatier, Paul, "An Advocacy Coalition Framework of Policy Change within Subsystems," Paper presented at the 1985 Annual Meeting of the Western Political Science Association, Las Vegas, NV.

_____, and Daniel Mazmanian, "The Implementation of Public Policy: A Framework of Analysis," *Policy Studies Journal*, vol. 8 (1980).

Schnapf, David, "State Hazardous Waste Programs under the Federal Resource Conservation and Recovery Act," *Environmental Law* (1982).

Seferovich, Patrick, "United States Export of Banned Products: Legal and Moral Implications," *Denver Journal of International Law and Policy* (1981).

Senkan, Selim M., and Nancy W. Stauffer, "What to Do with Hazardous Waste," *Technology Review*, vol. 84 (November-December 1981).

Shabecoff, Philip, "EPA Wants to Allow Burial of Barrels of Liquid Wastes," *New York Times* (March 1, 1982).

_____, "U.S. Plan Offered for Cleaning Up Toxic Dump Sites," *New York Times* (March 13, 1982a).

_____, "Rule on Reporting Waste Suspended," *New York Times* (March 15, 1982b).

_____, "U.S. Reversing Stand on Burial of Toxic Liquid," *New York Times* (March 18, 1982c).

Sheehan, Michael, "Economism, Democracy, and Hazardous Wastes: Some Policy Considerations," in Sheldon Kamieniecki, Robert O'Brien, and Michael Clarke, eds., *Controversies in Environmental Policy* (Albany, NY: SUNY Press, 1986).

Shue, Henry, "Exporting Hazards," *Ethics* (July 1982).

Shuman, Eric, "Potentially Hazardous Merchandise: Domestic and International Mechanisms for Consumer Protection," *Vanderbilt Journal of Transnational Law*, vol. 16, no. 2 (1983).

Steeler, J. H., *A Legislator's Guide to Hazardous Waste Management* (Denver, CO: National Conference of State Legislators, 1980).

Susskind, Lawrence, "The Siting Puzzle: Balancing Economic and Environmental Gains and Losses," *Environmental Impact Assessment Review* (June 1985).

Toffner-Clausen, John, "Danish Hazardous Waste System," in John Lehman, ed., *Hazardous Waste Disposal* (New York: Plenum Press, 1983).

"Toxic Waste Program is Being Scuttled," *Audubon Leader*, Vol. 22, No. 24 (December 18, 1981), pp. 1-2.

U.S. Comptroller General, *Hazardous Waste Facilities with Interim Status May Be Endangering Public Health and the Environment* (Washington, DC: General Accounting Office, 1981).

U.S. Environmental Protection Agency, Office of Water and Waste Management, *Everybody's Problem: Hazardous Waste* (Washington, DC: Government Printing Office, 1980).

U.S. Environmental Protection Agency, Office of Water and Waste Management, *Siting of Hazardous Waste Management Facilities and Public Opposition* (Washington, DC: Environmental Protection Agency, 1979).

U.S. House of Representatives, Committee on Interstate and Foreign Commerce, *Hazardous Waste Disposal Report* (Washington, DC: Government Printing Printing Office, 1979).

U.S. House of Representatives, Committee on Interstate and Foreign Commerce, *Hazardous Wate Disposal Report* (Washington, DC: Government Printing Office, 1979).

Van Horn, Carl, and Donald Van Meter, "The Implementation of Intergovernmental Policy," in Charles Jones and Robert Thomas, eds., *Public Policymaking in a Federal System* (Beverly Hills, CA: Sage, 1976).

Vogel, David, *National Styles of Regulation: Environmental Policy in Great Britain and the United States* (Ithaca, NY: Cornell University Press, 1986).

Walter, Benjamin, and Malcolm Getz, "Social and Economic Effects of Toxic Waste Disposal," in Sheldon Kamieniecki, Robert O'Brien, and Michael Clarke, eds., *Controversies in Environmental Policy* (Albany, NY: SUNY Press, 1986).

Weir, David, and Mark Schapiro, *Circle of Poison: Pesticides and People in a Hungry World* (San Francisco: Institute for Food and Development Policy, 1981).

Wells, Donald, "Site Control of Hazardous Waste Facilities," *Policy Studies Review* (May 1982).

Williams, Bruce A., and Albert R. Matheny, "Assessing the Assessors: Hazardous Waste Regulation in Florida," A Paper Prepared for Delivery at the 1981 Annual Meeting of the Midwest Political Science Association, Chicago, Illinois, April 22-24.

_____, "Hazardous Waste Policy in Florida: Is Regulation Possible?" in James P. Lester and Ann O'M. Bowman, eds., *The Politics of Hazardous Waste Management* (Durham, NC: Duke University Press, 1983).

_____, "Testing Theories of Social Regulation: Hazardous Waste Regulation in the American States," *Journal of Politics* (May 1984).

Wolbeck, Bernd, "Political Dimensions and Implications of Hazardous Waste Disposal," in John Lehman, ed., *Hazardous Waste Disposal* (New York: Plenum Press, 1983).

Worthley, John A., and Richard Torkelson, "Managing the Toxic Waste Problem: Lessons from the Love Canal," *Administration and Society*, vol. 13 (1981).

_____, "Intergovernmental and Public-Private Sector Relations in Hazardous Waste Management: The New York Example," in James P. Lester and Ann O'M. Bowman, *The Politics of Hazardous Waste Management* (Durham, NC: Duke University Press, 1983).

Wurth-Hough, Sandra, "Chemical Contamination and Governmental Policy-making: The North Carolina Experience," *State and Local Governmental Review* (May 1982).

PART I

THE LOCAL LEVEL

2

Rethinking Participation: Assessing Florida's Strategy for Siting Hazardous Waste Disposal Facilities

Albert R. Matheny and Bruce A. Williams

INTRODUCTION

The most enduring political problem in hazardous waste management is the siting of hazardous waste disposal facilities (O'Hare et al., 1983). The problem is political because a series of interrelated conflicts ultimately depend upon the siting issue for their resolution (Hadden et al., 1983). First is the conflict over the scope of regulation, joined by the public and private sectors. Second is intergovernmental conflict—problems of coordinating the regulatory efforts of federal, state, and local government. Failure to resolve conflicts at these levels exacerbates a third conflict: between individuals and communities over the distribution of risks, costs, and benefits associated with choosing a hazardous waste disposal facility (HWDF) site. For an affected population, siting concentrates risks and costs borne by a small segment of the population (typically residents near the site and local governments providing services for the site) and diffuses benefits among the remainder of the population. Risk-cost-benefit redistribution of this sort creates strong incentives for the risk-bearing population—an intense minority—to resist HWDF siting, while the remaining population is benefited only diffusely in the short run and therefore has no overwhelming counterincentive to force the siting decision upon the risk-bearing minority. As a result, nothing happens, and the urgency of the disposal problem grows unabated, thus increasing its risks and costs for the entire population in the long run. This political stalemate is often referred to as the NIMBY syndrome (for "not in my backyard").

Hadden et al. (1983: 197-198) argue that the interaction of these three conflicts combines with scientific uncertainties surrounding disposal technologies and produces classic conditions for the operation of Lowi's (1979) "interest-group liberalism" within state legislatures. As a result, many state legislatures delegate policymaking authority to administrative agencies, along with elaborate decision-making procedures and extensive provisions for public participation. According to Lowi, this preoccupation with procedural democracy enables the legislature to avoid making substantive political choices. Not only is the legislature delegating its political authority to the administrative agencies, but it is also delegating its representative function, so that "public participation" becomes a ubiquitous feature of agency mandates, appearing wherever conflicts are too intense for the legislature to resolve.

Passage of a siting law is itself an indication that the intensity of these conflicts had reached the critical point at which some political action was necessary. However, the difficulty of resolving the conflicts has led many states to pass complex, process-dominated siting laws. (Hadden et al., 1983: 209)

In fairness to the states, it must be said that they are effectively the victims of interest-group liberalism at higher levels of government. The federal Resource Conservation and Recovery Act of 1976 (RCRA) delegates much of the responsibility for regulating hazardous wastes to the states, leaving oversight to the federal Environmental Protection Agency (EPA). In particular, RCRA requires public participation in HWDF siting. In fulfilling this requirement, the EPA's definition of public participation once included engaging the public from "the beginning of facility planning . . . through the site selection and approval process. It should be accompanied by a broad-scale public education effort, since the public needs to be a knowledgeable partner in site selection decisions" (Costle, 1980: 7). Since the issuance of that statement, the EPA's approach toward public participation has changed dramatically (Rosenbaum, 1983), and the states have been left on their own to develop siting strategies to accommodate intense public interest in the hazardous waste issue and to combat the common perception that government has often failed to regulate hazardous wastes effectively (O'Brien et al., 1984; Elliott, 1984).

The public participation mandate has created problems for states in drafting siting legislation and in actually siting HWDFs for two closely related reasons. First, state HWDF siting has been unsuccessful because the NIMBY syndrome has replaced traditional public acquiescence regarding environmental policy. Second, the nature of "public participation" implied in state HWDF siting laws remains uninspired by any meaningful notion of democratic decision making.

For participatory processes to be meaningful in state policymaking, legislators must approach their design on both theoretical and practical levels, with one eye on democratic theory and the other on the potential problems posed by the structural realities of the policy involved. Such an enlightened approach to designing processes for siting HWDFs is particularly problematic—from theoretical and practical perspectives—because the issue lies at the nexus of what Alford and Friedland (1985) call democratic, managerial, and capitalist views of the state:

1. HWDF siting involves the maintenance of *capitalist* modes of production insofar as it attempts to remedy failures of the unchecked market to dispose of hazardous waste safely.
2. It concerns the *managerial* function of the state because the issue involves technical and scientific expertise, housed in public and private bureaucracies.
3. Most importantly, it invokes debate over *democratic* visions of the state as citizens and their elected representatives are called upon to make or ratify potentially risky decisions without clear-cut criteria for siting HWDFs.

We contend that in order to solve the NIMBY problem states must find new ways of addressing the participation problem. Florida has devised a strategy to overcome NIMBY through a statewide education program aimed at promoting public acceptance of government's handling of the hazardous waste problem. We examine this strategy, its partial implementation with the innovative "Amnesty Days" program, and the likelihood of its overall success in solving the siting stalemate. As a prelude to evaluating Florida's siting strategy, this article explores the issue of public participation in HWDF siting in the larger context of democratic theory.

SITING AND DEMOCRACY

Florida's innovative strategy should be placed in theoretical and empirical context before its chances of success are evaluated. In general, state siting programs vary along a dimension ranging from state-initiated, "proactive" siting to local-initiated, "reactive" siting (Hadden et al., 1983: 205). We refer to the extremes on this dimension as the *comprehensive* strategy versus the *case-by-case* strategy, respectively. As part of a more extensive study (Williams and Matheny, 1984), we have examined the siting programs of New Jersey and Ohio, finding the former in line with the comprehensive strategy and the latter conforming to the case-by-case approach. Each strategy and its problems are briefly described below.

New Jersey employs a centralized planning process using a blue-ribbon panel (the Hazardous Waste Siting Commission) made up of state environmental, industrial, and political leaders and experts. They analyze the state's hydrogeology, industry, and patterns of residence in order to determine the "best" sites for HWDFs in the state. Hearings are then held around the state to determine the suitability of these preselected sites, and finally, waste disposal firms are allowed to bid on specific sites. The assumption underlying this approach appears to be that siting decisions are inherently complex and scientific and thus should be based upon technical expertise in order to serve the public interest. The primary problem with this approach is that the designation of preferred sites is determined at the state rather than the local level, and local neighborhood and environmental groups in the state seem to have become skeptical of the panel's designation process precisely because of its heavily technical emphasis and the removal of the preliminary decision-making process from the affected localities. Apart from these considerations, the process is enormously time-consuming and tends, as a result, to alienate industry (including both waste generators and waste disposers).

Ohio's case-by-case strategy essentially allows for an expanded review of private disposal industry site applications before a special siting board (the Hazardous Waste Facility Approval Board). This process specifically involves the localities, but residents often feel that industry initiative in choosing sites causes only politically vulnerable (i.e., unorganized) areas to be targeted. As a result, public participation may be less than effective in conveying community concerns. The process in Ohio produced quick results (a major HWDF near Cincinnati, for example), but the initial advantages of speed and flexibility have traded on the built-in assumption of the case-by-case strategy: "too much" public participation leads to public rejection of proposed sites. Since the initial successes, these advantages have been lost, and in Ohio the public has become mobilized by a statewide network of local HWDF opponents. In the process, the legitimacy of the Ohio siting program has been severely damaged (cf. Kraft and Kraut, 1985).

The New Jersey and Ohio siting experiences indicate in different ways the breakdown of public participation strategies built into their HWDF siting laws, and prevalent in state HWDF siting laws generally. To understand why this breakdown has occurred, it is useful to reflect upon how governments approach the subject of public participation in administrative decision making. While such an inquiry might be hopelessly broad, the contributions of Shapiro (1982) make our inquiry both theoretically oriented and practically relevant. First, it should be understood that prevailing notions of public participation in administrative decision making are practically defined by judicial review of agency action. Shapiro argues persuasively that the doctrines of administrative law which emerge from judicial review of agency action are actually "the legal institutionalization of political theories . . . [and] not the political theory of court-agency relations but the more general theory of the liberal democratic polity" (Shapiro, 1982: 18). Accordingly, progressive theories of democracy, which emphasized the technical calculation of the "public interest" by experts, eventually led the courts to defer to agency expertise in reviewing administrative decisions during the decades of the 1940s and 1950s, thus minimizing the impact of public participation on agency decisions. Pluralist theories of democracy eventually developed to challenge the progressive approach (see Williams and Matheny, 1986). Under pluralist assumptions, a "good or 'public-interest-oriented policy was no longer defined as a technically correct policy designed by experts but as any policy that was the product of a decision-making process to which all the relevant groups had appropriate access" (Shapiro, 1982: 20).

Administrative law followed suit during the 1960s and 1970s, by expanding public access to agency decisions and by forcing agencies to ground their decisions upon ever more intricate procedural requirements aimed at respecting public input. These developments "constitute one long hymn to group access and to the underlying theme of procedural rationality. The true test of the rationality of a government policy is not its substance but whether or not it is the product of groups interacting with one another and with government" (Shapiro, 1982: 21). Shapiro's argument further applies to the administrative law of the 1980s and beyond, but its relevance for our inquiry should be obvious. Because judicial doctrines of administrative law are instrumental in the way agencies define their decision-making processes, public participation in administrative government has been conventionally viewed within the confines of the two versions of democratic theory already described by Shapiro. These competing views of democracy provide inspiration for the comprehensive and case-by-case HWDF siting strategies, as illustrated in New Jersey and Ohio, respectively. But if the experiences of these two states are generalizable to other states' siting problems, then the democratic underpinnings of their approaches deserve special scrutiny. We question whether either view is sufficient to produce meaningful public participation in the siting of HWDFs.

It may be that New Jersey's and Ohio's strategies have not met with success (and may have encouraged the NIMBY syndrome) because they delegitimize the HWDF siting process in the public's eyes. Essentially, we argue that existing efforts to promote public participation in the siting process, while guided by current standards of administrative law, are misguided in their assumptions about connections between public participation, political legitimacy, and democratic decision making. Typically, public participation in regulatory decisions had been either overwhelmed by expertise or buried in procedure, without regard for the substance of agency action. The latter problem echoes Lowi's (1979) condemnation of "interest-group liberalism," mentioned earlier in reference to HDWF siting (Hadden et al., 1983). But the former problem requires some more probing to clarify our point.

Our criticism focuses on structuring state siting processes in ways more consistent with or more sensitive to a range of democratic values. First, we consider the degree to which HWDF siting decisions involve *conflict* as opposed to *common concerns* among the parties to a siting dispute. As a point of departure for our critique, we turn to research conducted by

Mansbridge (1980) in which she distinguishes between "unitary" and "adversary" democracy. Adversary democracy assumes that legitimate decision making is the product of the equal representation of conflicting interests and is the hallmark of Shapiro's "pluralist" standard of judicial review of administrative actions like siting decisions. Less popular is the notion of unitary democracy, which stresses consensus as the basis for legitimate decision making. The former vision of democracy presumes that *selfish* interests can be aggregated into a substitute for some inestimable "public interest," while the latter identifies and attempts to embody an existing public interest growing out of a community of values and *shared* interests which encompass the population of those affected by political decisions.

Mansbridge's point is that some types of political decisions can be settled more legitimately using procedures inspired by adversary democracy, while others can be better solved through the process of unitary democracy. Where political decisions have redistributive consequences (clear winners and losers), the appropriate forum for making those decisions is an adversarial one which ensures that all interests are fairly represented, and the legitimacy of the result is determined by who has the votes rather than whether or not the "correct" solution is chosen. Unitary democracy assumes that a "correct" answer can be found to benefit all parties and, thus, emphasizes the comprehensiveness of *information* in the decision-making process (so that all relevant alternatives may be examined before choosing the "best" one to achieve a consensual goal) rather than the comprehensiveness of representation. Under unitary democracy, choice is a calculation following consent; under adversary democracy, it is a struggle.

Our argument is that hazardous waste policy in the United States is the product of inappropriate democratic processes, applied at different levels of decision making in the federal system. As a result, hazardous waste policy in general and HWDF siting decisions in particular are considered illegitimate by the public. As noted above, "interest-group liberalism" accounts for the general tendency of the legislative and executive branches to avoid difficult policy decisions by delegating them to administrative agencies. Characteristically, Congress, an "adversarial arena" designed ostensibly for making redistributive decisions, avoided making hard choices in passing RCRA by delegating political (i.e., redistributive) decision-making authority to the EPA. The EPA, for its part, stresses scientific and technical information in making its decisions and might ideally pursue a unitary process, although Mansbridge almost certainly did not intend *unitary democracy* to describe agency decision making. But if we may substitute predetermined political goals for political goals agreed upon by consensus, then the logic of unitary democracy applies to technical decision making. Ideally, the "political goals" of the EPA are identified by Congress through adversary means. But because it must make delegated redistributive decisions with unitary procedures, the EPA's conclusions are often (and accurately) viewed as political decisions cloaked in technical language (see Matheny and Williams, 1984; Williams and Matheny, 1983), particularly by those left out of the decision-making process. This can only complicate the agency's task of deciding technical issues made all the more difficult by incomplete or controversial scientific data.

A similar pattern has occurred at the state level, with state legislatures (adversary arenas) delegating redistributive decisions to state environmental agencies (unitary arenas). The residue of illegitimacy accumulates and is manifested in HWDF siting processes, where redistributive and technical issues collide. Since the choice of HWDF sites in a state is clearly a redistributive decision, equal representation of all interests in the affected population is essential for legitimate decision making. This is an obvious point, yet, in many cases, siting has been "successful" only when the process has ignored certain groups, such as poor and unorganized interests (U.S. GAO, 1983). In contrast, "too much" public participation may lead to the delay or vetoing of HWDF siting, even in the face of clear technical evidence supporting the need for HWDFs (Rosenbaum, 1983: 191-193). According to Rosenbaum, agencies caught up in the frustrations of NIMBY, sometimes retreat from public participation in siting decisions.

Some states appear to believe that "public participation" consists largely of informing the public about hazardous waste issues rather than soliciting public opinions and responding to them through policy formulation. It was this that EPA's consultants had in mind when they noted that among the states they studied . . . the tendency was to keep the public from providing "substantive input to technical and non-technical aspects of governmental decision-making" on hazardous waste. (Rosenbaum, 1983: 194; citing Centaur Associates, 1979: iv)

The wisdom of such a strategy seems questionable, if, as our argument asserts, the roots of NIMBY are in the failure of meaningful public participation. The states' dilemma is one caused by constrained choices among conventional democratic alternatives. In designing their siting processes, states have tended to emphasize either representation (e.g., public hearings or local veto) or information (i.e., technical expertise), without disentangling the redistributive and technical issues and assigning them to their appropriate decision-making processes. In fact, this separation is impossible.

The combination of unresolved redistributive (political) issues and scientific uncertainties surrounding the effects of hazardous wastes and their disposal technologies renders both adversary and unitary processes inappropriate for legitimate decision making. Another form of decision making must be developed to accommodate political indecision and technical indeterminacy. Since conventional approaches to democratic decision making have failed us, we turn to a vision of democracy which attacks conventional democratic theory as a possible inspiration for an alternate HWDF siting strategy.

STRONG PARTICIPATION

After developing a thoroughgoing critique of liberal democratic theory in its various forms, Barber (1984) suggests what he calls "strong democracy" in answer to the "conditions of politics," which include "a necessity for public action, and thus for reasonable public choice, in the presence of conflict and in the absence of private or independent grounds for judgment" (Barber, 1984: 120, emphasis deleted). These conditions seem promisingly similar to the dilemma facing the states in the siting of HWDFs. Barber's response to these conditions is even more promising.

[S]trong democracy is politics in the participatory mode where conflict is resolved in the absence of an independent ground through a participatory process of ongoing, proximate self-legislation and the creation of a political community capable of transforming dependent, private individuals into free citizens and partial and private interests into public goods. (Barber, 1984: 132, emphasis deleted)

Despite the flourish with which he introduces "strong democracy," Barber has some very concrete recommendations which simultaneously avoid the weaknesses of liberal democracy and ensure what he describes as legitimate, democratic governance. Relying heavily upon the democratic visions of Rousseau and Dewey, Barber details a theory which emphasizes *citizenship* and *community* as the basis for governance. They key to citizenship is education that goes beyond self-interest and transforms the "masses" into effective political actors (Barber, 1984: 154) who appreciate the public good. Citizens then act (or better, interact) through *participation* in community. "To participate *is* to create a community that governs itself, and to create self-governing community *is* to participate" (Barber, 1984: 155).

With this brief introduction to Barber's theory, we can focus on two aspects of legitimate decision making neglected in the conventional democratic theories underlying HWDF siting strategies. First, they generally assume that the public is too ignorant to understand the technical aspects of hazardous waste or its proper disposal (thus deferring to expert siting decisions). Second, they generally consider the interests involved in siting disputes to be necessarily antagonistic, such that, once a decision is made, values are permanently redistributed: winners and losers determined forever. The latter are comforted solely by the knowledge that they have had a "fair hearing."

Barber's "strong democracy" suggests two strategies to remedy the problems of the conventional approaches. First, substantive education for the affected public about hazardous waste, its long-term risks, and its safe disposal alternatives could conceivably bring the public's awareness of the issue beyond the NIMBY consciousness by engendering trust in those near the HWDF site and by mobilizing the rest of the indifferent public toward a realization of the long-term consequences of neglecting the problem. A by-product of such an educational effort might be an increasing public aware-ness of the technical complexities and uncertainties surrounding hazardous waste and its proper disposal. Second, the interests of the community surrounding a sited HWDF and the interests of the facility operator (whether public or private) need to be made compatible rather than competitive. In a sense, these adversaries need to be drawn into a "community of interest" in the operation of the facility, accomplished, perhaps, through joint management of the facility.[1] Attempting these proposals would invigorate public participation beyond its current token or negative presence in administrative government to a level of true public *involvement*.

However imperfectly, these two suggestions begin to address the en-tangled issues of technical uncertainty and redistributive politics plaguing HWDF siting. These suggestions have not, to our knowledge, been seriously pursued together in state HWDF siting processes, perhaps because of their preoccupation with satisfying conventional standards of democracy and judicial review in structuring their processes. Florida's strategy for HWDF siting addresses the first suggestion and represents a significant departure from other state siting processes. In the following sections of this article, we examine Florida's new program and discuss how it might accommodate aspects of "strong democracy" relevant to our second suggestion.

HWDF SITING IN FLORIDA: EDUCATION AND "AMNESTY DAYS"

In June 1983, the Florida legislature passed the Water Quality Assurance Act, a comprehensive bill representing state government's attempt to deal with the impact of Florida's phenomenal growth on the state's threatened water supply. A major portion of that bill (Part VI) was devoted to restruc-turing the state's existing hazardous waste regulation program, and particu-larly its HWDF siting process, which had proved woefully ineffective. That process contained a virtual local veto, and, as a result, facility operators never seriously pursued HWDF siting, nor were any permitted facilities operating anywhere in the state. The new siting provisions of Part VI were a remarkably consistent response to the problems in the old law. From its inception, clearly articulated assumptions guided the crafting of the new provisions:

1. Citizens fear the siting of HWDFs without appreciating that without them haz-ardous waste will be disposed of illegally and at comparatively greater risk to the locality.

2. Citizens do not believe that state government can handle safely the regulation of HWDFs.

3. Citizens thus resist local siting of HWDFs.

4. If citizens could be shown the extent of the local hazardous waste problem and if, simultaneously, state government could demonstrate its capacity to deal with such wastes safely, then citizens would be less resistant to facility siting in their localities.

5. Encouraged by accurate information about demand for HWDFs and by a more receptive local populace, facility operators would attempt to site facilities, and these attempts would be more likely to succeed.

In order to implement this strategy, the legislation required a small-quantity waste generator notification program, a hazardous waste survey and needs assessment, county-by-county hazardous waste storage facility area designation, and region-by-region facility site selection. All of these are being funded and implemented over a three-year period, beginning with the most populous regions in 1984 and covering progressively less populous regions in 1985, 1986, and 1987. In addition, the new siting strategy was bolstered by a revised facilities siting process which diminishes the possibility of local veto and enhances regional and state participation in siting decisions. While significant delay has occurred in the implementation of these programs, they remain funded, intact, and slightly expanded as of this writing.

The clear gamble in the new legislation is the state's attempt to raise public awareness of the hazardous waste problem to the point where citizens and industry alike can appreciate it as a shared concern. The state runs the risk of stirring a quiescent public to a level of negative awareness (NIMBY) and losing the chance to site HWDFs anywhere in the state. It is a gamble of knowledge versus NIMBY, and effective education is the key.

The primary educational vehicle in the state's new siting strategy is the "Amnesty Days" program. In this state-funded scheme, a privately operated mobile storage and transfer facility travels to different regions of the state and collects small quantities of hazardous waste from citizens, small businesses, schools, and local governments on a one-time-only, free, and no-questions-asked basis. The wastes are analyzed on-site and then shipped out of state for proper disposal.

The first phase of Amnesty Days ran simultaneously with the first phase of the notification and needs assessment programs in the densely populated and heavily industrialized areas of the state (the Tampa Bay, Miami, Orlando, and Jacksonville regions). Local media in these regions were encouraged to publicize Amnesty Days by the Office of Public Information in Florida's Department of Environmental Regulation (DER), which is charged with administering the new legislation. Press releases, radio and television spots, newspaper advertisements, inserts in utility bills, and a toll-free hotline were provided to inform the public. At the end of the first phase, Amnesty Days was considered a success. It cost the state roughly $800,000 (Burke, 1984). The mobile collection facility visited thirty-seven different sites in twenty-one counties and gathered nearly 610,000 pounds of hazardous wastes from approximately 6,500 contributors (DER, 1984). More than 80% of these sources were private households (Malkin, 1984). When participants brought wastes into the collection centers, they were given surveys to fill out (to be analyzed by DER) and extensive information on proper hazardous waste disposal. Interestingly, the rate of participation in Amnesty Days, which exceeded expectations throughout its first phase, actually increased over time, even though the mobile collection facility moved from more densely populated regions to less densely populated regions as the first phase progressed.

As of January 1987, Amnesty Days has visited all but ten of Florida's sixty-seven counties, with those remaining to be covered in May 1987. The program has gathered nearly 1.5 million pounds of hazardous wastes from nearly 11,000 participants, 78% of whom were private citizens disposing of hazardous household products (mostly old paint and pesticides).[2] Local press coverage of the various Amnesty Days visits has been remarkably thorough in both rural and urban areas. The statewide Amnesty Days toll-free hotline is averaging about twenty-five calls per day, and owing to state-sponsored workshops and media coverage, there is growing awareness among citizens and local governments of waste recycling and exchange possibilities, according to DER. In addition, the state legislature amended the Water Quality Assurance Act in 1985, making available temporary $50,000 grants to counties for establishing local hazardous waste transfer stations.

It is still too early to determine whether or not Amnesty Days has had a positive effect on public attitudes toward HWDF *siting*. County storage facility area designation is still underway as of this writing. When interviewed in November 1983, DER officials implied that regional planning councils and counties would assume responsibility for planning public education and participation campaigns beyond DER's Amnesty Days effort. But when contacted later in the implementation process (1984), regional and county officials in charge of implementing the new legislation in their jurisdictions gave vague and unsystematic responses to questions about their plans for public involvement. Since then, the state (DER) has taken a leadersahip role in the educational aspects of HWDF siting. Despite the state's efforts, the educational program is slated to end following the last collection operation in May 1987, although DER is lobbying to keep this program alive.

If Florida's new siting strategy is to succeed, the problem of continuing public education about hazardous waste disposal must be addressed by the state legislature. The public goodwill potentially generated by a successful

Amnesty Days program may be lost if consistent follow-up activities are not implemented. In our judgment, correcting this problem will not be sufficient to ensure successful HWDF siting. There are other problems with Florida's siting strategy which are not directly associated with its innovative educational efforts. These deal with public participation in the management of HWDFs once they have been sited.

PUBLIC PARTICIPATION VERSUS PUBLIC INVOLVEMENT

Perhaps, as Florida's strategy assumes, public education can address the problem of legitimacy in HWDF siting insofar as public participation in siting decisions is an adversary phenomenon. But we contend that successful siting is a two-stage process of public involvement, inspired by Barber's (1984) "strong democracy." Public participation deals only with the first, or redistributive, stage. The second stage of the process goes beyond education about the decision to site an HWDF and involves the prospect of the *legitimate operation* of the HWDF, once it is sited. Most of the literature on siting has ignored the public's concern over management questions surrounding HWDFs, focusing instead on siting politics (e.g., fair hearings) or technical issues (e.g., site-related risk prediction and prevention). Yet a recent study by Elliott (1984) indicates that a key element in establishing an acceptable HWDF site is *community control* of the facility, with an emphasis on risk detection and mitigation, rather than risk prediction and prevention. Public trust is the issue here—trust that facilities are run in the community's interest (Greenberg and Anderson, 1984)—and we believe that this requires procedures which foster citizen participation in the management of such facilities. We argue that the issue of public trust and second-stage legitimacy follows closely the tenets of "strong democracy."

A discussion of Elliott's findings lends support to our argument. He designed a simulation in which community representatives likely to be involved in HWDF siting decisions were confronted with proposals from three mythical waste management companies and asked to rank them in preference order. All three proposals involved the same site and equivalent expenditures. Two companies stressed technological approaches to risk management—one emphasizing advanced risk prevention technology, and the other stressing advanced risk detection technology. The third company ("Environmental Management Incorporated," or EMI), in Elliott's words,

argued that the risks of hazardous waste treatment developed not so much because of inadequate technology, but because of less-than-ideal management practices. They offered to open the operations of the company to public scrutiny and to subject safety decisions to community review. The core of their proposal was a safety board on which community residents would sit. The board would oversee the safety of the plant, manage its own annual budget for making improvements, and have emergency powers should hazards develop. The facility and its records would be inspected by an engineer hired by the town. Payments would be made to the town fire department so that it would have the specialized equipment and training to cope with emergencies. Agreements on how to resolve disputes would also stipulate the creation of emergency action trust funds to ensure the availability of necessary funds. Finally, EMI indicated that it would own all delivery trucks, specifying the routes they could travel and the hours they could operate. By carefully attending to issues of liability, accessibility and open management, Environmental Management offered reassurances that no shortcuts would be taken that might undermine the safety of the plant. (Elliott, 1984: 399-400)

While Elliott mentions several interesting findings about the community respondents and their preference orderings, the one most important for our concerns is that nearly half (48%) preferred EMI's proposal to the more technological proposals, and the least preferred (61%) of all proposals was the risk prevention option. This indicates to us that second-stage legitimacy in HWDF siting is largely a matter of community *involvement* in management rather than the *delegation* of management to experts. The incentives of the facilty operator typically contradict this community sentiment.

The risks that the firm seeks to minimize, however, are not the same risks that a potential host community might want to minimize. The incentives for the sponsoring firm to limit its own uncertainty help explain why discussion is [so often] restricted to technological alternatives. By restricting the debate to issues of technology, the firm can isolate a whole range of risk related issues from public scrutiny. . . . The firm retains control over its future and precludes the town from shifting uncertainty back onto the firm. (Elliott, 1984: 404)

The key to legitimacy under these conditions is the structuring of facility management to conform to the dictates of "strong democracy," with residents and facility operators developing a *shared* interest in the safe disposal of hazardous wastes. Elliott calls this the "coproduction of safety" (Elliott, 1984: 408). The emphasis is on openness, access to information, and adaptation, undergirded by extensive liability provisions unifying the facility operator's interest in safety with that of the community, effectively forging that "community of interests" mentioned earlier as crucial to legitimate HWDF siting. While the risks faced by the surrounding community may not actually be reduced by joint management of the facility, the community will have, in a sense, *shifted* its perception of the risks from an "involuntary" to a "voluntary" consciousness. Such a shift is crucial to overcoming the NIMBY syndrome, if we are to believe the Fischhoff et al. (1981) finding that public perceptions of voluntary risks are apparently much lower than those of equal involuntary risks.

It should be noted here that the notion of public involvement, as opposed to mere public participation, carries with it the "populist" spirit that inspires much of Barber's (1984) "strong democracy." Joint management of HWDFs means directly involving those members of the community who are affected most by the operation of the site. These are the "citizens" whose education is so crucial to combating NIMBY and whose actions will determine the success of any joint management scheme. Often, in situations of administrative stalemate like the HWDF siting dilemma, the use of environmental mediation or regulatory negotiation are suggested as solutions. While these suggestions should not be automatically excluded from the decision-making process, the tasks of citizenship should not be delegated wholesale to an elite of experts. These are essentially "corporatist" strategies of administrative decision making, too far removed from the citizens who must bear the burdens of HWDF siting decisions. The issues of siting and management must be addressed at the grass roots for a public involvement strategy to work.

CONCLUSION

With their emphasis on technical complexity and conflicting interests, conventional public participation strategies cannot comprehend the community's desire to seek control of its own future, nor can they adjust the facility operator's incentive to escape responsibility for that future. States have ignored the possibility that the siting process itself can affect the public's perception of how siting decisions are produced and how their relative risks are affected. As a result, only part of the NIMBY syndrome is being addressed in state HWDF siting programs. Participation and education are important, but together they cannot overcome the part of the syndrome that is ignored.

While it is still too early to evaluate fully Florida's attempts to address the NIMBY syndrome, we have specified a dual logic of public involvement which provides useful criteria for judging Florida's efforts in the future. Given more time and greater funding, the public education campaign required by the Water Quality Assurance Act of 1983 and implemented through Amnesty Days, small-quantity generator notification, and needs assessment programs potentially creates an informed public that can participate intelligently in siting decisions. Such participation can satisfy our requirement of educating the citizenry about HWDF siting and, thus, can contribute some legitimacy to Florida's siting process.

But Florida's and other states' siting plans fall short by ignoring the other aspect of public involvement. Without clearly identified structures for community control of HWDFs and without strong measures to ensure facility operators' responsibilities, a shared interest in safe hazardous waste disposal cannot emerge, and, therefore, an important piece of the legitimacy puzzle is missing. Without it, in our judgment, HWDF siting will continue to be resisted at the local level or, if not resisted, then resented by those who must bear the increased risks. Such resentment (expressed, for example, in declining property values surrounding HWDF sites) can only have a cumulative effect, leading other communities to resist siting efforts even more strenuously. Were structures of public involvement to be developed, community resistance and resentment might diminish, and the cumulative effect would work in the opposite direction, encouraging other communities to avoid the risks of illegal dumping by confronting their hazardous waste problems with safe disposal techniques and responsible facility management.

NOTES

1. Making a moral appeal to the facility operator's sense of community might be one way to achieve this, but a more realistic approach would be to build strict liability provisions into the facility's charter, requiring operators to assume *any* liability for damages upon the establishment of a prima facie case of contamination, and thus forcing the operator to share in the fate of the community. Unfortunately, one state's (Minnesota's) effort to establish strict liability for facility operators in the case of accidents met with such resistance from insurers that the effort was abandoned. This case suggests that a more appropriate arena for such liability legislation might be the federal government, perhaps using a federal insurance scheme. Federal courts have already taken the lead in tightening liability standards on hazardous waste generators and disposers in their interpretation of the Superfund act, applying both strict and "joint and several liability" standards to defendants in many hazardous waste cleanup cases (Grunbaum, 1985).

2. To place these results in perspective, roughly 0.1% of Florida's population deposited roughly 0.1% of the hazardous wastes generated annually in Florida! Of course, the primary purpose of Amnesty Days is not to solve the hazardous waste problem, but to educate the public about responsible, governmentally managed hazardous waste disposal.

REFERENCES

Alford, Robert R., and Roger Friedland, *Powers of Theory: Capitalism, the State, and Democracy* (Cambridge: Cambridge University Press, 1985).

Barber, Benjamin R. *Strong Democracy: Participatory Politics for a New Age* (Berkeley: University of California Press, 1984).

Burke, Tony, "Kirkpatrick Discusses Waste Hunt," *Gainesville Sun* (November 11, 1984), 1A.

Centaur Associates, Inc., *Siting of Hazardous Waste Management Facilities and Public Opposition* (Washington, DC: U.S. Environmental Protection Agency, 1979), doc. no. SW-809.

Costle, Douglas, Memorandum to State Governors (Washington, DC: U.S. Environmental Protection Agency, July 23, 1980), 7.

DER, "Participants Turn in 610,000 Pounds of Hazardous Waste during First Year of Collection Program," *Florida's Environmental News* 7 (1984) 5: 2.

Elliott, Michael L. Poirier, "Improving Community Acceptance of Hazardous Waste Facilities through Alternative Systems for Mitigating and Managing Risk," *Hazardous Waste* 1 (1984): 397-410.

Fischhoff, Baruch, et al., *Acceptable Risk* (New York: Cambridge University Press, 1981).

Greenberg, Michael R., and Anderson, Richard F., *Hazardous Waste Sites: The Credibility Gap* (New Brunswick, NJ: Center for Urban Policy Research, 1984).

Grunbaum, Werner F., "Developing a Uniform Federal Common Law for Hazardous Waste Liability," *Policy Studies Journal* 14 (1985): 132-139.

Hadden, Susan G., et al., "State Roles in Siting Hazardous Waste Disposal Facilities: From State Preemption to Local Veto," in James P. Lester and Ann O'M. Bowman, eds., *The Politics of Hazardous Waste Management* (Durham, NC: Duke University Press, 1983), 196-211.

Kraft, Michael E., and Ruth Kraut, "The Impact of Citizen Participation on Hazardous Waste Policy Implementation: The Case of Clermont County, Ohio," *Policy Studies Journal* 14 (1985): 52-61.

Lowi, Theodore J., *The End of Liberalism*, 2d ed. (New York: W. W. Norton, 1979).

Malkin, Jonathan, "Amnesty Days Praise Echoing a Week Later," *Gainesville Sun* (November 24, 1984), 1C.

Matheny, Albert R., and Bruce A. Williams, "Regulation, Risk Assessment, and the Supreme Court: The Case of OSHA's Cancer Policy," *Law & Policy* 6 (1984): 425-449.

Mansbridge, Jane J., *Beyond Adversary Democracy* (New York: Basic Books, 1980).

O'Brien, Robert M., et al., "Open and Closed Systems of Decision Making: The Case of Toxic Waste Management," *Public Administration Review* 44 (1984): 334-340.

O'Hare, Michael, et al., *Facility Siting* (New York: Van Nostrand, 1983).

Rosenbaum, Walter A., "The Politics of Public Participation in Hazardous Waste Management," in James P. Lester and Ann O'M. Bowman, eds., *The Politics of Hazardous Waste Management* (Durham, NC: Duke University Press, 1983): 176-195.

Shapiro, Martin, "On Predicting the Future of Administrative Law," *Regulation* (May–June 1982): 18-25.

U.S. GAO, Siting of Hazardous Waste Landfills and Their Correlation with Racial and Economic Status of Surrounding Communities (Washington, DC: U.S. General Accounting Office, June 1, 1983).

Williams, Bruce A., and Albert R. Matheny, "Hazardous Waste Policy in Florida: Is Regulation Possible?" in James P. Lester and Ann O'M. Bowman, eds., *The Politics of Hazardous Waste Management* (Durham, NC: Duke University Press, 1983), 74-101.

_____, "Testing Theories of Social Regulation: Hazardous Waste Regulation in the American States," *Journal of Politics* 46 (1984): 428-458.

_____, *Regulation and the Search for the Public Interest* (unpublished manuscript in progress 1986).

3

The Role of Economic Factors in Lay Perceptions of Risk

Kent E. Portney

One of the important questions that states are apparently feeling an increasing need to address is how to deal with the disposal of substances produced by industry which are known to be hazardous and toxic. State governments are increasingly becoming aware that the methods of the past, largely confined to unregulated landfills, simply defer the day when the substances must be dealt with. Yet at the same time, the general public has grown to distrust attempts to find ways, new and old, of disposing of such substances. Indeed, the opposition of the general public to siting facilities is so pervasive that it now bears the label of a social malady: the not-in-my-backyard (NIMBY) syndrome (Amour, 1984). Underlying much of the NIMBY syndrome is a thought process which people use to estimate the benefits and risks of accepting different siting proposals. This thought process results in what are often termed "lay perceptions of risk."

Various states have attempted to establish procedures for siting facilities (Ryan, 1984). Wells (1982) suggests that among the states, three basic approaches have been developed for hazardous waste facility siting. Each of these approaches treats the concept of lay perceptions of risk, and consequently public opposition, differently. The first of these is Michigan's approach, where a state hazardous waste site approval board is, in effect, given preemptive authority over local government and public opposition (Wells, 1982: 730). The second approach is that found in New York State, where the guiding statute requires a state siting board to deny siting permission if the facility conflicts with local ordinances. Somewhere in the middle of these is the Massachusetts siting approach, where a state board attempts to mediate any conflict between a local community and a developer who proposes to site a facility in that community. According to

Ryan (1984: 4), at least three states other than Massachusetts have established this type of process.

The Massachusetts approach carries a certain appeal because, at least theoretically, it permits facility siting without the direct preemption of local authority (Morell and Magorian, 1982; Hadden, Veillette, and Brandt, 1983). This approach relies heavily on the theory of compensation, which prescribes that communities receive negotiated benefits in exchange for permission to site a facility (Portney, 1984). This approach's appeal comes from the idea that the state, a developer, and the people of a local community can all benefit from facility siting. The approach attempts, in practice, to produce a positive-sum result (Hansen, 1984). The idea is that lay perceptions of risk can and will be balanced by providing an opportunity to allow the benefits to exceed the costs implied by perceived risk.

Although this theory and the processes prescribed by it sound appealing, we need to understand more about the role of economic incentives in that net risk perception calculation. I say this because there is little evidence that it produces successful siting. I read this as prima facie evidence that perhaps economic incentives do not play the role ascribed to them. This paper examines some public opinon data from five Massachusetts communities and from a nationwide survey to attempt to discover how much potential this theory of compensation has for such successful siting. Before we examine these data, we should explore the theory of compensation in a little more detail.

THE THEORY OF COMPENSATION IN HAZARDOUS
WASTE TREATMENT FACILITY SITING

The theory of compensation in siting facilities which are perceived by nearby residents to present risks is based on the provision of economic incentives. It starts with the assumption that public opposition stems from a basic imbalance in people's individual benefit-risk calculations (Hadden and Hazelton, 1980; Mitchell and Carson, 1986). The idea is that opposition to the siting of facilities comes from people in close proximity to the site because these people are being asked to bear the high personal costs (in the form of risk) while the benefits of the facility accrue to a larger outside population.

O'Hare's important theoretical work delineated the role of compensation in redressing this imbalance (1977). His analysis argues that economic incentives could be offered to local residents so that perceived benefits would eventually outweigh the perceived risks. Thus, the imbalance would be redressed, and public opposition would abate. Evolving from this argument are numerous discussions of techniques designed to mitigate or manage social risk assessment. Thus, the focus has become one of attempting to devise methods of altering people's subjective assessments of the risks associated with living near potentially noxious facilities (Elliott, 1984; O'Hare, Bacow, and Sanderson, 1983).

Although the Massachusetts state hazardous waste treatment facility siting law attempts to establish a process whereby this result would be achieved, to date no facilities have been sited. In every instance where a developer has proposed to construct a facility, public opposition has prevented construction. This raises the question of whether the theory of compensation is somehow flawed or whether the Massachusetts process is at fault.

Attempting to find an answer to this type of question, the Citizen Survey Program at the Lincoln Filene Center for Citizenship and Public Affairs conducted two major survey research projects to analyze residents' attitudes toward hazardous waste treatment facility siting. The first of these focuses on the potential for economic incentives in specific cities and towns (Portney, 1983; 1985). During the month of April 1983, the Citizen Survey Program conducted in-depth interviews with over 300 randomly selected residents from each of five communities in the state. Brockton, Chelsea, Newton, Sturbridge, and Ware residents were chosen for this project. We designed this survey to be community-based because the theory of compensation has implications for the way people in specific communities will react to economic incentives. Thus, we wanted to ensure that the results obtained reflect an assessment of how the people in given communities respond.

The second project conducted by the Citizen Survey Program, during July 1984, consisted of interviews with over 500 citizens from a nationwide telephone survey. This survey focused on the contiguous forty-eight states and the District of Columbia. The main purpose of this study was to develop a base of comparison for the Massachusetts results and to begin an assessment of how generalizable the findings are.

PUBLIC ATTITUDES TOWARD HAZARDOUS WASTE TREATMENT FACILITY SITING IN MASSACHUSETTS COMMUNITIES AND THE NATION

Our purpose in interviewing these residents was to develop a fairly clear picture of their benefit-risk calculations and to assess the potential for compensation in altering these calculations. Our method of trying to achieve this was to ask respondents first whether they would favor or oppose construction of a hazardous waste treatment facility somewhere in their state. Then, for those who said they favored or mostly favored such construction, we asked whether they would favor or oppose the siting of a hazardous waste treatment facility in their communities.[2]

Overall in the Massachusetts survey, we found that nearly 62% of the people we interviewed opposed or mostly opposed facility siting in the state or in their neighborhoods. Table 3.1 presents a breakdown of how the five

Table 3.1
A Town-by-Town and National Summary of Respondents' Attitudes
toward Building a Hazardous Waste Treatment Facility in Their Community

| City or Town | Respondents' Attitudes Toward Siting | | | |
	Favor or mostly favor	Oppose or mostly oppose	Don't know	Total
Brockton	44.6%	54.2%	1.2%	100.0%
Chelsea	34.9%	55.9%	8.2%	100.0%
Newton	35.4%	62.3%	2.3%	100.0%
Sturbridge	20.8%	77.2%	2.0%	100.0%
Ware	22.8%	75.9%	1.3%	100.0%
Nation	17.8%	54.6%	27.6%	100.0%

Source: Survey by the author

cities and towns and the nationwide sample differed with respect to opposing the construction of such a facility. These data suggest that each of cities and towns starts in a somewhat different position; the communities range in opposition from a little over half of the people (in Brockton) to over three-quarters (in Ware). In the nationwide sample, nearly 55% of the people opposed such a facility.

Respondents who opposed siting a facility in their city or town were asked to tell us how they would feel if various economic incentives were provided.[3] We focused on nine economic incentive proposals which had been discussed in various siting negotiations in Massachusetts and which are expected to be linked directly to the benefit portion of people's personal calculus.

We also made an effort to ask people who opposed a facility to tell us how they would feel if measures were taken to decrease the risk portion of their calculus. We specifically focused on safety precautions to get an idea of how much potential affecting the risk portion the personal calculation might possess. The proposals we put to the respondents who said they opposed facility construction are summarized in Table 3.2. Here we can see the proposal, the problem immediately associated with facility construction, and the broader problem, not necessarily associated with the facility, that each proposal is designed to address. The first nine of these are economic incentive proposals, where the focus is on providing financial benefit or overcoming financial loss. The last two proposals are the proposals directed at alleviating people's fears or reducing people's assessment of high risks.[4] Overall, in the Massachusetts samples we found that some 43.9% of those who opposed or mostly opposed siting a facility in their community changed their minds under one or another of these eleven proposals. Nationally, we found that some 33.6% of such people changed their minds under one or another of the proposals. Table 3.3 provides a breakdown of the percentage of respondents initially opposing the facility who changed their minds under one or another of these proposals.[5]

Table 3.2

Eleven Proposals and the Immediate and Broad Problems Each Addresses

Proposal	Immediate Problem Addressed by the Proposal	Broader Problem Addressed by the Proposal
Economic Incentive Proposals		
1) Have the developer pay all property taxes for ten years.	The fear that the facility would increase the need for services, thereby increasing financial burden on the city or town.	Long-term increases in local property taxes.
2) Have the developer pay a surcharge to the city or town based on the amount of waste processed.	Make company's payments to the city or town commensurate with the demands on the plant and surrounding community.	Again, long-term increases in local property taxes.
3) Have the developer hire at least 15 local residents.	Fear that plant workers may not have sufficient stake in the effects of the plant on the community.	High unemployment.
4) Have the developer pay for improved fire protection.	Increased reliance on the local fire department to deal with the danger of explosion and accidental spills.	Fire department cuts brought about by a statewide property tax limitation passed in 1980.
5) Repave the city's streets.	Deterioration of streets because of heavy truck traffic around the facility.	Deterioration of streets because of statewide property tax limitation.
6) Have the developer provide five full college scholarships to local high school seniors each year.	Lack of local technical expertise to monitor plant operation.	Rapidly increasing costs of higher education.
7) $50 direct payment to each family in the city or town.	Residents' personal inconvenience and risk to personal property.	None
8) Have the developer pay the amount of any decrease in property values.	Decreases in the market values of homes because of proximity to the facility.	None

Source: Survey by the author.

Table 3.2 *(continued)*

Proposal	Immediate Problem Addressed by the Proposal	Broader Problem Addressed by the Proposal
9) Have the developer purchase a life or health insurance policy.	Fear of risk of personal injury or loss from accidents not covered by existing insurance.	None
Risk Mitigating Proposals 10) Have public officials and local citizens conduct regular safety inspections in the facility.	Low confidence in internal plant managements' dedication to safety over profit.	None
11) Have state and local officials do their best to prevent groundwater contamination and accidental spills.	Risk from contaminated water supplies and potential accidents.	None

Table 3.3
The Percentage of Respondents Initially Opposing the Facility Who Changed Their Minds under One or Another Proposal, by Community and for the National Sample

City or Town	Responses to Proposals		Total
	Percent Who Changed Their Minds to Favor	Percent Who Still Opposed	
Brockton	43.1%	56.9%	100.0%
Chelsea	46.4%	53.6%	100.0%
Newton	37.3%	62.7%	100.0%
Sturbridge	32.9%	67.1%	100.0%
Ware	56.4%	43.6%	100.0%
Nation	33.6%	66.4%	100.0%

Source: Survey by the authors.

THE RESULTS OF THE SURVEYS

First of all, none of the proposals induces any sort of massive shift in public sentiment. The data in Table 3.4, which reflect the number of people who changed their minds as a percentage of the number of people who initially opposed the facility, show the basic patterns of change. While we would not necessarily expect people in every city or town to react identically

Table 3.4
The Percentage of Respondents Opposing a Facility in Their Community
Who Changed Their Minds in Response to Each of Eleven Proposals
(Numbers in parentheses are rankings)

| | City, Town or Nation | | | | | |
Proposals	Brockton n=336	Chelsea n=326	Newton n=334	Sturbridge n=303	Ware n=316	Nation n=564
Economic Incentive Proposals						
Pay all property taxes	7.5%(10)	10.5%(9)	10.2%(3)	5.6%(6)	17.9%(8)	5.3%(11)
Surcharge	12.0%(3)	11.4%(8)	10.2%(3)	9.4%(3)	16.6%(10)	9.2%(6)
Hire 15 local residents	11.3%(8)	12.2%(7)	7.4%(8)	4.7%(9)	25.9%(5)	9.9%(5)
Improved fire protection	12.8%(2)	13.8%(4)	9.1%(5)	4.7%(9)	26.2%(3)	12.2%(3)
Repave city streets	10.6%(9)	12.9%(6)	6.8%(9)	6.6%(5)	22.1%(7)	8.4%(7)
Five College Scholarships	12.1%(5)	15.4%(2)	5.7%(10)	9.4%(3)	24.8%(6)	6.9%(8)
$50 per family direct payment	6.0%(11)	7.3%(11)	5.7%(10)	2.8%(11)	15.2%(11)	6.9%(6)
Pay decreased property value	12.8%(2)	8.9%(10)	7.9%(7)	5.6%(6)	26.2%(3)	10.7%(4)
Buy health or life insurance policy	12.8%(2)	13.0%(5)	8.5%(6)	5.6%(6)	17.9%(8)	6.9%(8)
Risk Mitigating Proposals						
Regular safety inspections	15.1%(1)	15.4%(2)	15.9%(1)	16.0%(1)	30.4%(2)	23.7%(1)
State and local efforts to prevent groundwater contamination and accidental spills	12.1%(5)	16.2%(1)	12.5%(2)	15.1%(2)	31.8%(1)	22.1%(2)

Source: Survey by the author.

to each proposal (because local conditions could well affect the marginal utility of various economic incentives), we do see remarkable similarity across communities. And the patterns are remarkably similar to those for the nation.

Perhaps the most useful way to examine the data in Table 3.4 is to compare the proposals within communities and to assess the relative rankings given to proposals across communities. We can also compare the ranking results from each city or town to those from the nationwide sample.

Comparing the percentages themselves across towns can be somewhat problematic. We see that in Ware, for example, all of the proposals changed a larger proportion of people's minds than in other communities. This is probably due to the fact that a relatively large proportion of people in Ware initially opposed the facility compared to the other communities. While the differences among the other communities seem much smaller, the interpretation of these percentages across communities exhibits the same type of problem.

With this in mind, we can see that except in Brockton the risk-mitigation proposals (safety inspection and prevention of groundwater contamination) seem to exert more influence on peoples' benefit-risk assessments than any of the economic incentives. Even in Brockton, the safety inspection proposal seems to have been the most influential among the proposals, although three of the economic incentives produced slightly greater change than the prevention-of-groundwater-contamination proposal. This result for the nationwide sample is nearly the same. The pattern seems striking. Clearly, the risk-mitigating proposals consistently produce greater changes of public sentiment than almost any economic incentive.

WHAT ARE THE IMPLICATIONS OF THESE FINDINGS?

The results presented above are suggestive of several important conclusions. First, the focus on the theory of compensation on economic incentives probably underestimates the role of magnitude of people's risk assessments in the overall benefit-risk calculation. In other words, it would appear that, in general, people assess the risks associated with living near a hazardous waste treatment facility as being so great that virtually no reasonable amount of compensation, by itself, can have much impact. Clearly, economic considerations do not seem to play the kind of role we would expect on the basis of the theory of compensation. Consequently, none of the economic incentive proposals to affect these considerations made a great deal of difference. Indeed, this is somewhat analogous to conclusions reached with regard to nuclear power plant siting and related issues (Sorenson et al., 1987).

Second, dealing with the risk portion of the calculation through attempts to mitigate problems shows somewhat greater potential. Although such mitigation may never fully be able to allay people's fears, attempts to do so by themselves seem to be able to produce greater changes in people's assessments.

These results are fairly consistent with recent studies using very different methodologies (Elliott, 1984). The obvious conclusion to be derived from these findings is that public policy toward siting hazardous waste treatment facilities must address the techniques of mitigating risk and of convincing people that those risks have in fact been mitigated. In particular, major attention needs to be given to the role of such factors as the risk communication process, public participation in facility siting, and lack of confidence in political and social institutions on the formation of people's perceptions of risk (Kasperson, 1986). Until this is addressed directly, the potential for affecting public opposition to treatment facility siting through compensation would seem to be quite low.

NOTES

1. A full description of the methodology employed in selecting these cities and towns may be obtained from the author. Also see Portney (1984).

2. For specific question wordings, see Portney (1984).

3. This, of course, presents respondents with a purely hypothetical situation about which they must speculate. Although some respondents might act differently if actually faced with such a facility siting attempt, these data are clearly better than any other available information on the subject in that they provide us with responses to specific questions never before asked of people.

4. We rotated the presentation of these proposals to respondents to attempt to neutralize the possible influences exerted by question order on responses.

5. Obviously, this is a multiple response question set, so that the percentages of people changing their minds under the specific proposals reported later do not necessarily sum to the total percentage of people who changed their minds.

REFERENCES

Amour, A., ed., *The Not-In-My-Backyard Syndrome* (Downsview, Ontario: York University Press, 1984).

Elliott, Michael L. Poirier, "Improving Community Acceptance of Hazardous Waste Facilities through Alternative Systems for Mitigating and Managing Risk," *Hazardous Waste* 1 (1984) 3: 397-410.

Hadden, Susan G., and Jared Hazelton (1980) "Public Policies toward Risk," *Policy Studies Journal* 9 (1980) 1: 109-117.

Hadden, Susan G., Joan Veillette, and Thomas Brandt, "State Roles in Siting Hazardous Waste Disposal Facilities: From State Preemption to Local Veto," in James P. Lester and Ann O'M. Bowman, eds., *The Politics of Hazardous Waste Management* (Durham, NC: Duke University Press, 1983).

Hansen, Susan B., "On the Making of Unpopular Decisions: A Typology and Some Evidence," *Policy Studies Journal* 13 (September 1984) 1: 23-43.

Kasperson, Roger, "Six Propositions on Public Participation and Their Relevance for Risk Communication," *Risk Analysis* 6 (1986) 3: 275-281.

Mitchell, Robert Cameron, and Richard T. Carson, "Siting Hazardous Facilities: Property Rights, Protest, and the Siting of Hazardous Waste Facilities," *AEA Papers and Proceedings*, 76 (May 1986) 2: 285-290.

Morell, David, and Christopher Magorian, *Siting Hazardous Waste Facilities: Local Opposition and the Myth of Preemption* (Cambridge, MA: Ballinger, 1982).

O'Hare, Michael, " 'Not on My Block You Don't'—Facilities Siting and the Importance of Compensation," *Public Policy* 25 (Fall 1977): 407-458.

O'Hare, Michael, Lawrence Bacow, and Debra Sanderson, *Facility Siting* (New York: Van Nostrand, 1983).

Portney, Kent E., *Citizen Attitudes Toward Hazardous Waste Facility Siting: Public Opinion in Five Massachusetts Communities* (Medford, MA: Lincoln Filene Center for Citizenship and Public Affairs, Tufts University, 1983).

_____, "Allaying the NIMBY Syndrome: The Potential for Compensation in Hazardous Waste Treatment Facility Siting," *Hazardous Waste* 1 (1984) 3: 411-421.

Portney, Kent E., "The Potential of the Theory of Compensation for Mitigating Public Opposition to Hazardous Waste Treatment Facility Siting: Some Evidence from Five Massachusetts Communities," *Policy Studies Journal* 14 (September 1985) 1: 81-89.

Ryan, Anne Sprightley, *Approaches to Hazardous Waste Facility Siting in the United States*, Report to the Massachusetts Hazardous Waste Facility Site Safety Council, Boston, September 1984.

Sorenson, John, Jon Soderstrom, Emily Copenhaver, Sam Carnes, and Robert Bolin, *Impacts of Hazardous Technology: The Psycho-Social Effects of Restarting TMI-1* (Albany, NY: SUNY Press, 1987).

Wells, Donald T., "Site Control of Hazardous Waste Facilities," *Policy Studies Review* 1 (May 1982) 4: 728-735.

4

Citizen Participation and Hazardous Waste Policy Implementation

Michael E. Kraft and Ruth Kraut

INTRODUCTION

During the 1970s, the federal government adopted new and ambitious public policies directed at the problem of hazardous waste disposal. Implementation of those policies, particularly the Resource Conservation and Recovery Act of 1976 (RCRA), has proved to be an enormously difficult and slow process. There are many reasons for this outcome, including the scope and complexity of the statutes, scientific disagreements and uncertainties over the risks of hazardous waste and the safety of disposal methods, insufficient funding, requirements for intergovernmental coordination of decision making, and sharp political controversy, particularly at the state and local levels (Lester, 1983; Cohen, 1984; Carnes, 1982). Although delay and limited success in policy implementation are hardly unusual, the risk to public health and environmental quality in this policy area suggests the importance of understanding the major constraints on this process. This chapter examines one factor that is critical for successful implementation of post–Love Canal hazardous waste policy: public participation in facility siting and operating decisions.

Public participation is important for a number of reasons. First, the public is clearly concerned about living near hazardous waste facilities. As awareness of hazardous waste disposal grows, and as implementation of RCRA begins to touch more local communities over the next few years, one can expect increased demand for public involvement in such decisions.

We wish to thank the A. W. Mellon Foundation for supporting this research. Its grant to the Environmental Studies Program at Oberlin College provided funds for student support and research that greatly aided the collection and analysis of the data presented in this case study.

Second, the record of disputes over siting decisions strongly indicates that local citizen groups will react adversely to attempts to locate waste disposal facilities in their communities (U.S. EPA, 1979; Morell and Magorian, 1982). They are likely to challenge assurances of safety offered by the regulatory agency or the waste management firm, and to oppose recommendations for site location and procedures regardless of the kind of site proposed. Third, federal law and the United States Environmental Protection Agency (U.S. EPA) regulations require some form of public participation before a permit is granted for a disposal facility or recertified for an existing one. Section 7004 of RCRA requires that public participation in the "development, revisions, implementation, and enforcement of any regulation, guideline, information, or program" under RCRA be "provided for, encouraged, and assisted" by the EPA administrator and the states. Such provisions encourage the growth of local citizen activism; they provide legal opportunities and political access despite a history of limited governmental support for public participation (Rosenbaum, 1983).

These conditions create a dilemma for environmental administrators. Disposal facilities (at least for the near term) must be located somewhere, and technical considerations may dictate placement in an area where local opposition is strong. Hence, administrators responsible for siting and operation decisions must somehow reconcile these competing demands. The constraint of public opposition is likely to continue despite regulatory changes being considered in 1986 that would bar most land-based disposal of hazardous wastes. In revising RCRA in 1984, Congress declared its intentions to prohibit disposal of hazardous waste on land except under very narrow circumstances. In early 1986, the U.S. EPA proposed rules to implement the new law that were described by agency officials as "fundamental changes" in the way hazardous wastes are handled in the United States. Yet congressional staff members who helped draft the law and spokespersons for various environmental groups objected, saying that the U.S. EPA rules wre not stringent enough and that they ignored the clear intent of Congress (Shabecoff, 1986). These developments indicate that land-based disposal will only be phased out slowly and that controversies over the risks posed by hazardous wastes and public opposition to facility siting will continue.

Disputes over the safety of disposal methods, and the costs to industry and the economy, extend to the alternatives to land-based disposal being considered in both the United States and other nations. An example of the kind of conflict that may arise frequently in the future occurred in Philadelphia in early January 1986. Citizens attending a public hearing on a U.S. EPA proposal to test ocean incineration of chemical wastes protested vigorously against the plan. In this case, the wastes were to be shipped to Philadelphia by train, collected in holding tanks, loaded on board a specially designed incinerator ship, and carried some 140 miles out to sea for incineration. Spokespersons for the city and a number of environmental groups complained that each step of the plan contained unacceptable risks. Some one thousand people gathered to sing "God Bless America," recite the Pledge of Allegiance, and urge that the wastes be shipped from another port some distance from Philadelphia (Gruson, 1986).

As the Philadelphia protest illustrates, public resistance to plans for the disposal of hazardous wastes may occur whenever the public fears that risks to its health or environmental quality are unacceptably high. Much the same is true for disposal of high-level radioactive waste, evident in the mid-1980s as the Department of Energy (DOE) began what will surely be a long and controversial process of selecting a site for permanent disposal of spent fuel from commercial reactors. In part out of recognition of the familiar NIMBY (not in my backyard) reaction, the DOE has proposed a process of "consultation and cooperation" to provide opportunities for public participation in such decisions. In both cases, the public is obviously concerned about the risks; scientific data are limited, and thus uncertainty exists over the degree of risk; and pressures are directed by citizens, and often by state and local government officials, to shift the risk to another geographical area and population, whatever the distribution of the benefits.

Such public resistance to facility siting (and in cases where a facility is already in place, resistance to continuation of its operation) is understandable. But it also threatens to delay or block implementation of hazardous waste policy for years as public officials seek acceptable locations and try to devise acceptable operating conditions. Delays themselves may pose risks to public health or environmental quality, or may add measurably to the costs of disposal. Thus, officials of regulatory agencies increasingly are forced to chart a difficult course between professional management of hazardous waste problems and responsiveness to a concerned public.

Meeting this challenge is integral to the process of policy legitimation as described by Jones (1984), which in turn contributes significantly to effective implementation of hazardous waste policy. But precisely how such a challenge might best be met is not at all clear. Political processes for making "acceptable risk" decisions are not well defined and have not been studied to any great extent (Fischhoff et al., 1981; Kraft, 1986; Flores and Kraft, 1987). In particular, there has been little empirical study of public participation programs, their effect on regulatory agency decision making, and the way in which the behavior of agency officials affects the extent and type of public participation. The case study reported here may shed some light on these relationships and suggest some of the conditions for achieving acceptable and effective solutions to local hazardous waste problems.

Case studies are necessarily limited in comparison with studies using aggregate data, but one can make use of an analytic framework that facilitates comparison across cases. Mazmanian and Sabatier (1983) offer a comprehensive framework for the study of policy implementation, and their model identifies several factors related to citizen participation. As indicated in Figure 4.1, among the statutory variables are specification of the degree of "formal access by outsiders" in implementation decisions, and among the nonstatutory or political variables are "public support" and the "attitudes and resources of constituency groups." One might add that these two nonstatutory variables are likely to be influenced by the degree and type of media coverage of pertinent events and issues.

Together, public opinion and media coverage affect the policy agenda, the issues policymakers and agency officials consider important. They also influence officials' perceptions of relevant constituency groups and the legitimacy of their demands. Finally, the model suggests that the "commitment and leadership skill of implementing officials" is likely to affect public perception of the officials' actions and the mode of participation chosen by the public. As Mazmanian and Sabatier note, among other things, officials need to develop good working relationships with policymakers, convince target groups and opponents that they will be treated fairly, and mobilize support among other constituency groups and the public at large. Their ability to present the agency's case effectively in the mass media and to promote various kinds of public participation to build legitimacy for administrative decisions may be crucial for successful policy implementation.

To highlight the role of such variables we examine the impact of public participation in three distinct periods over a thirteen-year period: 1972-1985. The case study focuses on a "state-of-the-art" hazardous waste management facility in Clermont County, Ohio, and a series of decisions authorizing the facility to handle increasing amounts of hazardous material. Local opposition developed in the late 1970s concurrently with rising public concern nationwide over toxic and hazardous waste. Yet in 1981, officials at the Ohio Environmental Protection Agency (OEPA) believed the facility—one of the nation's largest toxic waste dumps—to have been managed responsibly and to offer "safe operation" (*Clermont Sun*, 1981a). By 1985, they shared some of the citizens' concerns. The account below is drawn from local newspaper archives, interviews with selected participants, hearing records, and other official documents.

FROM LANDFILL TO HAZARDOUS WASTE SITE: INCREMENTAL DECISION MAKING, 1972-1978

In the late 1960s, Clermont County, like many other local governments across the nation, discovered it needed a sanitary landfill to handle its growing volume of solid waste. Unfortunately, the county lacked sufficient financial resources to construct and operate a publicly owned facility, and in addition, every siting proposal for the landfill met with opposition from nearby residents. The county continued to transport its waste to neighbor-

Figure 4.1
Variables Involved in the Implementation Process

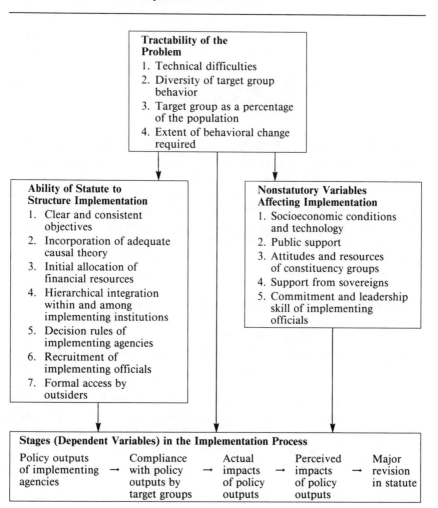

Tractability of the Problem
1. Technical difficulties
2. Diversity of target group behavior
3. Target group as a percentage of the population
4. Extent of behavioral change required

Ability of Statute to Structure Implementation
1. Clear and consistent objectives
2. Incorporation of adequate causal theory
3. Initial allocation of financial resources
4. Hierarchical integration within and among implementing institutions
5. Decision rules of implementing agencies
6. Recruitment of implementing officials
7. Formal access by outsiders

Nonstatutory Variables Affecting Implementation
1. Socioeconomic conditions and technology
2. Public support
3. Attitudes and resources of constituency groups
4. Support from sovereigns
5. Commitment and leadership skill of implementing officials

Stages (Dependent Variables) in the Implementation Process

Policy outputs of implementing agencies → Compliance with policy outputs by target groups → Actual impacts of policy outputs → Perceived impacts of policy outputs → Major revision in statute

Source: *Implementation and Public Policy* by Daniel A. Mazmanian and Paul A. Sabatier. Copyright 1983 by Scott, Foresman and Company. Reprinted by permission.

ing counties, but the increasing volume of waste necessitated development of a more acceptable, long-term solution.

Largely because the county had been unable for several years to finance the building of a sanitary landfill, it was receptive to overtures from a private developer, Clermont Environmental Reclamation Company (CER), to build and operate such a facility for the county. The landfill was to be developed on a 211-acre parcel in Jackson Township. As might be expected, area residents and township officials opposed the landfill, but the township lacked legal authority to prevent it; it had no zoning regulations, and the decision rested with county and state officials. County officials applauded the efforts of the developer and supported its request for an operating permit from the Ohio Department of Health. In March 1972, the department granted CER a permit to operate a sanitary landfill in Jackson Township.

The controversy over the 1972 permitting decision led to an important change in the township ordinances. Discovering that they were without influence, township trustees immediately proposed zoning regulations to create what they thought was sufficient authority to affect any similar decisions in the future. The new proposals were placed on the ballot at the next local election and were approved by a narrow margin. The most critical change was a zoning regulation that made clear how landfills would be treated: "*Privately* owned or operated landfills and dumps are prohibited in Jackson Township" (emphasis added). The site owned by CER began operation one week before the zoning proposal was voted into law, and was exempted from the new regulation as a "nonconforming user."

Although resigned to the existence of the CER-owned sanitary landfill in the township, citizens were neither prepared for nor aware of a second decision that occurred four years later. CER wanted to expand its activity to include the handling of limited quantities of industrial waste. While such a change in the status of the site would likely have provoked a strong reaction among township residents had it been widely publicized, it received little notice in the community. The OEPA's Division of Solid Waste, which supervised such landfills, was required to file a formal legal notice announcing a public hearing on the proposed change in CER's operating permit. That notice appeared in the *Cincinnati Enquirer* and the *Clermont Sun* in the spring of 1976. The hearing was advertised as one that would discuss granting a "solid waste" permit, leading citizens to believe CER was merely requesting authority for an expansion of the quantity of household waste then handled at the facility. The new permit request, however, was for "unwanted residual solid or semisolid material as results from industrial, commercial, agricultural, and community operations," as stipulated in OEPA solid waste regulations (OEPA, 1976).

In part because of confusion over the meaning of "solid waste," the public hearing was poorly attended. The permit request and the general subject of hazardous waste had not reached the community's political agenda, and there was little discussion of the implications of the expanded site operations for public health and environmental quality. Indeed, few realized what the implications were. In November 1976, the OEPA approved a permit for handling limited industrial waste at the CER site.

In effect, what began as a modest sanitary landfill, established without any opportunity for participation by area residents in the permitting decision, was converted through an incremental decision process into a far more significant industrial waste site. By early 1979, the site was the only secure landfill for hazardous waste in Ohio licensed for general commercial use, and one of about thirty in the United States capable of handling toxic and hazardous wastes on this scale.

HAZARDOUS WASTE REACHES THE LOCAL AGENDA: CITIZEN PROTEST, 1978–1981

Over the period 1972-1978, Jackson Township residents seemed to adjust to the existence of the landfill, although they continued to regard it as a nuisance. However, public concern over the site and fear of the risk of hazardous waste increased sharply in early 1978. At that time residents discovered that the CER site was accepting contaminated soil from Kentucky and other hazardous waste from West Virginia because the arrival of these materials was reported prominently in the local press. Following a series of protest rallies and petitions to try to shut the landfill down, concerned residents incorporated themselves as Independent Citizens Associated for Reclaiming the Environment (I-CARE).

For over a year they engaged in what might be termed unfocused and generalized protest over the continued operation of the site. Without much knowledge of the pertinent scientific facts and with no public forum or administrative process on which to rely, citizen action in this early phase was characterized by bewilderment over what might be done, the issuing of unfounded allegations, and expressions of anger. The main public concern was possible contamination of groundwater, a fear dismissed by the OEPA as unwarranted. CER responded to public concern by asserting it was accepting mere "paint sludge"; like the OEPA, CER downplayed the risks and said that residents' fears were unjustified. They made repeated references to the facility's state-of-the-art design and to the fact that the landfill was "uniquely suited" for waste disposal because of its impermeable clay soil. During this period, neither the OEPA nor CER appeared to make a serious attempt to educate local citizens on the issues or to encourage an informed dialogue on the OEPA's regulatory program.

That some basis for citizen concern existed, however, was suggested by a representative of the OEPA, who acknowledged in March 1979 that the agency lacked adequate staff to regulate hazardous waste dumps statewide.

(Only two employees worked full time in this area.) Because of the "enormous" public resistance to establishment of such facilities, he advised the OEPA that "a major public relations effort" would be required to establish any new facility (*Cincinnati Enquirer*, 1979a). To judge from available evidence, then, the OEPA had insufficient staff and resources to measure the risk posed by hazardous waste facilities and to monitor their operations closely enough to ensure that public health was protected adequately. Without such resources, OEPA officials were unable to convince residents that risks were indeed negligible and to mobilize citizen support for the agency's regulatory program, which is designed in part to keep risks at an acceptable level. As noted above, such actions are directly related to effective implementation of hazardous waste policy.

After one year of citizen protests and largely ineffective results, Jackson Township officials attempted to intervene directly. In early February 1979, they asserted that CER was in violation of its nonconforming user status for having changed the kinds of waste the landfill accepted without asking for a zoning variance. They tried to close the landfill, fining CER $100 for every day the company continued to accept hazardous waste. CER responded one week later by filing a million-dollar suit against Jackson Township trustees and I-CARE; they also sued township and I-CARE officials as individuals. I-CARE countered with a suit of its own against CER, alleging that the company was trying to prevent further investigation of its activities. The underlying issues were ignored as the antagonists resorted to legal maneuvers and largely symbolic posturing. Such actions did little to foster public understanding of technical and administrative concerns or to create more constructive processes for citizen participation.

As a further complication, by this time CER had merged with a nationwide waste management company, Chemical and Environmental Conservation Systems (CECOS), and was generally referred to as CECOS/CER. Mergers and sales of waste treatment facilities of this kind make more difficult the tasks of public education and building of public trust that facilitate citizen participation in hazardous waste decision making. In this case, by early 1983 there was yet another change in ownership as Browning-Ferris Industries (BFI), one of the nation's largest hazardous waste disposal companies, bought the Clermont County facility. As these mergers continued, the owners literally grew more distant from Clermont County; whereas the first owners of the landfill lived in the area, BFI is based in Texas. One possible consequence of these changing patterns of ownership is that the company perceived that it had less of a stake in the community, and in southwest Ohio in general, and it was less motivated to promote a dialogue with community leaders and citizens' groups.

Aside from disappointment over the lawsuits and other ineffective local actions, township residents were frustrated with developments in the state legislature in late 1979 and 1980. In October 1980, complying with requirements under RCRA, the Ohio legislature passed SB 269, establishing procedures for regulation of hazardous waste and replacing previous rules affecting solid waste. The law clearly provided for state preemption of local zoning ordinances:

No politicial subdivision of this state shall require any additional zoning or other approval for the construction of a hazardous waste facility authorized . . . pursuant to this chapter . . . nor shall any political subdivision adopt or enforce any law . . . that in any way . . . limits the authority granted in the permit by the board. (SB 269)

The law also included a "grandfather clause" that automatically granted CECOS/CER a permit from the OEPA's Hazardous Waste Facilities Approval Board, without any public hearings, because it was previously operative and "substantially" in compliance with previous laws. SB 269 left Jackson Township's zoning ordinance without any clout, and it meant that CECOS won the lawsuit.

Cooperative solutions to continuing disputes over the CECOS/CER site seemed more remote when township trustees decided in December 1981, against the advice of the prosecuting attorney, to appeal the judicial ruling (of March 1981) against the township's zoning ordinance. In doing so the township rejected a conciliatory move by CECOS/CER which would have allowed for independent monitoring of the landfill. The company offered what it considered to be an attractive package to the township: It would purchase expensive fire equipment for the town and set up a citizen complaint board *if* the trustees would agree not to appeal the court decision, would cease making public accusations over landfill operations, and would no longer object to further landfill expansion, including acceptance of PCB (polychlorinated biphenyl) wastes. The township declined the offer. In December 1982, the Ohio Supreme Court ruled against the township, saying that the state law prohibiting local regulation of "properly licensed" hazardous waste disposal sites was constitutional (*Cincinnati Enquirer*, 1982).

Having failed to reassure local residents of the facility's safety, the director of the OEPA, Wayne Nichols, in what was termed "an unprecedented move," announced in August 1981 that he would assign a full-time inspector to monitor the landfill on a daily basis to "at least try to maintain public confidence." "I found," Nichols said, "that we didn't have that at this particular site" (*Cincinnati Post*, 1981). The inspector began work in October, and by December 1981 reported in an interview with the local paper that the landfill was "a good operation." "They [CECOS/CER] don't hide a thing from me," he said. "They're kind of glad to see someone there" (*Clermont Sun*, 1981b). The article appeared on the front page of the paper under the headline "Landfill Safety Praised by State EPA Inspector."

One other decision affecting CECOS/CER's operating permit further aroused citizen suspicion of the site's threat to public health—and also demonstrated the citizens' continued ineffectiveness in trying to influence hazardous waste policy implementation. In September 1978, the company was granted permission by the U.S. EPA to accept limited quantities of PCBs for some of its cells (self-contained storage units within a hazardous waste facility). A second request for expansion of its PCB disposal permit was made in April of 1980, which was also approved. Following aproval by the Ohio-Kentucky-Indiana (OKI) Regional Council of Government of a loan for additional construction, the company opened a sixth hazardous waste cell in April 1981. The following month it requested permission to bury PCBs in the rest of the cells. Citizens were entitled to write to the U.S. EPA's Chicago regional office to comment on the third request, and many from the township did so. They argued against this further expansion of the site's activity. Nevertheless, the EPA granted CECOS/CER's permit, noting that the landfill was meeting all current state and federal standards. However, this time the Clermont County Board of Commissioners, which had generally sided with the company, opposed the landfill's expansion, and opposed funding it through the OKI Regional Council of Government. After some legal maneuvering and threats by the company to challenge the county on the state preemption issue, the commissioners backed away from direct opposition and settled for a symbolic vote of protest against the site. They voted against the landfill expansion but not to withhold funding of the landfill.

Township residents increasingly realized that they could make little headway with their attempts to affect policy implementation at the local level. Although they won the support of the township trustees, there was little the trustees could do. While at least some of the county commissioners sided with township residents in their battle with CECOS/CER, the county was also constrained by state preemption of regulation over hazardous waste sites. Even when assured by the OEPA that the landfill was one of the best managed sites in the nation and substantially in compliance with both state and federal regulations, I-CARE members and their supporters (who, to judge from its mailing list, numbered at least 300 individuals from the rural area) considered additional political action imperative. They approached several state legislators but made little progress. One representative, Harry Malott, with whom they worked from the beginning of the dispute, was sympathetic but without much influence in the legislature; he introduced legislation to return control of landfills to local governments, but the effort failed. Another, State Senator Cooper Snyder, was described by the group as "pro-landfill." Intervention by U.S. Representative William Gradison, who wrote to the U.S. EPA on the PCB permit, was also ineffective; his letter to the EPA, which arrived during the height of the turmoil over Anne Gorsuch's and Rita Lavelle's management of toxic and hazardous waste programs (see Cohen, 1984), was never answered.

NEW POLITICAL STRATEGIES AND INCREASING
CITIZEN IMPACT: 1981-1985

Because of the events described above, relationships between citizen groups and the OEPA, and between citizens and CECOS/CER, were poor and provided little basis for constructive dialogue. Each party had become mistrustful of the other and somewhat bitter. The citizens did not trust the OEPA and rejected its assurances that there was no evidence of groundwater contamination. For its part, CECOS/CER believed the citizen groups to be "unreasonable" and unreceptive to the company's overtures. Relationships deteriorated further when, after two leaders of I-CARE publicly condemned the company at a local Sportsman's Club meeting, CECOS/CER filed a suit against them for slander. They had insinuated that there was a connection between poor health in the area and CECOS/CER's operation of the facility. The suit had three important effects: It increased citizen hostility toward the company, it discouraged further activity by I-CARE in Jackson Township, and it led to a new strategy of statewide coalition building and political pragmatism.

Believing it could accomplish little at the local level, members of I-CARE worked increasingly with a statewide network of similar groups, Voting Ohioans Initiating a Clean Environment (VOICE), and with other groups at the state level. In support of I-CARE, VOICE refused to deal directly with CECOS/CER. The OEPA served as a mediator at times and also worked with an emerging coalition of industry and environmental groups. While much of the focus of these efforts was on revision of the 1980 state statute for implementing RCRA, there were other implications not so directly tied to that legislation. For example, the company began an educational campaign to explain its operation, and it began to respond more fully to some of the citizen complaints. With increasing national attention being given to alternatives to land-based disposal of hazardous waste (e.g., recycling and incineration), CECOS/CER developed a ten-year plan for moving away from landfilling. The plan noted explicitly that the company would initiate a series of programs to "improve community relations." Its objectives included creating a more "favorable awareness of CECOS and its services," establishment of the "credibility and reliability of CECOS to safely handle the disposal of hazardous waste," development of a "communication package of materials and programs for industry and the public," and provision to the public of the "best available information to address any concerns that may arise regarding CECOS." A wide range of strategies were proposed to achieve those objectives, from design of community education programs, a speaker's bureau, a newsletter, and public service announcements on hazardous waste to establishment of an "active and responsive Office of Public Information" (CECOS International, 1981). The citizens who worked with VOICE also adopted a more realistic and cooperative stance on the issues. Compared with those active in the earlier period, they were better informed and more sophisticated in their discussion of the problems and possible solutions. A review of their literature and public comments in the two periods indicates a striking change in both knowledge of technical issues and style of political participation. In effect, citizen groups shifted from protest and confrontation, typically using highly emotional language, to informed participation and accommodation, where their knowledge and use of technical information and terminology was noticeably greater. As a result, they earned kudos from both industry and state government officials, and by the mid-1980s, they were in frequent contact with the director of the OEPA and the governor. While CECOS/CER officials continued to maintain that citizen fears were groundless, they made a greater effort to explain company operation and to treat public concerns as legitimate.

Particularly on a statewide level, there was evidence that a process of cooperation and coalition building could effectively resolve conflicts over the operation of local facilities such as the one in Clermont County. The Ohio Manufacturers' Association (OMA), convinced that groundwater contamination would be a major issue in Ohio, joined environmental groups (including VOICE and the Ohio Sierra Club) and members of the Ohio legislature in formulating and supporting enactment of HB 506. This industry-environmental group coalition preceded by several years the formation of similar coalitions at the national level, such as Clean Sites, Incorporated, which was established in 1984, to help speed the cleanup of toxic waste dumps. By the mid-1980s, environmental mediation had become increasingly popular as an alternative to protracted and costly litigation (e.g., Talbot, 1983). The U.S. EPA has turned to mediation for resolving conflicts in areas as diverse as pesticide regulation and motor vehicle emission control. The use of mediation in this case in Ohio corroborates the general findings of recent research on environmental mediation (Bingham, 1986; Bacow and Wheeler, 1984; Sullivan, 1984), namely, that negotiation, consensus building, and joint problem solving can lead to quicker, less costly, and more successful resolution of conflicts in cases of facility siting than might be obtainable through more conventional forms of decision making.

Signed into law on August 1, 1984, HB 506 is widely viewed as a substantial improvement over the 1980 SB 269 in the siting of hazardous waste facilities. In particular, it includes provisions for greater citizen participation in decisions and stipulations that facilities must be located farther away from homes and schools. For example, it required changes in the public notice process and the availability of materials related to the public hearing on an application, including a statement on environmental impact, and it adds the board of township trustees of the township in which the facility is to be located to the groups previously included in an adjudication hearing on the application. The law also authorizes any individual who is aggrieved or adversely affected by the violation of the statute or rules, permits, or orders issued under it to file a civil action in court. The new law broadens a requirement that the facility represent a "minimum risk" not only of contamination of ground and surface water by leachate and runoff but by any other means as well; and not only by "improper" treatment, storage, or disposal methods but from "any" of these methods. The bill adds a requirement that a facility represent minimum risk of impact on public health and safety, of air pollution, and of soil contamination. It stipulates also that facilities with a large capacity for hazardous or toxic waste not be located or operated within 2,000 feet of any residence, school, hospital, jail, or prison; within any naturally occurring wetland; or within any flood hazard area with which the facility is not equipped to deal. Whereas under SB 269 a permit was permanent, the new law specifies that permits are limited to a five-year period. An installation and operation renewal permit is subject to similar requirements for public notice and comment and may be denied by the director of the OEPA on the basis of application materials, facility inspection reports, performance tests, the history of compliance with its existing permit, or other relevant information.

Although the practical effects of these new provisions on public partici-pation and the level of permissible risk will depend upon administrative interpretation and implementation decisions, the changes over the 1980 law were quite significant. Moreover, the target industries and other constituency groups, as noted, have adopted a more cooperative stance in recent years, and this is likely to promote a more effective citizen voice in implementation decisions. As of late 1986, it is difficult to describe precisely how the new legislation will affect disputes over the CECOS/CER facility. But several developments in 1984 and 1985 suggest that conflict over the landfill's operation will continue despite the generally improved atmosphere and statutory changes.

For example, the temporary permit held by CECOS/CER was due to be replaced in 1984 with a permanent permit, the granting of which requires a public hearing. The company requested of the OEPA, and received, permis-sion for a one-year extension on the interim permit. Some citizens believe that delay in conducting the public hearing may be yet another attempt by CECOS/CER to avoid responding to citizen concerns. In another action, on November 9, 1984, the OEPA temporarily closed the facility, by now one of the country's biggest toxic waste dumps, after discovering that ·contaminated water was knowingly pumped into a creek supplying drinking water to a nearby town (Shabecoff, 1984). The contamination was discovered by the inspector assigned to the site by the OEPA. Although the landfill was reopened about three weeks later under strict new regulations, the OEPA sought an independent hydrogeologist to survey the area. That action had been suggested several years earlier by VOICE.

In May 1985, the landfill was closed again, this time because of indications (in a study by an independent hydrogeology firm) that groundwater contamination might be occurring. However, test results indicated that there was only low-level, minor contamination for several of the oldest cells; there was no evidence of off-site contamination. Early data were misleading owing to the way test wells were drilled. The landfill reopened in mid-August 1985 but was allowed to accept non-RCRA wastes only. That was because Cell Number 9 (currently in use) does not meet the newly tightened RCRA requirements. However, the landfill may continue to accept wastes that fall under the Toxic Substances Control Act (TSCA), which include PCBs and nonhazardous industrial wastes. CECOS/CER has applied to the U.S. EPA for a waiver to RCRA's requirement for a double liner for Cell Number 9, which was already in use when the new RCRA requirements went into effect in May 1985.

Although the OEPA had stated earlier that no groundwater was flowing through the site, the agency now characterized the area as "saturated." The Ohio Department of Health initiated a survey of potential health effects as CECOS/CER conceded that the two oldest cells in the facility (the only ones without plastic liners) might have been leaking. As an outgrowth of these recent disputes, the OEPA indicated it was not satisfied with data the company had been keeping on its operation. Of even greater significance was an announcement by the OEPA in mid-1985 that it was reevaluating its basic support for hazardous waste landfills. The deputy director of the agency's hazardous waste management program, Virginia Aveni, explained the OEPA's new posture: "People should know that we are moving to a policy of discouraging landfilling in the state" (*Cincinnati Enquirer*, 1985).

Given these recent developments, it is perhaps not surprising that the OEPA has created a citizens' committee, headed by the mayor of Williamsburg (whose jurisdiction overlaps Jackson Township). Although there are no members of VOICE on the committee, it includes citizens who have been active at the local level. The committee meets with company officials in an effort to resolve differences over the operation of the facility. At this time, it is too early to assess the impact of the committee on the company or on the OEPA. But it is worth noting that the committee's creation is evidence that the OEPA has recognized the importance of working with citizen groups.

CONCLUSIONS

We have examined the role of citizen participation in decisions affecting the Clermont County facility during three time periods. The impact of citizens on implementation of Ohio's hazardous waste policy varied considerably across these three periods. In the first, 1972-1978, hazardous waste was something of a nonissue in Clermont County. The lack of zoning regulations at the local level and the incremental change in the landfill's permit from sanitary landfill to hazardous waste dump resulted in few opportunities for citizen participation, and hence little impact. In the second period, 1978-1981, hazardous waste issues reached the political agenda in Clermont County as a variety of controversies over the operation of the site erupted and media coverage of them increased sharply. Yet during this period the citizen role was largely one of protest, accompanied by ineffective attempts by the township to assert authority over the site. While the impact of citizen participation in the late 1970s was somewhat dysfunctional, these more organized and persistent citizen efforts did move both the OEPA and CECOS/CER to take public concerns more seriously than they had previously. Organized citizen protest also paved the way for a change in both strategy and effectiveness in the third period. Between 1981 and 1985 there was greater effort at coalition building and cooperation as political participation shifted to the state level. Citizen groups were able to change state law and establish the basis for longer-term influence over policy implementation.

The analytical framework developed by Mazmanian and Sabatier (1983) suggests a number of factors that help to explain these varied forms of participation and their impact on policy implementation. Statutory provisions for citizen access were clearly important in this case. Had greater opportunity for participation been provided, an earlier resolution of disputes over the site might have been possible, and citizen distrust of the OEPA and CECOS/CER might have been lessened. The framework also calls attention to the impact of generalized public support on the agency's decisions and the role of organized citizen groups (among other constituencies). Persistent public fears and opposition to the facility constrained policy implementation, particularly when extensive media coverage helped to mobilize citizens and increase their effective political influence. One result was that the OEPA was forced to devise new ways to build public confidence, most evident in the assignment of two inspectors to the site. The leadership skills of agency officials become significant when they must educate citizens on the nature of toxic substances, the risks posed, the standards for regulating facilities, and the alternatives available in a given locale. By 1985, the OEPA at least recognized the importance of working with local citizens and established the citizens' committee in Clermont County.

Rosenbaum (1983) has noted that there has been "little institutional learning about the impact of citizen concern with hazardous substances and the procedures for coping with citizen involvement." The Clermont County case suggests that some degree of institutional learning did take place, within both the OEPA and industry. This case suggests also that local conflicts of this kind may be resolved best with state-level mediation, which may provide for more effective representation of citizen concerns.

Looking beyond this particular case study, there are other implications for both scholars and governmental decision makers. Policy implementation analysis in general may contribute to knowledge of why policies succeed or fail and the conditions for effective implementation (Mazmanian and Sabatier, 1983; Williams et al., 1982). A particular focus on public participation holds the promise of learning more about the way in which both formal and informal mechanisms of citizen input promote policy legitimation, or ensuring that administrative decisions are broadly responsive to public preferences and needs. In the case of hazardous waste policy and other policies involving technological risks (e.g., nuclear waste disposal), policy legitimation includes the special and difficult decisions that establish acceptable levels of risk under conditions of uncertainty and with evident public fear of potential risks.

As noted early in this chapter, there is every reason to believe that such decisions will continue to be as important in the future as they are at present. The United States alone produces between 56 and 264 million metric tons of toxic and hazardous wastes each year, depending on the definition used and the particular study relied upon; 90% of it has been disposed of improperly in the past, that is, in ways considered "unsafe" (Conservation Foundation, 1984). Even as disposal shifts from land burial to treatment or incineration, questions will be raised, as they were in Philadelphia in early 1986, about risks to public health and environmental quality. Given the obvious need to find suitable methods of disposal, we would benefit from further knowledge of how public participation can be fostered and can contribute to effective siting and operating decisions.

Rosenbaum (1983) has observed that public involvement programs may become a gamble against public prejudices or an act of faith in the possibilities of public education, often with considerable risks to the agencies promoting them. Yet studies of local opposition to hazardous waste facilities suggest that a strategy of cooperation and negotiation (and sometimes compensation) that allows active participation by citizen groups may be the only feasible alternative (Morell and Magorian, 1982; Bacow and Milkey, 1982; Pitney, 1984). Comparative case studies, particularly of state and local decisions where public involvement has played a major role, might illuminate the conditions facilitating effective citizen participation.

State and local governments will be assuming added responsibilities for environmental protection, including hazardous waste policy, in the late 1980s and 1990s as a result of "new federalism" initiatives of the Reagan administration and federal budgetary cutbacks (Kraft, Clary, and Tobin, 1987). We know little about the resources and capabilities of these governments to make such decisions in a rational and responsive manner. The challenge of designing workable public participation programs is especially consequential given the enormity and complexity of the hazardous waste permitting process, the limited resources available to environmental protection agencies, and political dynamics that offer few incentives to policymakers to deal seriously with the problem (Pitney, 1984). Hence there is a clear need to examine how well equipped state and local governments are to make such decisions and to learn more about the factors influencing successful policy formulation and implementation. The case study here indicates some of the important questions deserving of further inquiry.

REFERENCES

Bacow, Lawrence S., and James R. Milkey, "Overcoming Local Opposition to Hazardous Waste Facilities: The Massachusetts Approach," *Harvard Environmental Law Review* 6 (1982): 265-305.

Bacow, Lawrence S., and Michael Wheeler, *Environmental Dispute Resolution* (New York: Plenum Press, 1984).

Bingham, Gail, *Resolving Environmental Disputes: A Decade of Experience* (Washington, DC: Conservation Foundation, 1986).

Carnes, Sam A., "Confronting Complexity and Uncertainty: Implementation of Hazardous-Waste Management Policy," in Dean E. Mann, ed., *Environmental Policy Implementation: Planning and Management Options and Their Consequences* (Lexington, MA: Lexington Books, 1982).

CECOS International, "Executive Summary, Ten-year Technology Plan," Prepared for the New York Department of Environmental Conservation, 1981.

Cincinnati Enquirer, March 1, 1979a, p. B-3.

Cincinnati Enquirer, October 9, 1979b, p. D-1.

Cincinnati Enquirer, December 16, 1982, p. D-2.

Cincinnati Enquirer, May 11, 1985, p. C-1.

Cincinnati Post, "EPA to Watch," August 7, 1981, p. B-3.

Clermont Sun, October 14, 1981a, p. 1.

Clermont Sun, December 16, 1981b, p. 1.

Cohen, Steven, "Defusing the Toxic Time Bomb: Federal Hazardous Waste Programs," in Norman J. Vig and Michael E. Kraft, eds., *Environmental Policy in the 1980s: Reagan's New Agenda* (Washington, DC: CQ Press, 1984).

Conservation Foundation, *State of the Environment: An Assessment at Mid-Decade* (Washington, DC: Conservation Foundation, 1984).

Fischhoff, Baruch, et al., *Acceptable Risk* (New York: Cambridge University Press, 1981).

Flores, Albert, and Michael E. Kraft, "Determining the Acceptability of Risk in Regulatory Policy: Ethics, Politics, and Risk Analysis," in James S. Bowman and Frederick A. Elliston, eds., *Ethics, Government, and Public Policy* (Westport, CT: Greenwood Press, 1987).

Gruson, Lindsey, "Philadelphians at Hearing Protest Plan to Store Hazardous Waste for Ocean Burning," *The New York Times*, January 14, 1986, p. 8.

Hadden, Susan, ed., *Risk Analysis, Institutions, and Public Policy* (Port Washington, NY: Associated Faculty Press, 1984).

Jones, Charles O., *An Introduction to the Study of Public Policy*, 3rd ed. (Monterey, CA: Brooks/Cole, 1984).

Kraft, Michael E., "The Political and Institutional Setting for Risk Analysis," in Vincent T. Covello et al., eds., *Risk Evaluation and Management* (New York: Plenum Press, 1986).

Kraft, Michael E., Bruce B. Clary, and Richard J. Tobin, "The Impact of New Federalism on State Environmental Policy: The Great Lakes States," in Peter Eisinger and William Gormley, eds., *The Midwest's Response to the New Federalism* (Madison: University of Wisconsin Press, 1987).

Lester, James P., "The Process of Hazardous Waste Regulation: Severity, Complexity, and Uncertainty," in James P. Lester and Ann O'M. Bowman, eds., *The Politics of Hazardous Waste Management* (Durham, NC: Duke University Press, 1983).

Mazmanian, Daniel A., and Paul A. Sabatier, 1983. *Implementation and Public Policy* (Glenview, IL: Scott, Foresman, 1983).

Morell, David, and Christopher Magorian, *Siting Hazardous Waste Facilities* (Cambridge, MA: Ballinger, 1982).

Ohio Environmental Protection Agency, *Solid Waste Disposal Licenses and Regulation*, OAC-3745-27, July 29, 1976.

Pitney, John J., "Bile Barrel Politics: Siting Unwanted Facilities," *Journal of Policy Analysis and Management* 3 (Spring 1984): 446-448.

Rosenbaum, Walter A., "The Politics of Public Participation in Hazardous Waste Management," in James P. Lester and Ann O'M. Bowman, eds., *The Politics of Hazardous Waste Management* (Durham, NC: Duke University Press, 1983).

Shabecoff, Philip, "Officials in Ohio Shut Key Dump for Toxic Waste," *The New York Times*, November 14, 1984, p. 10.

Shabecoff, Philip, "E.P.A. to Propose New Toxic Rules," *The New York Times*, January 10, 1986, p. 12.

Sullivan, Timothy J., *Resolving Development Disputes through Negotiations* (New York: Plenum Press, 1984).

Talbot, Allan R., *Settling Things: Six Case Studies in Environmental Mediation* (Washington, DC: Conservation Foundation, 1983).

U.S. Environmental Protection Agency, *Siting of Hazardous Waste Management Facilities and Public Opposition* (Washington, DC: U.S. Environmental Protection Agency, Office of Water and Waste Management, 1979).

Williams, Walter, et al., *Studying Implementation: Methodological and Administrative Issues* (Chatham, NJ: Chatham House, 1982).

5

Locals versus Metropolitans: The Community Dynamics of Groundwater Protection

John D. Powell

INTRODUCTION

The process of coming to grips with the problems of hazardous wastes in America has been characterized by its severity, complexity, and uncertainty (Lester, 1983). These characteristics reveal themselves in local politics when groundwater contamination is seized on the local governmental agenda in one form or another. Recognition of the problem of public and private well contamination has grown rapidly as groundwater testing has occurred under federal, state, and local sponsorship. The extent of the problem in eastern Massachusetts led the New England River Basins Commission (1981) to label it an "assault on a precious commodity." As problem recognition has grown, so have policy approaches to prevention of contamination and ways of dealing with it when detected. Of the three related policy process cycles involved—the problem cycle, the policy cycle, and the political cycle (Kingdon, 1984)—the last has proven decisive to when and how groundwater contamination has been brought onto the local governmental agenda. And once it is on the agenda, the political dynamics of individual communities prove decisive in how, and how well, contamination incidents and threats are handled.

The purpose of this study is to explore political dynamics in local communities, which over the past decade have dealt with groundwater contamination threats and actual incidents in strikingly different ways. It is based on data from seven small-to-medium-sized towns on the outer fringe of the high-growth, high-technology industrial corridor of eastern Massachusetts (see Powell, 1984). While there are some differences among these communities in terms of natural resource configurations and patterns of growth, the institutional arrangements of local government are essentially identical, which removes this factor as an explanatory variable and permits concentration on more interesting dynamic factors.

THE PROBLEM

Within this group of seven communities, all of which depend on their own groundwater resources, some startling contamination threats and incidents have occurred. One town's historic industrial park found its way into the top ten of Superfund's national list of priority hazardous waste dumpsites. In a second community, two of three municipal wells were shut down due to organic chemical contamination. In a third town, state officials studying the residual effects of past uses of the herbicide silvex detected significant levels of dioxin contamination near a public well. In other instances, private wells have been closed because of petroleum product or organic chemical contaminations, illegal dumpsites have been discovered, and a variety of industrial accidents involving hazardous chemicals have occurred. Yet the responses of local governments to these events have varied widely. Three of the seven towns were measurably less responsive than the remaining four towns to the growing problems in their own and neighboring communities. I have divided the study group, therefore, into four "more responsive" and three "less responsive" towns.

LEVELS OF LOCAL ENVIRONMENTAL RESPONSIVENESS

What makes one town more responsive to the problem of groundwater contamination than another for purposes of this study? Towns were placed in one group or the other according to a set of three criteria. One criterion consisted of a town's adoption, or failure to adopt, specific recommendations for groundwater protection policies stipulated by the Boston Metropolitan Area Planning Council. More responsive towns adopted one or more recommended protective measures in advance of contamination incidents or threats. Less responsive towns either never adopted any protective measure or did so following major contaminations of municipal wells. A second criterion was the response of local officials to laboratory test results showing chemical contamination in drinking water or within the cone of depression of a municipal well. Officials in more responsive towns closed their wells forthwith. Officials in less responsive towns awaited further testing and, even upon verification of initial results, refused to shut down the contaminated well until forced to by state orders. A third criterion was the pattern of communication between public officials and the citizens in their communities. More responsive town officials immediately communicated, through personal contact and the local media, the nature of the contamination incident or threat to public health. This occurred even when state officials advised against divulging test results, pending another round of verification tests (which typically took several months for the results to be known). Officials in less responsive towns did not willingly communicate testing results to their local publics until forced to do so by the intervention of local environmental interest group pressures.

THE CHARACTER OF MORE AND LESS RESPONSIVE TOWNS

I have already pointed out that the governmental structures of these seven communities are essentially identical (one has a representative town meeting form of government, the other six an open town meeting). In addition, citizens in these seven towns, it can be expected, reflect the same high levels of general concern over the health menace of toxics found throughout the country (Mitchell, 1984). Furthermore, detailed information on the various contamination threats and disasters which have occurred over the past decade within the study group area have been chronicled in the local-oriented news media. One might reasonably expect, therefore, that the steadily rising problem and policy cycles within these seven communities ought to have produced a more or less homogeneous cycle of political activities to deal with the manifest assault on the study area's groundwater quality. What explains the fact that they did not?

Patterns of Community Growth

Thirty years ago, regardless of the differences among them, all seven towns in the study were more rural, less densely populated, and less industrialized than they are today. About then, however, two slightly diverging paths of growth began in today's more responsive and less responsive towns. A process of decay set in among the less responsive towns, marked by the loss of older, less competitive industries (bottling, shoes, watches) which in the more responsive communities had either never existed or been lost decades earlier. The more responsive communities, particularly in the decade from 1965 to 1975, gradually began to acquire the characteristics of bedroom communities for the area's professional and business work force.

These processes of socioeconomic evolution were reflected in time in distinctly different growth policy orientations in the more responsive and less reponsive groupings. Less responsive towns, seeking to protect their shrinking local job base, pursued policies to decrease unemployment, expand the municipal tax base, and make up for the loss of older industries. They consciously upgraded a policy of the pursuit of industrial and commercial growth in their communities. Boosterism among local elites waxed eloquent. Meanwhile, the more responsive communities pursued a less visible growth control policy. Arguments over zoning policy and enforcement came in time to be increasingly dominated by consideration of residential property values, rather than preserving or promoting jobs and business investments in the community. Table 5.1 shows that as a result the more and the less responsive towns have come to differ markedly with respect to six selected community characteristics. These two types of towns undoubtedly differ on many other characteristics as well. But these six serve to illustrate how different they are.

This kind of divergence in outlook toward industrial growth versus protection of residential amenities is, of course, commonplace in small-town America (Lingeman, 1980). Studies of local politics routinely reveal factional conflict within leadership strata (Scoble, 1960). The story of local politics is often one of the gradual acceptance of one of these factions over another; while never settling permanently, the existing balance of forces within a local community usually crystallizes into measurably divergent pathways of growth.

Localism and Cosmopolitanism

The concept of a continuum stretching between the poles of localism and cosmopolitanism is a venerable one in the social sciences, stretching back to Ferdinand Tönnies' distinction between *Gemeinschaft* and *Gesellschaft*. In recognizable variants, it has proven fruitful in understanding and explaining differences in American villages (Johansen & Fuguitt, 1984), towns (Martindale & Hanson, 1969; Lingeman, 1980) and city neighborhoods (Crenson, 1983) and comparative differences among cities, suburbs, and

Table 5.1
**Indications of Divergent Patterns of Community Growth in
Seven Massachusetts Towns**

Indicators	Mean Measure in the *more responsive* group of four towns	Mean Measure in the *less responsive* group of three towns
Population density	440/square mile	986/square mile
Household income	$28,509	$21,993
Residential Parcel Value	$109,540	$81,754
Industrial Parcel Value	$290,528	$310,314
Single-resident housing starts as a percent of all housing starts	100%	61%
Unemployment Rate	2%	4%

Sources: U.S. Bureau of the Census, Census of Population and Housing, 1980, updated; FY 1985-1987 Assessor's property tax data; and 1948-1986 building permits.

small towns (Ladd, 1972). In his classic discussion of the concept, Robert
Merton defines two types of influentials (Merton, 1968):

The chief criterion for distinguishing the two is found in their *orientation* toward
Rovere [the town under discussion]. The localite largely confines his interests to this
community. Rovere is essentially his world. Devoting little thought and energy to the
Great Society, he is preoccupied with local problems, to the virtual exclusion of the
national and international scene. He is, strictly speaking, parochial.
Contrariwise with the cosmopolitan type. He has some interest in Rovere and must
of course maintain a minimum of relations within the community, since he, too,
exerts influence there. But he is also oriented significantly to the world outside
Rovere, and regards himself as an integral part of that world. He resides in Rovere
but lives in the Great Society. If the local type is parochial, the cosmopolitan is
ecumenical. (p. 447)

At the most general level, the higher degree of localism among officials in
the less responsive towns helps explain their resistance to preventive
planning, their reluctance to act on information regarding chemical
contamination of drinking water, their reluctance to communicate with
their fellow townspeople, and the subsequent conflict they encountered with
local environmental activists. Correspondingly, the higher degree of cosmopolitanism among local officials in the more responsive towns helps explain
their contrary behavior.

Localism is consistently linked in the literature with lengthier residence in
a community (native born, old-timers, insiders) than for cosmopolitans
(newcomers, outsiders) and with lower levels of education, occupational
status, and a variety of other socioeconomic indicators. The data in Table
5.2, drawn from preliminary interviews with officials in the seven towns, are
typical of such differences.

DYNAMICS OF LOCAL ENVIRONMENTAL
POLICYMAKING

It is not surprising to find that officials (more locally oriented) in less
responsive towns resisted recommendations to adopt a variety of water
protection controls such as aquifer protection zoning, site review planning
requirements, and the like. Local businessmen and potential industrial
developers consistently complain before town boards and among their fellow
townsmen about the burdens of federal and state regulatory agencies and
programs. They argue against additional regulatory controls being placed
on them at the local level. Officials in the less responsive towns, being more
locally oriented, tend to agree with these arguments, since they are characteristically sensitive to personal relations with local business influentials
(Wildavsky, 1964). More cosmopolitan officials in the responsive towns,
attuned to national media reports of inadequacies in the EPA's Superfund

Table 5.2
**Indications of Localism and Cosmopolitanism among Local Officials
in Seven Massachusetts Towns** *(N = 131)*

Indicators	Officials in the *more responsive* group of four towns *(N = 79)*	Officials in the *less responsive* group of three towns *(N = 52)*
Residence:		
average length	16 years	24 years
native born (%)	10	35
Education: (%)		
HS, some college	24	35
BA/BS	39	40
MA/MS	27	25
PhD	10	0
Occupation: (%)		
professional, executive, managerial	56	46
supervisory, worker/clerical, small business	40	54

Source: Survey by the author.

program and aware of shortages of funds for state-level efforts to protect groundwater quality, reject these arguments and feel compelled to take local preventive action.

The generally higher level of information and awareness of public life beyond the locality is typical of cosmopolitans and is closely linked with their higher levels of education. An additional indication of local-cosmopolitan dynamics has to do with these local officials' notions of what responsibilities their local offices entail, as opposed to other levels of government. Parochials often argue that it is the federal or state government's responsibility to worry about toxics and groundwater contamination, since they have "more expertise" and "more resources." Anomalously, cosmopolitans argue that town officials are best informed about and most responsible for local realities. If asked directly which level of government ought to be responsible for improving the protection of groundwater against toxic assault, 41% of those interviewed in the more responsive towns say "local government," while only 20% of the officials in the less responsive towns point the finger at themselves.

As Table 5.2 indicates, leaders in the more responsive towns are more likely to have executive and managerial occupations than their counterparts in less responsive towns. This factor, when combined with the cosmopolitans' more recent (they are younger) and higher levels of education, seems to be the explanation for their relative confidence and assertiveness in closing down wells upon receipt of initial testing results indicating imminent or actual contamination. In comparison, parochials in the less responsive towns were reluctant to act in the face of the scientific and health risk uncertainties. In fact, they resisted pressure from environmental activists to take action. Occupational experience involving the making of difficult and high-impact decisions under conditions of uncertainty, it can be argued, should reinforce other factors which would incline cosmopolitan officials to take local responsibility for action. Conversely, parochials in less responsive towns might feel less inclined to challenge the advice of state technicians or industrial spokesmen who emphasize the comparative uncertainties in all such situations (see Regens, Dietz, and Rycroft, 1983).

Locals and cosmopolitans also differed in their policies of communication of the risks involved to their fellow citizens. Locals did so grudgingly, and cosmopolitans routinely and voluntarily communicated. At the root of these differences lie two quite different understandings of (and attitudes toward) risk assessment in the kind of complex situations upon which we are focusing. In reporting on his innovative research in two Massachusetts communities, Elliott (1984) categorized respondents as proponents, guardians, or conservationists. These orientations were derived from differing approaches to the risks involved in the hypothetical siting of a hazardous waste treatment facility in these communities. Proponents favored the siting, based on a narrow, technical risk approach of quantitative prediction of risk and reliance on preventive technologies. Guardians accepted the idea of siting only if the proponent's approach were broadened to focus more on the human factor: monitoring of risk indicators and prevention equipment, operator training and procedures, documented management oversight, accident mitigation planning, and plant accountability to local officials. Conservationists believed that the risks could be neither predicted nor managed and rejected the siting proposal altogether. The localities in the study towns essentially adopted a proponentlike posture toward situations in which complex risk was an issue. They tended to "let the engineers and experts who know" define the appropriate decisions to be made. Localites, therefore, did not feel they had much to say to their neighbors and did not communicate. The cosmopolitans fit the picture of Elliott's guardians. Skeptical of mechanistic assurances from the proponent's experts, they focused on a rational, reasonable, comprehensive approach to the management of risk in their communities. Cosmopolitans seemed to define communication with their publics regarding risks as a kind of educational responsibility.

Finally, we come to the most overtly "political" of the dynamics differentiating the two groups of towns, namely the emergence of environmental activism in the less responsive towns. The leaders of these public interest groups fit into the cosmopolitan pattern. But living in towns dominated by parochial leadership, they expressed policy positions akin to Elliott's conservationists, arguing against voluntarily assuming any additional risk to health and welfare in the local community. While there were also environmental activists in the more responsive towns, the events under discussion failed to bring them into political conflict with their local officials, who acted as guardians.

In the less responsive towns, local environmentalists, frustrated with the lack of interest and communication from local officials concerning contamination and health threats, formed organizational pressure groups. They attended and spoke up in meetings of local boards, held public protest meetings bringing in outside political leaders (state representatives) and media, and in one case successfully contested the reelection of the chairman of the local Board of Health (Powell, 1984). Given the norm of volunteerism which operates in small communities (low turnout, uncontested elections, voluntary entry into and exit from local governmental service), this was dramatic evidence of political tension within these towns (see Prewitt, 1970).

CONCLUSION

Two groups of towns, differing measurably in their patterns of growth and responsiveness to groundwater contamination issues, were compared in this study. The political dynamics which helped account for these differences were explored through the concept of localism-cosmopolitanism. Characteristics of local officials, including residential longevity, level of education, and occupational status, were linked to policy differences in preventive planning, well closures and communications patterns with citizens.

The local-cosmopolitan dimension proved to be a helpful tool to augment our conventional ways of studying the agenda-building stage of policy processes, particularly when looking at smaller-scale units of government (Cobb and Elder, 1972; Kingdon, 1984).

REFERENCES

Cobb, R., and C. Elder, *Participation in American Politics: The Dynamics of Agenda Building*. (Baltimore: The Johns Hopkins University Press, 1972).

Crenson, Matthew A., *Neighborhood Politics* (Cambridge: Harvard University Press, 1983).

Elliott, Michael L. P., "Improving Community Acceptance of Hazardous Waste Facilities through Alternative Systems for Mitigating and Managing Risk," *Hazardous Waste* 1(1984) 3:397-410.

Johanson, H., and G. Fuguitt, *The Changing Rural Village in America* (Cambridge, MA: Ballinger, 1984).

Kingdon, John W., *Agendas, Alternatives, and Public Policies* (Boston: Little, Brown, 1984).

Ladd, Carll E., Jr., *Ideology in America: Change and Response in a City, a Suburb, and a Small Town* (New York: W. W. Norton & Co., 1972).

Lester, James P., "The Process of Hazardous Waste Regulation: Severity, Complexity, and Uncertainty," in James P. Lester and Ann O'M. Bowman, eds., *The Politics of Hazardous Waste Management* (Durham, NC: Duke University Press, 1983), 3-22.

Lingeman, Richard, *Small Town America* (New York: Putnam, 1980).

Martindale, D., and R. Hanson, *Small Town and the Nation* (Westport, CT: Greenwood Press, 1969).

Merton, Robert K., *Social Theory and Social Structure* (New York: The Free Press, 1968).

Mitchell, Robert Cameron, "Public Opinion and Environmental Politics in the 1970s and 1980s," in N. Vig and M. Kraft, eds., *Environmental Policy in the 1980s* (Washington, DC: CQ Press, 1984).

New England River Basins Commission, "Well Contamination: Assault on a Precious Commodity," *Waterfacts* 2 (1981) 2: 1-2.

Powell, John Duncan, "The Changing Local Scene: Protecting Groundwater from Industrial Contamination," *Hazardous Waste* 1 (1984) 3: 323-332.

Prewitt, Kenneth, "Political Ambitions, Volunteerism and Electoral Accountability," *The American Political Science Review* 64 (1970) 1: 5-17.

Regens, J., T. Dietz, and R. Rycroft, "Risk Assessment in the Policy Making Process: Environmental Health and Safety Protection," *Public Administration Review* 43 (1983) 2: 137-145.

Scoble, Harry, "Leadership Hierarchies and Political Issues in a New England Town" in Morris Janowitz, ed., *Community Political Systems* (Glencoe: The Free Press, 1960): 117-145.

Wildavsky, Aaron, *Leadership in a Small Town* (Totowa, NJ: Bedminster Press, 1964).

PART II

THE STATE
AND REGIONAL LEVELS

6

Longitudinal and Catastrophic Models of State Hazardous Waste Regulation

C. K. Rowland, S. C. Lee, and D. B. Goetze

INTRODUCTION

Most students of environmental regulation recognize explicitly or implicitly that such regulation is the product of three factors: objective toxic externalities; the subjective severity or perceived risk associated with these externalities; and the quantity and quality of group political pressures engendered by these objective and perceived market failures (Wilson, 1980; Voegel, 1981; Weingast, 1984). Thus distal threats become perceived risks and serve as the basis for group demands. The quantity and quality of these demands define the set of politically rational options open to policymakers. For a given policy decision these options tend to be dichotomously divided into proregulation and prodevelopment policy choices. Accordingly, group competition tends to be between those who would impose stringent environmental regulation at the cost of economic development and those who would promote development at the cost of stringent regulation. Over time the group struggle is over the balance between protection and development in response to objective and subjective environmental risks.

This potential interaction between perceived externalities and relative group influence is typified by the politics of hazardous waste regulation at the state level. The relative influence of prodevelopment groups promoting material benefits (Salisbury, 1969) and proenvironment groups promoting diffuse environmental benefits should vary across states over time and among states at the same point in time in response to variance in the

This work was supported by a grant from the University of Kansas Graduate Faculty Research Fund. The authors gratefully acknowledge the help of John W. Falley in designing and depicting the catastrophe models.

perceived threat of waste externalities. The quantity and quality of this variation define the temporal and spatial complexities of hazardous waste politics as well as the political structure of waste regulation in a given state at a given time. Consequently, we offer a framework for the analysis of the politics of hazardous waste regulation at the state level that posits variation in group influence as the proximate effect on variance in regulatory effort.

ANALYTIC FRAMEWORK

Our proposed framework is offered as a supplement to, not an alternative to, extant theoretical work. As a supplement it is designed to expand extant work in two ways. First we present a four-stage longitudinal theory that posits group activity, subjective waste severity, and, during its later stages, regulatory capacity as the causes of interstate variation in regulatory response to waste deposition.[1] Second, because some assumptions of contemporary quantitative models are incompatible with our theoretical expectations, we derive from catastrophe theory a cross-sectional descriptive model as a framework for testing empirically the expected pattern of state response for the most recent stage of the regulatory process. As the first step in the presentation of our framework its assumptions will be made explicit.

ASSUMPTIONS AND CONDITIONS

Our model of interstate variation in regulatory response to hazardous waste assumes the following decision-maker characteristics and regulatory conditions.

1. Waste-producing technologies combine the capacity for immediate, specific social benefits and potential, unspecified environmental costs.
   a) Awareness of social benefits precedes perception of social costs.
   b) Perception of social costs does not include deterministic knowledge of the biological or social risk associated with perceived social costs.
2. A positive correlation exists between waste deposition in a state and the contribution of waste generators to that state's economic development.
3. Hazardous waste generators seek to maximize profits; profit-maximizing producers are free to shift resources among political subdivisions.
4. State policymakers seek to achieve economic development and a clean environment; subject to minimum standards established by the central government, states are free to vary the marginal costs of government imposed on producers in their subdivisions.

RANGE OF REGULATORY RESPONSE

Table 6.1 depicts a range of possibilities given different levels of public perception of issues and problems. From our posited range of group influ-

Table 6.1
Values, Public Knowledge, and Environmental Regulation

	Balance of Pro-Environment Groups Favor	Balance of Pro-Development Groups Favor	Public Perceptions of Problems and Severity	Expected Change in Levels of Regulation
(1)	Environmental Protection	Environmental Protection	Low	Steep Rise
(2)	Industrial Development	Industrial Development	Low	Steep Decline
(3)	Environmental Protection	Environmental Protection	High	Steep Rise
(4)	Industrial Development	Industrial Development	High	Steep Decline
(5)	Environmental Protection	Industrial Development	Low	Modest Decline
(6)	Industrial Development	Environmental Protection	Low	Modest Rise
(7)	Environmental Protection	Industrial Development	High	Modest Rise
(8)	Industrial Development	Environmental Protection	High	Modest Decline

Source: Compiled by the authors.

ence and public awareness we derive three independent variables. One is the relative importance to proenvironment groups of environmental protection values versus economic development values associated with attracting industry to the state. A second is the relative importance to prodevelopment groups of environmental protection values versus values associated with attracting industry to the state. Prodevelopment groups may include private-regarding waste generators and public-regarding groups concerned with jobs, tax base, and other indicators of economic development. A third variable is public perception of hazardous waste deposition and its consequences. The sole dependent variable identified is level of regulatory effort, defined as the commitment of governmental resources to achieve net reductions in the deposition of waste externalities.

The table lists each permutation of the dichotomous values of the independent variables and associates each with the anticipated pattern of change in regulatory stringency. Distinguishing between concern for the interests of prodevelopment and proenvironment groups does not preclude the possibility that a given regulatory action could simultaneously benefit both sets of groups. Some prodevelopment groups, for example, may place a high value on environmental protection because it enhances the state's quality of life and, therefore, makes it more attractive to new producers. Permutations 1 through 4 are instances where the predominant values held by environmental and developmental groups are the same. Since there is no conflict in values between sets of groups, the question of whose concerns enter most demonstratively in the calculi of decision makers is moot. Regulatory levels should rise if both groups place a relatively high value on environmental protection.

Permutations 5 through 8 are instances where values held by public- and private-regarding groups are in conflict. The conflictual balance should be determined by public perceptions of the diffuse risk posed by hazardous waste externalities relative to the perceived contribution of waste generators to economic development. If perceived risk is high then diffuse values held by public-regarding environmental groups are of proximate concern to decision makers. Values held by developmental groups should be most important where public perception of risk is low. Value conflict also means that values held by the two sets of groups are not reinforcing and each may mitigate the other's influence on the regulatory actions of decision makers. If so, the predicted changes in regulatory levels should be less dramatic than in instances where values are congruent.

These eight permutations indicate some of the elements from which a political theory of waste regulation can be constructed to explain the relative effects of group activity and public perceptions on state regulation at a given point in time. However, the likely incidence of particular combinations of values of independent variables affecting waste regulation in a given jurisdiction varies over time. In recognition of this temporal variance, we posit four stages of state hazardous waste regulation.

TRENDS IN THE VALUES OF INDEPENDENT VARIABLES

The four stages evolve by reference to vectors of independent-variable values that occur simultaneously at a given point in time and define a particular stage in the evolution of regulatory effort. Projections must be made about the values assumed by independent and dependent variables through time, that is, in each of the four stages. In this section, therefore, we discuss how values for the dependent and each independent variable are expected to change from one stage to the next.

Objective levels of hazardous waste are expected to increase uniformly in stages 1 and 2; then, depending on a state's regulatory activity in prior stages, to decline or increase in stages 3 and 4. Thus, we expect states to differ in levels of absolute waste at a given point in time but to experience similar patterns of change in the direction and rate of waste growth over time. Continuous growth over time in the magnitude of hazardous waste deposition in the environment is likely to create a corresponding growth in the magnitude of physical contamination problems; however, because the benefits of chemical technologies are apparent long before their associated costs, we anticipate that the public will not perceive social costs until well after the physical problems become evident. When the magnitude of the physical problems reaches a critical point, usually marked by catastrophic revelations such as Times Beach or Love Canal, the public's perception of social costs should become ubiquitous. We note this behavior in our theory by positing that public perception of waste deposition and its associated risks remains low for all states in stages 1 and 2, increases unevenly among states in stage 3, and becomes uniformly high during stage 4.

We also expect that the configuration of group influences will vary across stages and among states during a given stage. Groups favoring the interests of waste-generating firms should be uniformly influential in early stages because prodevelopment and private-regarding groups representing waste generators should be influential when public knowledge of waste externalities is low, as expected in the first two stages. Hence, groups representing waste generators and promoting the developmental benefits of waste-generating production are expected to dominate the regulatory process throughout the first two stages. The low level of public knowledge about hazardous waste implies that environmental groups are relatively inactive on the question of waste regulation during stages 1 and 2. The political activity of these groups increases in stage 3 in accord with the increase in public awareness posited for that stage and, although their relative influence is constrained somewhat by the head start gained by private-regarding groups during the previous stages, remains at a high level during stage 4. Moreover, when perceived risk becomes ubiquitous in stage 4 many prodevelopment groups can be expected to reduce their opposition to waste regulation and to focus their attention on the problem of achieving waste reduction without destroying economic development.

Thus, the theory implies that for regulatory effort to be maximized in a state, the balance of that state's groups must anticipate securing relatively high levels of benefit from enhanced environmental protection and that the balance of group influence will shift in response to change in public awareness of waste externalities. The derivation of this expectation is presented below.

ANTICIPATED VECTORS OF VALUES OCCURRING IN PARTICULAR STAGES

We construct our theory of regulatory levels from the sets of relationships, as depicted in Table 6.1, anticipated for each stage of the regulatory process.

Stage 1. In stage 1, we posit for the case of hazardous waste that a rapid growth of new waste-generating technologies creates important social benefits (products and employment) and introduces unprecedented threats to the environment from waste deposition. For the public interest to be served, a rise in regulatory levels should accompany the rise in the volume of generated waste. However, at this stage, dissemination of knowledge to the public and to policymakers about the environmental risks posed by introduction of the new waste-generating technologies is poor—lagging far behind dissemination of knowledge about the benefits of the new waste-generating technologies (Rushefsky, 1982; Rowland and Feiock, 1983). Moreover, in the absence of publicly perceived social costs, the only groups organized at this time to engage in political activity are prodevelopment groups. Without public-regarding group activity in support of social regulation, policymakers are expected to welcome waste generators and the social benefits of waste-producing technologies. A glance back at Table 6.1, rows (2) and (5), indicates that, since regulatory programs have not previously been established in most states, we can expect either no regulation or symbolic regulation that imposes virtually no costs on waste generators to prevail throughout this stage for most states. Firms should be free to maximize profits by allocating resources among states on the basis of markets, feedstocks, tax benefits, and other factors without considering marginal costs of regulation.

Stage 2. In stage 2, most states place a relatively high value on industrial economic development. Public knowledge of waste issues continues to be low in this stage, so the goals of prodevelopment groups should continue to dominate. What distinguishes stage 2 from stage 1 is a growing dependence of states on the economic benefits (e.g., value added, new capital, employment) of attracting waste producers and a growing reliance on reductions in costs of government to compete with other states to attract waste-generating production. By stage 2, new or expanding waste-generating firms must allocate resources among states with comparable markets, feedstocks, and other incentives. Without public perception of social costs, states with comparable extralegal resources (e.g., feedstocks, labor pool) can be expected to compete for the benefits of production by lowering the cost of government, including the cost of regulation. Even if decision makers in these competing states were placing a high value on environmental concerns, the absence of perceived risk and the dominance of prodevelopment groups should make them susceptible to groups representing waste-generating firms, a susceptibility exacerbated by their growing economic dependency on waste-generating producers.

The anticipated interstate competition to attract waste-generating firms by adjusting regulatory levels implies a decline in mean levels of regulatory spiral among those states involved in the competition (Rowland and Marz, 1981). Thus, circumstances defining stage 2 reinforce the posited decline in regulatory levels for states whose balance of groups place a relatively high value on industrial development. Since these states had previously eschewed social regulation, the prediction is for a devolution to the promotion of waste-generating production at the expense of environmental protection throughout stage 2.

Stage 3. Stage 3 is distinguished primarily by the paradoxical combination of burgeoning public perception of waste externalities, nascent environmental group activity, and the continued interstate competition for waste-generating industries. Incidents such as Love Canal elevate public awareness of hazardous waste issues and activate public-regarding environmental groups in some states; however, public perception of risk is not ubiquitous. Moreover, firms may close down or shift resources to other states if states impose unacceptable costs of regulation, leaving behind the wastes generated during their stay. Because regulation is not retroactive, it cannot restore the supply of land and water lost from contamination. Hence, although the elevated perception of biological risk and the associated increase in proenvironment group activity should engender an increase in regulatory effort, this effort may be mitigated by the fear of losing producers while keeping their toxic legacy. At the federal level, elevated public perception of risk moves hazardous waste onto the policy agenda, but federal policy during this stage remains unformulated, and states must rely on their own fiscal and organizational capacities to meet the costs of regulation.

The sharpest inclines in regulatory stringency should occur in states that had avoided or been unsuccessful in the cycles of intense competition for waste-generating firms. Without dependence on waste generators, the interests of environmentally aware publics in these states take precedence in the calculi of regulatory decision makers, environmental groups organize, and their political influence reinforces outcomes favorable to a rise in regulatory levels. Moreover, given low levels of waste depositon and limited dependency on waste generators, the cost to the states is relatively low. This outcome is consistent with row (3) in Table 6.1.

States that participated in the competition are expected to increase regulatory stringency but less dramatically and less adequately. A rise in the level of public knowledge about waste deposition pushes environmental interest concerns onto the agenda in calculations of regulatory levels, but countervailing concerns about economic costs constrain the effects of public perceptions and effectiveness of environmental groups. In states with conflicting environmental and developmental concerns, organizational and fiscal capacity to pursue environmental goals without imposing unacceptable costs on waste generators appears as a mitigating determinant of relative group influence. However, in the absence of ubiquitous risk perception, many states should continue to use lax regulation as a lure in the competition for waste-generating industry.

Stage 4. Four important changes in the regulatory setting make stage 4 qualitatively different from its predecessors. First, the public perception of waste severity and associated risk becomes ubiquitous. This is not to say that perceived risk does not vary among states; objective and subjective severity continue to differ from state to state. But hazardous waste is perceived everywhere as a policy problem worthy of a place on the policy agenda.

Second, the ubiquity of risk perception should engender a realignment of group pressures. Many prodevelopment groups can be expected to reduce opposition to regulation or to support waste regulation because firms are hesitant to shift resources to states where environmental degradation threatens the quality of life and creates potential legal and tax liabilities. Active opponents of regulation designed to achieve a net gain in waste deposition should be limited primarily to private-regarding groups representing waste generators.

Third, because the elevated perception of risk recognizes implicitly that state programs have failed to control toxic waste deposition, the federal government assumes primary responsibility for formulating hazardous waste policy. Legislation such as the Resource Conservation and Recovery Act (RCRA) creates a model federal program and imposes minimum federal standards on state programs. A state may retain primary authority over waste regulation if it formulates a program judged by the U.S. Environmental Protection Agency (EPA) to be essentially equivalent to the federal model. However, state programs that fail to meet minimum federal standards or fail to implement and enforce their program as formulated may be preempted by the federal government.

Finally, the importance of fiscal and organizational capacity as control factors mitigating group influences increases dramatically during this stage. This is so because federal standards make it difficult for even the most prodevelopment states to use lax regulation as a major tool in the interstate competition for developmental resources. To do so would be to invite federal preemption and lose state control over implementation and enforcement. States remain free, however, to allocate the costs of regulation between private and public sources and to organize their own implementation and enforcement efforts. Under these circumstances, the organizational and fiscal capacity to pay for regulation without imposing its costs on sources of employment and taxes make the state more receptive to demands for regulation. By contrast, states with inferior organizational and fiscal capacity should be less receptive to similar group demands under similar conditions of perceived severity.

In combination with the assumptions specified in the introduction, stage 4's conditions would seem to predict a convergence of state effort around a national norm responsive to perceived severity. This expectation is mitigated, however, by two factors. First, scarce federal resources limit the threat of federal preemption to the most recalcitrant states. Second, although state programs are constrained by the federal model and EPA oversight, states retain substantial discretion over the specifics of implementation and enforcement and remain free to promulgate regulations more stringent than the federal standard. Thus, although interstate variance should diminish, substantial variance in regulatory effort should remain as some states continue to face trade-offs between economic and environmental priorities.

Because stage 4 represents a qualitative change in the regulatory climate, we expect a qualitative change in the pattern of regulatory response. Given the assumed and observed conditions of stage 4 regulation, we expect a bimodal response to waste severity. A bimodal response pattern suggests that states respond to similar stimuli in different ways. When faced with comparable stimuli, some are expected to respond to ecological priorities, others to economic priorities. Ecological responses achieve adequate regulation and net environmental gains—that is, net waste deposition is reduced. Economic responses ensure that waste deposition will continue to increase but minimize the possibility that waste generators will "punish" the state and impede economic development by shifting resources to other states in response to regulatory costs (Lindblom, 1983).

Implicit in this expectation is the question: What determines which path a state will follow? The answer for stage 4 is rooted in the assumed desire of policymakers to accommodate both developmental and environmental demands where possible, the assumed freedom of producers to shift resources among states in response to unacceptable costs of government, and the observation that under the conditions defining stage 4, groups promoting economic development and environmental protection may both favor an increase in regulatory effect. Given these conditions, all states want to regulate hazardous waste; however, stringent regulation may be irrational for some states with a high level of waste and a high level of dependency on waste-generating producers. This irrationality derives from the ironic fact that, beyond a certain unspecified point of waste deposition, it may not be possible for states whose fiscal capacity (Davis and Lester, 1984) to regulate is dependent on the economic contribution of waste-generating industries to finance adequate regulation without imposing unacceptable marginal costs of government on these producers. These marginal costs are exacerbated if the state's organizational capacity must be expanded to accommodate the demands of the federally approved program. For such states the pursuit of stringent regulation engenders market punishments that simultaneously impede economic development and reduce their capacity to achieve adequate regulation. Thus, the ecological path is environmentally futile as well as economically disastrous. Compromise or "middle-road" paths are equally irrational because, although they may slow environmental degradation, they too require the imposition of unacceptable costs of government on mobile producers and lead inevitably to a destruction of economic benefits without a commensurate cleanup of toxic residues. By contrast, states less dependent on waste generators can achieve new gains without incurring the debilitating spiral of market punishments if they have the fiscal capacity to socialize the cost of an adequate regulatory effort (Williams and Matheny, 1984) and the organizational capacity to accommodate new programmatic demands without incurring new costs. For these organizationally and fiscally capable states it becomes irrational to spend less than the amount required to achieve net reductions in waste deposition. To continue the competition in laxity would be to invite federal intervention and incur political punishments. To compromise by reducing waste deposition without achieving net gains would be to spend money without achieving net environmental protection or developmental benefits. Thus, institutionally capable states should respond to severity, and this response should reflect the degree of severity.

The conditions of contemporary waste regulation,therefore, create two sets of policy calculi. In fiscally capable states policymakers can be responsive to perceived waste severity and the demands of proregulation groups without incurring net developmental losses. Because policymakers value development and protection, we would expect in these states a positive correlation between public awareness, waste severity, and regulatory effort. In other states, those without the capacity to socialize the cost of regulation, we would expect policymakers to be relatively unresponsive to perceived severity and the demands of environmental groups. To respond would be to incur net losses in economic development without reducing net waste severity, because to regulate is to lose the financial base of regulation. Since environmental priorities would destroy the resources necessary to achieve net environmental gains, states can be expected to eschew such priorities and maintain the minimum effort required to achieve federal enforcement grants. To do more would lead to self-inflicted market punishments; to do less would lead to federal preemption and allow the feds to impose costs of government that would do to the state what it will not do to itself.

EMPIRICAL APPLICATION

If our theory proposes accurately the evolution of state hazardous waste policy and the interstate distribution of regulatory effort, the anticipated patterns of state responses should be apparent in empirical examinations of regulatory patterns. Although an empirical test of the theory is beyond the scope of this effort, we shall examine the congruence between our posited bimodal response patterns and extant empirical work, suggest some limitations of extant quantitative models, and offer an alternative, cross-sectional framework derived from catastrophe theory as a descriptive model to guide future empirical efforts.

Research to Date

Extant research into the contemporary distribution of state regulation offers tentative support for our anticipated bimodality and illustrates the limitations of conventional quantitative models. For example, Lester and his collaborators (Lester et al., 1983) found that, as anticipated by the assumed preferences of policymakers for a clean environment, states responded positively to the severity of waste deposition. However, their best linear model left approximately half the interstate variance unexplained. By contrast, Rowland and Feiock (1984) found that states' regulatory efforts were negatively related to their dependency on waste-generating industries. Like that of Lester et al., their conventional statistical model left substantial variance unexplained. More recently, Williams and Matheny (1984) found that a state's fiscal capacity was the best predictor of its expenditures for clean land and water (a questionable surrogate for hazardous waste regulation) but that under controls for overall state expenditures environmental group activity and problem severity were the best predictors of public expenditures. Private expenditures, on the other hand, were best predicted by measures of economic dependency, all of which were negatively related to costs imposed on producers. Again, under controls for state budget, conventional statistical techniques explained about 50% of the variance.

In combination, the work summarized above supports our theoretical expectations by suggesting that group influence, perceived severity, institutional capacity, and economic dependency all influence regulatory decisions. However, its inconsistencies and tendency to explain half the variance among states suggest that the combined influence of groups and severity under control for independent fiscal capacity may engender a bimodal response pattern not susceptible to conventional linear measurement because the pattern is not susceptible to the assumptions of linearity and continuity associated with such measurement. In response to this possibility we offer a supplemental descriptive model derived from catastrophe theory. Before presentation of the model, we specify each independent variable's anticipated effect on waste regulation.

Anticipated Effects on Bimodality

Our conceptualization of stage 4 posits five systemic dimensions of concern. Four of the dimensions are seen as independent variables: the balance of influence between proenvironment groups and prodevelopment groups (a), fiscal capacity to socialize the cost of regulation (b), the level of public attention devoted to the deposition of waste in the state (c), and organizational incapacity to respond to waste problems (d).[2] The fifth dimension is viewed as the dependent variable: the level of state regulation (x). For methodological convenience, we assume that x can have either positive or negative values. Positive values of x achieve net reduction in waste deposition; negative values do not.

Thus, for the contemporary stage, the level of state regulatory stringency, x, can be given by the equation

$$x = F(a, b, c, d) \qquad \text{(Eqn. 1)}$$

where *F* is a function describing the relative importance of causal variables to the dependent variable. The anticipated effect of each independent variable is presented below.

The Balance of Influence between Public-Regarding
and Private-Regarding Groups (a)

This variable can assume either positive or negative values in the following way:

$a > 0$: dominant influence of proenvironment groups
$a < 0$: dominant influence of prodevelopment groups

The midpoint ($a = 0$) of this continuum is the transition point of influence. Because groups more concerned with environmental protection than with economic development would express preferences or exercise pressure for higher, more stringent levels of regulation, our dependent variable is a monotonic, but not necessarily linear, function of *a*. This case is shown in Figure 6.1.

Figure 6.1
The Relationship between the Level of State Regulation (*x*) and the Balance of Group Activity (*a*)

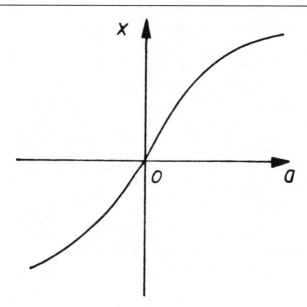

Source: Compiled by the authors.

Fiscal Capacity to Socialize the Cost of Stringent Regulation (b)

We anticipate a nonlinear bifurcating effect on regulation defined by an unspecified critical value of this variable. Above that value regulator costs can be socialized and states can achieve net gains without incurring market punishments. However, for states whose fiscal capacity falls below the splitting values, stringent or compromise regulation will be irrational; therefore, these states follow a "developmental" mode. Given this situation, a positive increase in *a* will have little or no effect on *x* until a certain threshold point is reached (see Figure 6.2).

Public Perception of Risk (c)

Public knowledge or perception of biological risk functions as the distal determinant of the proximate balance of group influence. Like the cost of stringent regulation, this variable has little effect on the level of state regulation when its value is low. However, when public perception of the risk associated with deposition of waste in the state increases, then values held by proenvironmental groups are of increasing concern to state decision makers.

Organizational Capacity to Respond to Waste Problems (d)

After federal intervention into the regulatory arena, the organizational capacity of state and local governments is expected to have a significant effect on the level of state regulation. Because of the complexity and inter-

Figure 6.2
The Threshold Effect on *x* for a High Value of *b*

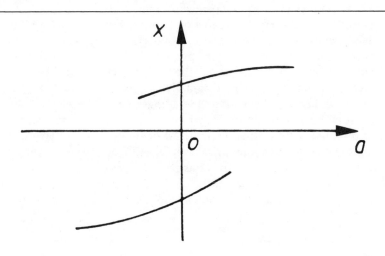

Source: Compiled by the authors.

actability of waste regulation, the level of organizational capacity is hypothesized to have a positive relationship with x. That is, the higher the value of d, the lower the level of state regulation. However, below an unspecified level of fiscal capacity, organizational capacity may be rendered irrelevant.

So far, we have examined the anticipated effects of independent variables (a, b, c, and d) on the level of state regulation. In the following section, their interactive effect on x will be discussed within the framework of catastrophe theory and the butterfly catastrophe model.

CATASTROPHE THEORY

Motivated by the inability of traditional mathematics, grounded in assumptions of continuous or linear change, to explain recurring patterns of discontinuities in natural and social settings, Rene Thom developed catastrophe theory as an alternative framework. The basic elements of the theory have been summarized in several sources (Zeeman, 1976, 1978; Thom, 1975; Saunders, 1980); however, because catastrophe theory is rather new to the policy sciences, we will briefly introduce the theory and the fundamental models derived from it. The use of catastrophe theory in social science can be most easily introduced by outlining three special characteristics that make it attractive for the study of discontinuous social phenomena. First, because catastrophe theory rests upon topological mathematics, the theory can accommodate the qualitative properties of most social problems. Second, catastrophe theory can provide a basis for a classification of diverse responses to similar stimuli. Third, its mathematical system can effectively describe large variatons or sudden, discontinuous structural changes of social equilibria in one or more dependent variables caused by small, smooth changes in independent variables.

The discontinuities that engender qualitative shifts in social equilibria can be modeled as one of seven general geometric models, which Thom (1975) calls the elementary catastrophes, possible in our dimensional control (or parameter) space. They are called the fold, the cusp, the swallowtail, the hyperbolic umbilic, the elliptic umbilic, the butterfly, and the parabolic umbilic. Because our theory and the findings of extant research suggest that states respond differently to similar ecological and economic stimuli, and state response patterns may be bimodal or multimodal, reflecting discontinuous choice between alternative risk/benefit equilibria, we adopt as our regulatory model the butterfly catastrophe; however, the applicability of this elementary catastrophe will be clarified by considering first the topological properties of its less complex predecessor, the cusp catastrophe.

The Cusp Catastrophe

Given the classification theorem of catastrophe theory, the only way mathematically a bimodal distribution can emerge from a unimodal one is by means of the cusp catastrophe. The cusp catastrophe, which requires two control factors, is the unfolding of the function.

$$fa, b(x) = 1/4 \times^4 - ax - 1/2 bx^2 \qquad \text{(Eqn. 2)}$$

The qualitative properties of two control factors, a and b, are drawn in Figure 6.3. In this figure, a is called the *normal factor* and b the *splitting factor* because a small change in b can engender qualitative changes in the value of x, the dependent variable. Such discontinuous changes may, for example, literally "change the direction" of regulatory policy.

The behavior surface (G) shown in Figure 6.4, is derived from the potential function (Eqn. 2), and can be expressed as

$$x^3 = a + bx \qquad \text{(Eqn. 3)}$$

The projection of G (the behavior space) into $a - b$ space (or, in the language of catastrophe theory, "control space") has similarities which project to the unique cusp curve $b^3 = 27/4\, a^2$. For $b > 0$ the sections are equivalent

Figure 6.3
The Cusp Catastrophe and Singularities

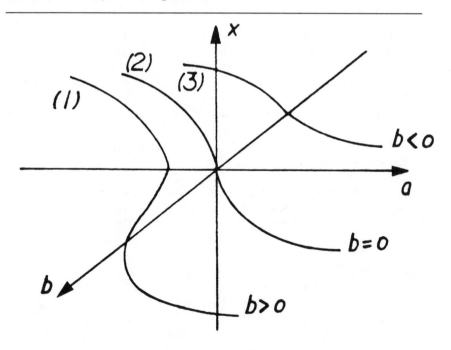

Source: Golubitsky, 1978: 368.

to the graph (1) in Figure 6.3 and for $b < 0$ to the graph (3). If the value of b (the splitting factor) is less than the splitting value, the normal factor (a) "pushes" x on the surface of G in a unimodal pattern (A_1 or B_1). However, if b equals or exceeds the splitting value—that is, at or beyond the cusp—the combination of normal and splitting factors produces a bimodal pattern (A_2 and B_2) in which similar normal values engender qualitatively dissimilar values in the dependent variable.

The cusp model accommodates nicely the earlier stages of waste regulation (Lee, 1985). However, because the fourth stage of waste regulation is marked by qualitative changes in regulatory climate and the emerging importance of fiscal and organizational capacities as controls on regulatory effort, its conditions cannot be accommodated by the cusp model. We turn, therefore, to the butterfly catastrophe.

The Butterfly Catastrophe

Since we are dealing in stage 4 with four causal variables, the functional form of F can be written as

$$F(x, a, b, c, d) - x^6 - dx^4 - cx^3 - bx^2 - ax \qquad \text{(Eqn. 4)}$$

where x is the level of state regulation and (a, b, c, d) are independent variables discussed above.

The functional equivalence between the model (Eqn. 4) and our conceptualization of variables can be illustrated first by examining interactive effects of a and b on x. With two control variables and one dependent variable, Eqn. 2 is reduced to the cusp catastrophe of fourth-degree polynomials, $F(x, a, b) = x^4 - bx^2 - ax$, as depicted in Figure 6.5.

The path 1 in Figure 6.5 is functionally equivalent to the graph in Figure 6.2. That is, when b remains at a low level, the value of x is a smooth function of a. Path 2 in Figure 6.5 corresponds to the phenomenon described in Figure 6.3; that is, when the value of b is high, there is a bimodal pattern of x with increasing value of a. In the second case, since the cusp in the control plane is bifurcated by b, b is called the splitting factor in catastrophe theory. Bifurcation occurs "catastrophically" beyond a splitting value of b. Therefore, beyond a certain value of (b) anticipated state responses to similar levels of the balance of group influences (a) exhibit quite dissimilar, alternative response patterns, depending on the fiscal capacity of states.

Figure 6.6 illustrates variations of the bifurcation locus for the butterfly catastrophe. Note the effect of c, risk perceptions. As is shown in the figure, risk perception alters the position and shape of the bifurcation locus. The value of c also exacerbates the effects of a, thus moving the level of x up and down. This effect of c is expected because the level of public perception

Figure 6.4
The Cusp Catastrophe and Most Probable Behavior Modes

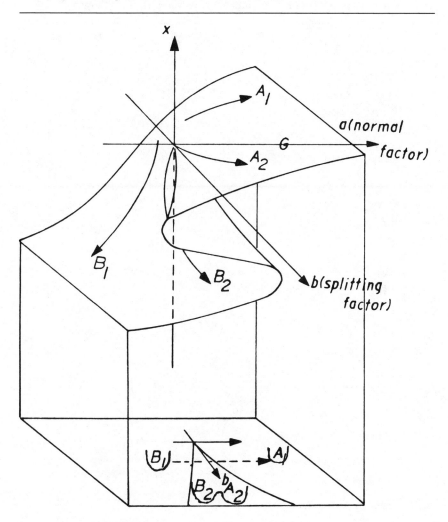

Source: Compiled by the authors.

Figure 6.5
Interactive Effects of *a* and *b* on *x*, illustrated by the Cusp Catastrophe

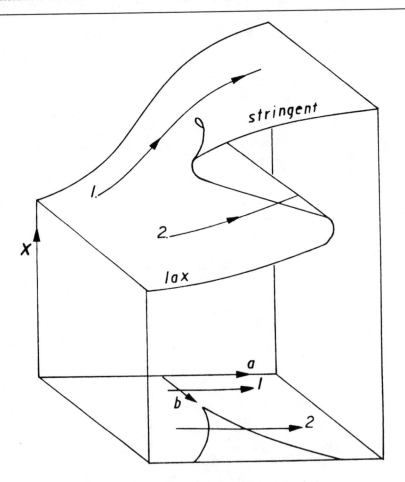

Source: Compiled by the authors.

Figure 6.6
Sections of the Butterfly Catastrophe Bifurcation Set

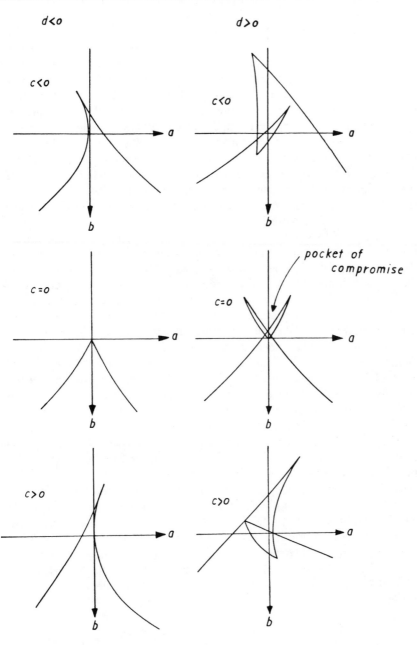

Source: Compiled by the authors.

functions as the pivotal determinant of the balance of group influence (a), thus changing the level of regulation (x).

Now consider the effect of d, organizational capacity (incapacity). As the value of d increases, it creates three cusps: the upper, the middle, and the lower sheet. The middle sheet is called the "pocket of compromise" in catastrophe theory. This middle sheet can thus be viewed as a third mode in the level of x. However, the existence of a compromise region is dependent on the interaction of c and d factors. A rapid change in the value of c (perceived risk) or a small decrease in the value of d (organizational incapacity) may render much of this region inaccessible. Most important, only at indifference (zero) levels of perceived severity do changes in d create a zone or "pocket" of compromise. Under stage 4's condition of ubiquitous risk perception the acceptability of compromise and, therefore, the pocket of compromise are closed. Thus, beyond unspecified levels of risk perception and fiscal capacity (or incapacity), the interaction between perceived risk and organizational capacity (or incapacity) should reinforce the bimodal response pattern.

Now the hypothesized pattern of state regulation during stage 4 can be depicted on the behavioral surface of the butterfly model (see Figure 6.7). The bifurcated response pattern, with roots in T_{-1}, is accentuated by the ubiquity of risk perception and the preemptive constraints of federal intervention. Beyond a splitting value (V) of fiscal capacity (b), the group pressures (a) associated with perceived severity (c) will push states into the responsive (R) mode. Below that splitting value the pressures will be ineffective, because to regulate adequately (x) is to destroy the fiscal capacity to regulate. States whose fiscal capacity is below V will, therefore, be unresponsive and distributed within the U mode. Because the earlier disparity between perceived social benefits and perceived social costs of waste-generating technologies has led to catastrophic elevation of perceived risk, the compromise pocket that might have been available to organizationally capable states at one time is now closed. Catastrophic shifts ($T_1 - T_2$) from unresponsive (U) to responsive (R) modes become the only options for states whose unresponsiveness leads to continued net increases of waste deposition. Such catastrophic shifts are anticipated because prolonged fiscal dependence on waste generators to meet costs of regulation produces one of two outcomes as net deposition and the cost of meeting federal standards increase. Increases in the costs of government may drive major waste generators to fiscally capable states; refusal to improve such costs may lead to federal preemption. In either case the state's policy calculi shift, and a qualitative shift to environmental prerogatives, as depicted, can be anticipated.

Figure 6.7
Butterfly Model of Contemporary State Regulation

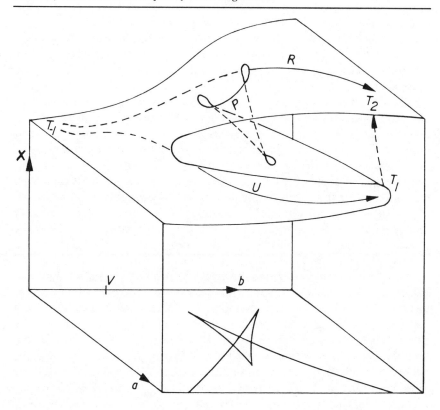

Source: Compiled by the authors.

SIGNIFICANCE

The models presented above should be viewed as heuristic devices designed to focus inquiry on specific determinants of waste regulation. Catastrophe models were chosen because they represent a tacit recognition that during the initial stages of waste regulation we have not been able to operationalize regulation and fit it persuasively to conventional qualitative models. As the regulatory environment continues to change, conventional linear models may become compatible with that environment. Indeed, if we are correct, the unresponsive mode will ultimately become irrational for all states. For now, however, the significance of the frameworks presented here will be determined by the degree to which they facilitate research into the effects of group activity and public perceptions of waste severity on state regulation of hazardous waste at each proposed stage of the regulatory process. If empirical tests confirm theoretical expectations of delayed and inadequate response to waste externalities in states with fiscal dependence on the targets of regulation, the long-term significance will be to suggest that, for analogous technological externalities in the future, federal intervention should anticipate and obviate the interstate competition for developmental benefits before the delayed but inevitable ecological costs become apparent.

Of course, neither this framework nor documented state-level inadequacies would necessarily tell us which governmental level is best able to regulate hazardous waste and analogous technological externalities. Federal policy could produce uniformly inadequate regulation without commensurate economic benefits of interstate competition. But any reasonably successful effort to capture the presumed benefits of autonomous state-level regulation must, at a minimum, reduce the lag between actual and perceived social costs of production so that states may calculate rationally the costs and benefits of production before they become trapped by their own link between economic dependency on waste producers and the capacity to regulate producer externalities.

The efficacy of future regulation will also depend on the ability of policymakers to find remedies for institutional failures where multiple government actors, in pursuing their individual states' perceived short-term economic interests, take actions that benefit none of their states in the long run. If this failure is analogous to a classic prisoners' dilemma game, then a sensible search for remedies ought to include consideration of the various cooperative solutions proposed for the dilemma (Axelrod, 1985). If such dilemmas occur within a sequence of regulatory events, then timeliness becomes crucially important in devising appropriate remedial actions, especially ones distinct from a federal takeover of regulatory responsibility. At a minimum, we need to understand the evolution of present policies as a means of anticipating, identifying, and resolving analogous future problems before they reach catastrophic proportions.

NOTES

1. This four-stage theory was introduced originally in a recent issue of *Policy Studies Journal* (Goetze and Rowland, 1985). Its presentation here is expanded to include explicitly the theory's assumptions and to accommodate states' fiscal and organizational capacity as control variables.

2. As we will see later, the term *incapacity*, rather than *capacity*, in variable d is used for mathematical purpose. The reader can regard d as the negatively transformed value of organizational capacity. For convenience, d will be referred to as capacity rather than incapacity in the remainder of the narrative.

REFERENCES

Axelrod, Robert, *The Evolution of Cooperation* (New York: Basic Books, 1985).

Davis, Charles, and James Lester, "Decentralizing Federal Environmental Programs: Problems and Prospects," Paper presented at American Political Science Association Meeting, Washington, DC, August 30, 1984.

Dubnick, Melvin, and Alan Gitelson, "National State Policies," in J. Hanus, ed., *The Nationalization of State Government* (Lexington, MA: Lexington Books, 1981).

Goetze, David, and C. K. Rowland, "Explaining Hazardous Waste Regulation at the State Level," *Policy Studies Journal* 14 (September 1985): 111-122.

Golubitsky, Martin, "Introduction to Catastrophe Theory and Its Applications," *Siam Review* 20 (April 1978): 352-387.

Lee, S. C., 1985. "A Catastrophe Model of State Hazardous Waste Regulation," Paper presented at the Southwest Political Science Association Meeting, San Antonio, March 22, 1986.

Lester, James P., James L. Franke, Ann O'M. Bowman, and Kenneth W. Kramer, "Hazardous Wastes, Politics, and Public Policy: A Comparative State Analysis," *Western Political Quarterly* 36 (June 1983): 258-285.

Lester, James P., and Ann O'M. Bowman, *The Politics of Hazardous Waste Management* (Durham, NC: Duke University Press, 1983).

Lindblom, Charles, "The Market as Prison," *Journal of Politics* 44 (1983) 324-336.

Rowland, C. K., and R. Marz, "Greshman's Law: The Regulatory Analogy," *Policy Studies Review* 1 (1981) 572-580.

Rowland, C. K., and Richard Feiock, "Economic Dependency and State Regulation of Hazardous Waste," Paper presented at the Southern Political Science Association Meeting, Birmingham, Alabama, November 4, 1983.

Rushefsky, Mark, "Technical Disputes: Why Experts Disagree," *Policy Studies Review* 2 (1982) 676-685.

Salisbury, Robert, "An Exchange Theory of Interest Groups," *Midwest Journal of Political Science* 13 (February 1969): 1-32.

Saunders, I. T., *An Introduction to Catastrophe Theory* (Cambridge: Cambridge University Press, 1980).

Thom, R., *Structural Stability and Morphogenesis*, English translation by D. H. Fouer (Benjamin, NY: Reading Press, 1975).

Voegel, David, "The New Social Regulation in Historical and Comparative Perspective," in T. K. McGraw, ed., *Regulation in Perspective* (Cambridge, MA: Harvard University Press, 1981).

Weingast, Barry, "The Congressional Bureaucratic System: A Principal-Agent Perspective (with Applications to the SEC)," *Public Choice* 44 (1984) 147-192.

Williams, Bruce, and Albert Matheny, "Testing Theories of Social Regulation: Hazardous Waste Regulation in the American States," *Journal of Politics* 46 (May 1984): 428-458.

Wilson, James Q., *The Politics of Regulation* (New York: Basic Books, 1980).

Zeeman, E. C., "Some Models from Catastrophe Theory in the Social Sciences," in L. Collins, ed., *The Use of Models in the Social Science* (New York: West-view Press, 1976).

————, *Catastrophe Theory: Selected Papers, 1972-1977* (New York: Addison-Wesley Publishing Company, 1978).

7

Hazardous Waste Facility Siting: State Approaches

Richard N. L. Andrews

Recent attempts to promote the siting of new hazardous waste facilities raise challenging questions in stark form. New facilities may provide safer treatment than many wastes are receiving now, but they too may lead to accidents, spills, leaks, and unwelcome emissions. As a matter of public policy choice, therefore, on what grounds can we distinguish between "good" and "bad" proposals? And at what level of government should such choices be made?

Prevalent traditions favoring local self-governance argue for continuation of local autonomy over land-use controls and related health and safety protection, so long as such controls are not weaker than federal and state mandates. The local government is closest to the issue, will experience most directly both the benefits and the costs of siting decisions, and is in principle most responsive to the will of the citizens most directly affected. If such facilities *are* especially hazardous, the local jurisdiction has a responsibility to ensure that its citizens' health and welfare are not sacrificed by more remote state or federal officials who are not at risk; and if they are *not* any more hazardous than other businesses that use the same materials, they should negotiate with local governments just like any other business, and not receive special help by invoking the power of state government.

A contrasting viewpoint, however, holds that there is a broad public interest in the establishment of safer facilities for the management of these materials, as well as a sometimes unwarranted pejorative power in the

The author gratefully acknowledges the contributions of Dr. Terrence K. Pierson, who co-authored an earlier version of this research, and of Philip Prete, who assisted in the updating of it.

"hazardous waste" label; and that such facilities shall not therefore be blocked by unfounded fears and "not-in-my-backyard" (NIMBY) politics at the local level. Advocates of this view argue that such facilities need some special protection simply to ensure that they are reviewed fairly on their merits and invoke the power of state government to override, preempt, or otherwise restrain local opposition to state-approved facilities.

Advocates of the latter view have in fact succeeded in enacting new state siting legislation in a substantial number of states over the past decade. While these actions represent an important and surprisingly widespread set of experiments, the scholarly literature on the subject is still relatively limited. The National Conference of State Legislatures published a summary of state laws in 1980 (NCSL, 1980), and Hadden et al. (1983) have published a more limited study of state siting laws; Bacow and Milkey (1982) also summarize these laws but apparently from their texts only, without attention to their interpretation and use in practice. Commentaries on particular approaches, and case studies, include work by Morell and Magorian (1982), Keystone Center (1982), O'Hare et al. (1983), Bingham and Miller (1984), Tarlock (1984), Elliot (1984), Susskind (1985), and several chapters in Lester and Bowman (1983). Empirical comparisons of the relative advantages and disadvantages of state and local siting approaches, however, and of their effects and effectiveness in practice, are still quite few; the primary one is Andrews and Pierson (1983).

This paper presents findings from two studies of state and local siting processes and their results to date (Andrews and Pierson, 1983; Andrews and Prete, 1987). The first study, conducted in 1983-1984, compared four primary approaches to the role of government—state preemption, state override, local veto, and state procedural restraints—using data derived from a survey of officials in all fifty states, followed by two rounds of telephone interviews. Data for this study also included face-to-face interviews of business, government, and environmental leaders in seven states to illustrate the major approaches to siting so far attempted. The second study, conducted in January 1987, used data from a second telephone survey of officials in all fifty states to update information on trends in siting and siting processes.

APPROACHES

Local governments are legally subdivisions of state government and may therefore exercise only such powers as are delegated to them by state law. Traditionally, however, most states have in fact delegated relatively broad autonomy (or "home rule") to local governments in matters of land-use control and moderate amounts in the regulation of health, safety, and nuisances.

The starting points for most state approaches therefore are the usual local requirements for zoning approval or special-use permits based upon general-purpose land-use controls, plus a new federal requirement (of the Resource Conservation and Recovery Act of 1976) that every hazardous waste facility obtain a federal or equivalent state operating permit. Few states or localities had specific statutes dealing with the siting of hazardous waste facilities before the late 1970s.

Beginning about 1980, more than half the fifty states enacted legislation that specifically addressed the siting of hazardous waste management facilities, and in most instances these laws specified the institutional arrangements and authority for siting decisions. These arrangements can be grouped into four primary approaches: state preemption, state override, local veto, and procedural restraints.

Preemption

In nine states the laws assign to state governments the initiative to identify appropriate sites, and in four of them to obtain and own them. At least one other (North Carolina, in 1984) added legislation to invoke state-initiated siting if private facilities were not proposed and approved before a statutory deadline. This approach will be referred to as *preemption*, since in such cases the state essentially takes unto itself full power over both selecting a site and authorizing its use for a hazardous waste management facility.

Override

A second approach was to create a state agency or board that had power to override local decisions that blocked proposed facilities, either with original jurisdiction or on appeal. In eight states such a board was given final authority over facility location decisions, without any members representing the local community affected; in eleven others the board included ad hoc representatives from the affected community. This approach is referred to as *state override*, since in such cases the state government does not take over the initiative for siting proposals but does intervene to override local government powers that might otherwise be used to block facilities.

Local Veto

In contrast, eight states' laws formally vested authority over facility siting in the local government affected; and the states that had not enacted siting legislation were presumed to have left control at the local level by default. This approach is referred to as *local veto*, since it leaves the primary power to approve or disapprove siting in the hands of local government. Note, however, that under this approach a facility can still be *dis*approved by state government; since it must also obtain a federal or equivalent state permit, the approach is sometimes referred to as a *"mutual* veto."

Procedural Restraints

Finally, a few states left primary control at the local level but added state restrictions on how that control could be exercised. Examples include prohibiting rezoning to block a facility after an application was received, or prohibiting disapproval unless the facility was shown more risky than other comparable ones already operating in the state. This approach is referred to as *procedural restraints,* since the state intervenes not by preempting or overriding the substance of the decision but by circumscribing the procedures and criteria by which local governments may make such decisions.

RESULTS

As of 1987, three-fourths of the states had established some form of explicit siting process. In twenty-eight of these thirty-seven states, the initiative must come from a private applicant; in the other nine, it may come from either a private applicant or state government. In no state was the initiative assigned solely to state government.

In all the states surveyed, the approaches attempted are still in progress. None has yet proven itself a model of success for all to adopt, at least if success is defined as actually siting new facilities sufficient for the state's waste streams; but each sheds light on some of the advantages and pitfalls of the various approaches. One pattern worth noting is a "grass is greener" phenomenon: Numerous states exemplifying *each* approach have at times become concerned that their approaches were not working and therefore shifted to others, often without careful attention to similar perceptions of failure on the part of states that had tried the other approaches. Real progress thus may or may not ensue.

Between 1980 and 1986 there were 179 identifiable attempts to site new hazardous waste facilities—46 proprietary and 133 commercial—not counting undeterminable numbers of on-site facilities that are not subject to federal RCRA regulations (for instance, treatment of hazardous wastewater). Of these, 22% (39) had been successfully sited, 25% (45) were not sited, and 53% (94) were still pending. Twenty-six of those sited were commercial facilities; the other 13 were proprietary (Holman, 1986).

Preemption

State preemption is usually advocated on two grounds: that there is a compelling statewide public interest in a facility, and that state government is the best judge of appropriate locations for it (for instance, by criteria of safety and "need" rather than profit). It has been attempted under two different sets of circumstances, to dispose of materials from state-mandated cleanup activities or to promote the siting of commercial facilities for future wastes.

In principle the state can probably assert its most compelling arguments for preemption in cleanup cases, invoking its authority and responsibility to remedy imminent hazards to public health. Even here, however, the record shows both successes and failures. North Carolina successfully sited a single-purpose landfill for disposal of soil contaminated with poly-chlorinated biphenyls (PCBs) from a roadside dumping event, though not without legal battles. Michigan, however, was blocked in its attempts to site a burial facility for PCB-contaminated cattle and ultimately had to ship them out of state to a licensed disposal facility. Similar controversies have arisen in other states.

State preemption to promote siting of commercial facilities has been attempted by a number of states but has rarely succeeded so far. In Arizona, the state legislature directed that a facility be sited, and it was in fact sited: a high-technology, full-service facility, located on purchased federal land in a thinly populated area thirty miles outside Phoenix and operated by a private firm (ENSCO) under contract to the state. Massachusetts attempted preemptive siting in the late 1970s but was blocked immediately by legislation introduced by representatives of the affected areas. New York in 1981 used a more sophisticated process including a statewide advisory committee and engineering feasibility study, but vehement public opposition led the governor to disavow and terminate the process almost as soon as a proposed site was announced.

Minnesota in 1980 undertook a diligent effort to identify appropriate sites, including explicit *a priori* criteria and extensive public involvement; but there too opposition intensified as the process narrowed toward particular sites, and the process was "put on hold" and ultimately replaced by a different approach: a negotiated process inviting county resolutions of interest in hosting one specific type of facility (stabilization) with financial incentives for acceptance. This process attracted at least ten nonbinding resolutions of interest; final results are not yet known. North Carolina in 1984 created a Hazardous Waste Treatment Commission charged to site and operate at least one treatment facility if no privately initiated one was approved by 1986; as of 1987 this commission had identified a list of potential sites for more detailed screening, but the results of this mandate are yet to be seen.

These anecdotal results suggest that state preemption is still a minority approach to the siting issue, with no clear evidence of success except in Arizona (where the availability of unpopulated federal land may have provided a factor not available to most other states). In most cases the preemptive use of formal state power probably is not sufficient to prevail against the real political power of aroused localities; and it may in fact have the undesirable side effect of exacerbating such opposition by attempting to defeat it by force.

More generally, as of 1987 only nine states had established siting processes that explicitly provided for state-initiated siting; six reported active siting proposals initiated by the state, and only four expected state-initiated proposals in the future. These results suggest that applications from private firms will continue to be the predominant approach to siting.

One further pitfall in the preemptive approach is that state agencies do not necessarily make good decisions about the viability of commercial facilities. Maryland, for instance, opened a state-of-the-art treatment facility on a state-owned site but discovered that without regulations mandating state-of-the-art treatment or requiring that waste flows be directed to it, it could not compete against older and cheaper facilities in nearby states. North Carolina experienced similar results in attempting to operate an oil re-refining facility; and even states that have attempted only to secure sites preemptively have often discovered that the sites they identify based upon their ideas of environmental protection, public acceptability, and "need" are not necessarily economically attractive to private-enterprise operators. Physical capacity and intrinsic site suitability are not a substitute for economic feasibility.

Override

Far more widespread than outright preemption are statutes authorizing state boards to override local powers that might otherwise block proposed facilities. The primary rationale usually given for this approach is to substitute more dispassionate state-level decision making for parochial NIMBY prejudices. A second consideration is the apparent concern of state legislators to show responsiveness both to established and prospective businesses that generate such wastes and to the governments of neighboring states to which these materials are now transported for disposal.

In practice this approach has taken at least three forms, which vary considerably in the degree to which the state intervenes. In the strongest form a state board that does not even include local representatives is authorized to make final decisions on all siting proposals: Pennsylvania and Washington provide examples of this approach, as does Florida, where the governor and his cabinet may override local vetoes. A more moderate form is illustrated by Maine, Michigan, and Ohio, whose state boards also exercise final decision authority but include ad hoc representatives of affected local jurisdictions. The least intrusive form is exemplified by California, Connecticut, and North Carolina, whose state boards do not decide on every siting proposal but can be asked to override on appeal by a rejected applicant.

State override has obviously been an appealing idea to many states and has been advocated as a model both by business groups and even by some local governments—mainly large cities, who apparently expect it to be used to override suburban and rural jurisdictions rather than themselves (see resolution adopted by National Association of Local Governments on Hazardous Wastes at its 1984 first annual meeting). The most significant finding about this approach so far, however, is how little impact it seems yet to have had. As of the end of 1986, Michigan and Ohio, for instance, had each sited two facilities under override procedures, but Michigan had also turned down five facilities and had two still pending; Ohio had turned down one and had six still pending. In many states the override procedures simply have not yet been used. In North Carolina, for instance, several proposals for facilities have been developed, but none so far has reached the point of invoking the override process, although one facility was approved without controversy or appeal, and several have been withdrawn due to political opposition or state regulatory disapproval prior to that point.

It is not clear, therefore, that state override procedures are necessarily any quicker or more effective a mechanism for siting decisions than the traditional procedures they replace. The experiences of Michigan and other states suggest that local opposition may arise not just from local ignorance or selfishness but from real uncertainties about the likelihood and significance of risks, questions that state boards may find just as difficult to answer as local governments.

Local Veto

Despite the wave of recent preemption and override laws, many states still leave primary siting control to local government, and a few have even reconfirmed that principle in new legislation. The primary arguments for this position include both traditional advocacy of local governance as more responsive to citizens and pragmatic belief that formal state power is not an effective substitute for real local acceptance.

Many of the states that have retained a local veto are those that simply have not yet enacted any formal siting legislation. Others, however, have consciously left local governments in control. Colorado, for instance, has repeatedly considered and rejected proposals for state preemption or override, primarily because of the strong opposition of the state association of county commissioners (though it did add a provision in 1983 allowing state action if the county failed to make a decision within a specified time period). California, a sophisticated and heavily industrialized state with the largest waste streams in the nation, also leaves primary jurisdiction over siting to its local governments, subject to a limited ad hoc appeal process (added in 1986) for commercial facility proposals. Kentucky retains a local veto power over land-disposal facilities, though it has also established a regional siting board without local veto power for facilities to serve regional markets.

The results so far in local-veto states are not sufficient to draw strong conclusions, but they do not necessarily suggest a less successful record than in states that have attempted more aggressive state intervention. California, for instance, by the end of 1986 had approved five facilities, three of which were commercial, and had rejected only two; twenty-one were still pending. Colorado had sited one, rejected one, and had three pending; Kentucky had sited two and had one pending. North Carolina sited a commercial treatment facility without controversy. To be sure, some proposed facilities *have* been blocked by political opposition at the local level. The point here, however, is that other sites have been approved even in states that have reaffirmed local control, and state preemption and override powers do not appear to have been any more effective in overcoming local blockage where it exists. Since state preemption and override powers represent significant changes from traditional decision-making prerogatives, the burden of proof must rest with their advocates.

Procedural Restraints

A final approach leaves primary authority over siting at the local level but under procedural restraints imposed by the state to assure fair treatment of each application on its merits. The main examples of this approach are requirements that siting decisions be reached through a formalized negotiation process between the developer and representatives of the host community. The rationale for this approach is to respect both the tradition and the practical necessity of local decision making, but at the same time to hold that process to reasonable standards of fairness and evidence. The override-on-appeal procedure (such as in North Carolina) is in a sense a form of this approach, since the threat of appeal is intended as an incentive for well-reasoned and equitable local decision making; but several other states have used procedural restraints and negotiated siting more directly as well. Wisconsin is probably the leading example so far; others include Rhode Island, Massachusetts, Illinois, and California.

The Wisconsin negotiated siting process was created in 1981 in the wake of judicial decisions overturning state preemption. It allows the local government to decide whether or not it wishes to enter a formal negotiaton process, but if it does not it must live with the results of the normal state permit process. If it does enter negotiations, the local assessment committee can negotiate any issue except the need for the facility or conditions less stringent than state requirements, but it risks severe penalties if it does not negotiate in good faith. Impasses can be subjected to binding arbitration by a state siting board. Two hazardous waste facilities have been sited so far under this system, along with seventeen nonhazardous solid waste facilities, and so far there has been no need to invoke the arbitration process.

Massachusetts adopted a locally based process but with state restraints after its attempts to impose siting preemptively were rejected by its legislature. State law requires a permit from the local board of health as well as from the state itself, and denial of the local permit cannot be overridden by a state agency; but it can be challenged in court if the board does not show a factual finding that the facility would be more hazardous than businesses already operating in the state using comparable processes or materials. In addition, the applicant must sign a siting agreement with a committee legally representing the local community, in which both operating and monitoring requirements and compensation may be openly negotiated; as in Wisconsin, if an impasse occurs a state oversight board may invoke binding arbitration. Five facilities have been proposed under this system, but none have been sited. The difference from the Wisconsin process appears to result at least in part from a more burdensome process and intense opposition to several of the initial proposals on their merits.

Illinois, similarly, initially sought to impose siting preemptively through a state pollution control board; but after several years of bitter opposition it shifted to a locally initiated approach with state restraints. Under its subsequent approach, application for a state permit does not even occur until after county or municipal location approval is obtained; but denial of this approval must be based on a public hearing, documented in a written record subject to state review, and can only be based upon specific grounds of need, safety, land-use compatibility, flood plain protection, or traffic impacts.

Finally, Rhode Island in 1986 also approved a treatment facility under a procedure requiring negotiation with a local assessment committee, with a provision for arbitration if an impasse occurred.

Like the other approaches discussed above, procedural restraints and negotiated siting have produced small numbers of anecdotal success stories as well as failures but do not provide sufficient numbers or consistency of results to permit strong generalizations. There appears to be a consistent pattern, however, by which states in which preemptive state approaches have been blocked have found negotiated siting procedures promising as alternatives.

CONCLUSIONS

The strongest conclusion that emerges from observation of all these approaches to date is that few facilities have so far been sited under any of them. One reason for this is undoubtedly their newness, another the general decline in economic activity during a significant portion of the same period, and a third the high level of regulatory and enforcement uncertainty as both federal and state governments geared up to deal with hazardous wastes. Two additional factors, however, have undoubtedly been the initial emphasis on landfill siting at a time when both the public acceptability and the economic attractiveness of landfills were rapidly declining and significant increases in source reduction and on-site management by large-quantity generators faced with stricter liability threats.

The real tests of siting approaches are probably yet to come. Recent surveys of both industry and state officials show expectations of a substantial number of new siting proposals, especially incinerators, in addition to the ninety-four proposals already pending but not yet resolved (Andrews and Prete, 1987). One major uncertainty is the degree to which tightened enforcement against small firms—as well as closures of noncomplying existing facilities—will increase the market for new facilities. Another is the question of whether or not future regulations will ban yet more classes of materials from landfills.

A second conclusion that may be tentatively suggested, however, is that the prejudice of many states in favor of state preemption and strong override authority may be misplaced. These approaches do sometimes succeed, but overall they do not appear to have better success records than locally based approaches, and they have sometimes inflamed opposition more than they have surmounted it. At least several states have turned back to locally based approaches—especially with some state procedural restraints or backup override authority, such as mandatory negotiation—after discovering the problems that come with more aggressive attempts to impose state control.

In principle, the combination of local control with state restraints to ensure fair procedures and reasoned criteria for decisions seems most consistent with the American political tradition of self-governance. If in practice its results are not demonstrably worse than other approaches, therefore, it may deserve some presumption of preference. Some clarification of fair procedures and criteria does seem necessary to restrain potential abuses and power plays on all sides; and if such clarification can establish an open and legitimate process for local negotiations over siting proposals, the actual costs and impacts of most such facilities probably are not so great as to prevent reasonable agreements on safe operation and compensation (Smith et al., 1986).

In short, state preemption and override procedures will probably be less effective than efforts to further refine and formalize the processes by which local governments, along with their citizens and existing and proposed businesses, may legitimately and fairly negotiate the terms of siting decisions. State governments may play important roles in this formalization, but they will probably play them more effectively as referees of the procedures' fairness—and in some cases, as a threat of override on appeal—than by unilaterally preempting or overriding traditional local governance.

An important problem for this approach, however, may have been created by Section 104(K) of the federal Superfund Amendments and Reauthorization Act of 1986, which threatens a cutoff of federal cleanup funds to states that do not assure the availability of future treatment capacity including (in the words of the sponsor) state procedures to override local vetoes. While well intentioned as a way to get states involved in planning for hazardous waste management, such a provision may also panic states into coercive approaches on behalf of poor proposals or even exacerbate opposition to all proposals. It will be important for states to compare carefully the results of coercive versus negotiative approaches before deciding what approach to adopt.

REFERENCES

Andrews, R. N. L., and T. K. Pierson, *Hazardous Waste Facility Siting: A Comparison of State Approaches* (Chapel Hill, NC: UNC Institute for Environmental Studies, 1983).

Andrews, R. N. L., and P. J. Prete, "Trends in Hazardous Waste Facility Siting and Permitting," Paper presented at the Conservation Foundation Workshop on Negotiating Hazardous Waste Facility Siting and Permitting Agreements, Arlington, Virginia, March 11-13, 1987 (forthcoming in proceedings).

Bacow, L. S., and J. R. Milkey, "Overcoming Local Opposition to Hazardous Waste Facilities: The Massachusetts Approach," *Harvard Environmental Law Review* 6 (1982): 265-305.

Bingham, G., and D. S. Miller, "Prospects for Resolving Hazardous Waste Siting Disputes through Negotiation," *Natural Resources Lawyer* 17 (1984): 473-489.

Elliot, M. L. P., "Improving Community Acceptance of Hazardous Waste Facilities through Alternative Systems for Mitigating and Managing Risk," *Hazardous Waste* 1 (1984): 397-410.

Hadden, S. G., J. Veillette, and T. Brandt, "State Roles in Siting Hazardous Waste Disposal Facilities: From State Preemption to Local Veto," in J. P. Lester and A. O'M. Bowman, eds., *The Politics of Hazardous Waste Management* (Durham, NC: Duke University Press, 1983).

Holman, H. F., *Siting New Hazardous Waste Facilities: Final Report* (Washington, DC: Office of Policy, Planning, and Evaluation, U.S. Environmental Protection Agency, 1986).

Keystone Center, *Siting Hazardous Waste Facilities in the Galveston Bay Area: A New Approach* (Keystone, CO: Keystone Center, 1982).

Lester, J. P., and A. O'M. Bowman, *The Politics of Hazardous Waste Management* (Durham, NC: Duke University Press, 1983).

Morell, D. L., and C. Magorian, *Siting Hazardous Waste Facilities: Local Opposition and the Myth of Preemption* (Cambridge, MA: Ballinger, 1982).

National Conference of State Legislatures, *Hazardous Waste Management: A Survey of State Laws* (Washington, D.C.: National Conference of State Legislatures, 1980).

O'Hare, L., L. S. Bacow, and D. Sanderson, *Facility Siting and Public Opposition* (New York: Van Nostrand Reinhold, 1983).

Smith, M. A., F. M. Lynn, and R. N. L. Andrews, "Economic Impacts of Hazardous

Waste Facilities," *Hazardous Waste and Hazardous Materials* 3 (1986): 195-204.

Susskind, L. E., "The Siting Puzzle: Balancing Economic and Environmental Gains and Losses," *Environmental Impact Assessment Review* 5 (1985): 157-163.

Tarlock, A. D., "Siting New or Expanded Treatment, Storage or Disposal Facilities: The Pigs in the Parlors of the 1980s," *Natural Resources Lawyer*, 17 (1984): 429-461.

Wright, J. W., *Managing Hazardous Wastes* (Lexington, KY: The Council of State Governments, 1986).

8

Superfund Implementation: Five Years and How Many Cleanups?

Ann O'M. Bowman

INTRODUCTION

"Shovels first and lawyers later" was the implementory promise accompanying Superfund, the federal program that makes money available for the cleanup of abandoned hazardous waste dumps. The federal governmental apparatus was to be mobilized behind an effort to prevent harm to public health and the environment—to drain lagoons brimming with liquid wastes, to haul away rusting and leaking waste barrels, to purify contaminated soil and groundwater. Four years into the program, however, implementation appeared to have taken the form of "lunch now, lawyers maybe, but shovels never" (Cohen, 1984: 285).

Many analyses of the federal Superfund program have reached a similar conclusion: its implementation has been a botched affair, and as the program neared its 1985 termination date, only a handful of cleanups had been completed (Novick, 1983; Davis, 1984). Observers point to the shaky compromise hammered out of a lame-duck Congress and a dissension-wracked Environmental Protection Agency (EPA) as factors that have impeded the process (Bowman, 1984). However, an even more basic problem plagued Superfund—inadequate data regarding the number of sites, the severity of the conditions, and the cost of the cleanups (U.S. GAO, 1984; 1985a). Such informational insufficiency raises doubt about the soundness of the theory and the clarity of the goals underlying the program. These conditions alone render implementation problematic (Mazmanian and Sabatier, 1983).

This chapter explores hazardous waste cleanup activity during the original Superfund authorization period (1981-1985). Four components of the Mazmanian and Sabatier implementation model guide the analysis: (1) the hierarchical integration among participating organizations, (2) the decision rules of implementing agencies, (3) the commitment and leadership skills of implementers, and (4) the role played by target groups. The difficulties that dogged the implementation of Superfund in the early years laid the foundation for the corrective actions taken by Congress in 1986 (*Congressional Quarterly Weekly Report*, 1986).

LEGISLATIVE HISTORY OF SUPERFUND

One of the externalities of industrialization has been the generation of hazardous by-products. These wastes are either handled on-site by the generators or transported to off-site locations for storage, treatment, or disposal. Unsafe storage and disposal practices coupled with undercapitalization of waste-handling firms has resulted in the abandonment of many waste sites across the country. Superfund, formally called the Comprehensive Environmental Response, Compensation, and Liability Act of 1980 (CERCLA), was aimed at alleviating this problem by cleaning up abandoned hazardous waste dump sites. The importance of the cleanup function stems from the potential environmental harm and threat to public health and safety posed by uncontrolled hazardous waste sites. Growing public awareness of the dangerous conditions posed by the sites (an awareness often triggered by accidental spills or explosions) provoked congressional reaction. After extensive debate, a Superfund bill emerged from Congress and was signed by President Carter.

The legislative battles surrounding Superfund foretold some of the sticking points that have developed in implementation. The bills (the Carter administration proposal, the House version, the Muskie-Culver Senate bill) raised several critical issues: the source of the funding, the amount of money to be accumulated in the fund, the type of cleanup activity covered, the functional role of the states in the cleanup effort, the extent of the liability and compensation provisions, and the extension of Superfund coverage to oil spills.

Industry groups representing business in general and the chemical industry in particular opposed the legislation, while those speaking for environmental interests tended to be supportive. With Republican party fortunes on the upswing after the 1980 elections, there was pressure from proponents for the lame-duck Congress to act on the measure. Proponents feared that the cleanup issue would fare poorly in an administration with an ostensibly lessened commitment to environmental protection. Numerous negotiations, compromises, and fortuitous events coalesced, and the departing Congress produced the Superfund bill in December 1980. The unusual circumstances that created the Superfund bill have led to an unending series of legal challenges. As chemical industry defense counsels have concluded, "The most charitable characterization of the legislative process that spawned CERCLA is that it was confused" (Freeman, n.d.: A-11).

This contention notwithstanding, the resolution of the aforementioned issues was as follows:

Funding source: Industry would contribute (through taxes on the manufacture or import of chemical feedstocks) 87.5% of the total fund; the remainder would come from general revenues.

Amount of the fund: $1.6 billion.

Type of cleanup activity: Both emergency and remedial covering not only abandoned chemical dumps but the leading, spilling, emitting, and injecting of hazardous wastes into the environment.

Role of the states: Negotiable; either EPA or a state's environmental control agency can be designated as the lead agency under a contract or cooperative agreement. Financially, states would contribute 10% of the Superfund expenditure for cleanup of a privately owned site, 50% for a publicly owned site.

Liability and compensation provisions: Victim compensation provisions were deleted from the final bill; "strict liability" provisions were diluted.

Oil Spills: Deleted from the final bill.

Superfund gave the federal government the authority to step in and clean up severe hazardous waste problems without first engaging in legal wrangling with the parties responsible for the conditions. As "shovels first, lawyers later" implies, when the hazard was under control, the federal government was to pursue legal actions against generators and transporters of the wastes and owners/operators of the site. The federal government was authorized to seek treble damages in these cost-recovery actions. Awards are to be used to replenish Superfund. Three types of cleanup actions can be undertaken through Superfund. Two of them, immediate removals and planned removals, are basically emergency actions taken to prevent imminent public health and environmental damage. During the first two and one-half years of the program, the EPA tackled over 100 removals of this nature. The third category of cleanup activity, the remedial actions intended to be permanent solutions to the problems at a hazardous waste site, is the area that has enveloped the EPA in controversy. It is these actions to which the remainder of this chapter is devoted.

THE EPA'S HANDLING OF SUPERFUND: PRELIMINARY ACTIVITY

The transference of Superfund from the legislative arena to the EPA sparked renewed debate and controversy. The EPA's rule-making performance under the Resource Conservation and Recovery Act (RCRA), the other major piece of hazardous waste legislation, has been highly criticized (U.S. GAO, 1981a, b). Several factors hindered optimal bureaucratic performance under RCRA: protracted lobbying and public participation, the intrusion of hazardous waste "accidents" that galvanized public opinion, legislative oversight and executive redirection of the program, and scientific/technological uncertainty (Carnes, 1982). Superfund was not immune to similar complications.

The EPA's initial task was, with the help of state governments, to inventory and prioritize abandoned hazardous waste sites nationwide. This inventory of sites, called the Emergency and Remedial Response Information System (ERRIS), contained close to 20,000 sites as of late 1984 (Reisch, 1984). Prioritizing the sites has proved to be somewhat imprecise.

When a state submits a site for ERRIS inclusion, it is assigned a priority for subsequent action. Assignment of the priority is based on professional judgment regarding conditions at the site, for example, the actual existence of hazardous waste at the site and its potential to contaminate. A U.S. Office of Technology Assessment study (1985) concluded that this "desktop" preliminary evaluation process offers little likelihood of nationwide consistency. At one point, the EPA had conducted preliminary assessments of conditions at 61% of the ERRIS sites and had determined that, of those assessed, one-third needed no further action, information was lacking for 18%, and site inspections were called for in half of the cases (U.S. GAO, 1985a). At that rate, over 10,000 sites will need inspection. After the preliminary assessment, high-priority sites receive immediate inspection while the rest are queued. The site inspection process determines whether a site will appear on the National Priorities List (NPL), thus qualifying it for Superfund money. The significance of the inspection process cannot be overstated. Through it, the 20,000 ERRIS sites will be narrowed to produce the 1,500 to 2,000 NPL sites. To make this determination, the Superfund law required the EPA to consider these factors: the population at risk, the hazard potential of the substances, the potential for contamination of drinking water supplies, the potential for direct human contact, the potential for destruction of sensitive ecosystems, and a state's ability to assume certain costs and responsibilities.

The EPA has operationalized these criteria through a "hazard-ranking system." A site is scored according to the quantity and nature of hazardous waste present, the proximity of the site to population concentrations and to sensitive natural environments, and the effect of the wastes on three migratory routes: groundwater, surface water, and air. The hazard-ranking system has been subject to criticism. The U.S. Office of Technology Assessment (OTA) (1985: 162) has identified some of the major problems with the system:

1. There is a very strong bias toward human health effects, with little chance of a site getting a high score if there are primarily environmental hazards or threats.

2. For human health effects, there is a strong bias in favor of high affected populations.

3. For the air route there must be documentation (e.g., laboratory data) of a release, but there is no such requirement for the water routes.

4. Scoring for toxicity/persistence may be based on a site contaminant, which is not necessarily one with a known or potential release.

5. A site with a very high score for one migration route but zero or very low scores for the other two routes can get a relatively low total score, while a site with moderate scores for all three routes might get a higher score; in other words, averaging the route scores creates a bias against a site.

6. Only the quantity and not the distribution of waste is considered, even though similar quantities over markedly different areas pose different threats.

These problems with the hazard-ranking system combined with the reported "low priority" that EPA places on the discovery of new sites (U.S. GAO, 1985a) suggest that Superfund represents only a fraction of the effort that will be required to resolve the waste site problem. For example, the General Accounting Office estimates that between 130,000 and 380,000 other sites of "potential concern" exist (U.S. GAO, 1985a). These include currently operating hazardous waste facilities (regulated under the Resource Conservation and Recovery Act), municipal and industrial landfills, mining waste sites, and leaking underground storage tanks. Gradually, discussions of the hazardous waste problem have evolved from an initial concern as to whether a threat exists to a generalized concern over the magnitude of the threat.

If a site scores the requisite number of points and if there is concurrence from the regional EPA, it becomes part of the proposed NPL update. (The EPA is required to update the NPL annually.) Listing the proposed sites offers an opportunity for public comment. *Public comment* is perhaps a misnomer, because most of the comments come from parties potentially responsible for waste at the site who are anxious to dispute the scores. In approximately 2% of the cases proposed sites are dropped from the list because of errors brought out in the comments phase (Melamud, 1984).

This system has produced an NPL that by the end of 1987 contained 964 sites. (The figure includes proposed sites as well.) The map of the United States in Figure 8.1 shows the distribution of NPL sites by state in 1985.

Figure 8.1 reveals a pattern of NPL concentration. Far from being evenly distributed across the nation, the site proportions are greatest in the Northeast and Midwest. New Jersey leads the lists with 98 sites on the NPL, followed by Michigan with 64 sites, California with 60, and New York and Pennsylvania with 59 sites each.

The presence of NPL sites is linked to a number of conditions in the states. The correlational analysis presented in Table 8.1 shows a link between the amount of hazardous waste generated in a state and the existence of abandoned waste sites with conditions serious enough to

Figure 8.1
National Priorities List of Sites, by State

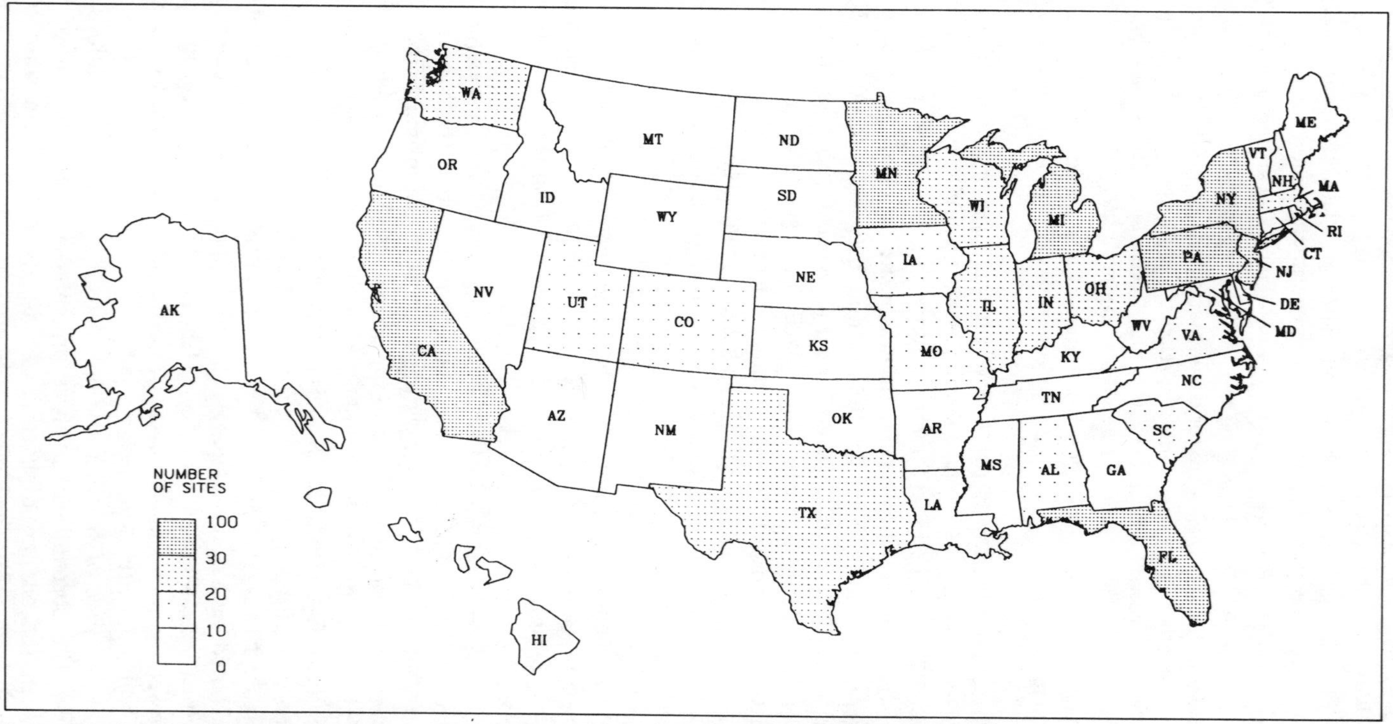

Source: Environmental Protection Agency, "National Priorities List Final and Proposed Sites through Update 4," (September 18, 1985), mimeo.

Table 8.1
Bivariate Correlations

	Number of NPL Sites
Independent Variables	*r*
Amount of Hazardous Waste Generated[a]	.75
Importance of Hazardous Waste to Economy[b]	.52
	Number of NPL Sites
Dependent Variable	
State Environmental Effort Score[c]	.48

All of the relationships presented in the table are significant at the $p < .001$ level.

[a]Amount of hazardous waste generated is measured in millions of metric tons, by state, for 1982. The source for the data is EPA, as reported in Michael R. Greenberg and Richard F. Anderson, *Hazardous Waste Sites: The Credibility Gap* (New Brunswick, NJ: Rutgers: Center for Urban Policy Research, 1984).

[b]Importance of hazardous waste industry to a state's economy is measured by the proportionate contribution of hazardous waste generating industry to a state's economy in 1977. The source for the data is Rich Feiock and C. K. Rowland, "Political and Economic Correlates of Regulatory Commitment: Interstate Variance in Hazardous Waste Regulation," a paper presented at the Annual Meeting of the Southern Political Science Association, Birmingham, AL: November 5-7, 1983.

[c]State environmental effort score is measured by state responses to a Conservation Foundation survey of pollution control policy. The source is Christopher Duerksen, *Environmental Regulation of Industrial Plant Siting* (Washington: Conservation Foundation, 1983).

warrant inclusion on the NPL ($r = .75$). Not surprisingly, the importance of the hazardous waste industry to a state's economy is another factor highly positively related to the presence of NPL sites in a state ($r = .52$). While those two variables seem linked to conditions that produce NPL sites, the sites themselves appear to be associated with an interesting state regulatory response. The greater the number of NPL sites in a state, the higher a state's score on the Conservation Foundation's environmental effort scale ($r = .48$). This suggests that the states facing the most severe toxic waste challenges are the states that are engaging in the most extensive protectionist policy.

THE EPA'S HANDLING OF SUPERFUND: CLEANUP ACTIVITY

One of the major criticisms of the EPA has been that it has dragged its feet at a critical juncture in implementation: site cleanup. One method of determining the legitimacy of the claim is to examine the number of cleanups that have occurred since the program's inception. The first two years of Superfund saw very little action. As of April 1983, planning for twenty-three remedial actions and the implementation of two of them had been completed (Cohen, 1984). The replacement of the political leadership of the EPA in 1983 produced a reorientation toward action. EPA staff proposed five sets of initiatives to increase Superfund program activity: streamlining Superfund rules and operating procedures, improving agency relationships with states, clarifying the role of enforcement in Superfund, responding to releases of hazardous substances at federal facilities, and improving agency management and relations with EPA regional offices (Cohen, 1984). Those efforts have borne some fruit. By the time a General Accounting Office investigation was conducted in late 1984, the number of completed cleanups had risen to four (GAO's figure) or ten (EPA's figure), Superfund-financed remedial activity was underway at 298 sites, responsible party-financed remedial activity was occurring at 30 sites, 12 sites were experiencing a Superfund removal action, and roughly 36% of the 538 sites on the NPL at that time had no removal or remedial Superfund-financed activity (U.S. GAO, 1985b). While those numbers appear impressive, it should be noted that of the 298 sites undergoing Superfund remedial work, only 62 were slated for cleanup. The other 236 remained at the remedial investigation/feasibility study phase.

Because of the additive nature of the NPL and its annual updates, another way of assessing the program's progress is to examine the status of the original sites on the first NPL list. The first list contained 110 sites, excluding the 5 located in U.S. territories. Five categories of response actions are possible: a voluntary or negotiated response in which responsible parties will take corrective actions at a site, a combined federal/state response, a federal enforcement action against parties responsible for waste at a site, a state enforcement action against responsible parties, and an "actions to be determined" category. For sites that belong to one or a combination of the first four action categories, an indicator of cleanup status is also available. There are three discrete possibilities: implementation activity is underway in one or more operable units, implementation is complete in one or more operable units with others underway, or implementation activity has been completed in all operable units. Table 8.2 displays the status of the original NPL sites as of September 1985.

The data in Table 8.2 demonstrate that 15.2% of the original NPL sites remained in the "actions to be determined" category. This means that at 84.8% of the "oldest" sites, some kind of response action was underway. It would be inaccurate to calculate percentages for the other categories because of the overlap in response actions. For example, at the Ottati & Goss/Kingston Steel Drum site in New Hampshire, all four of the action responses have occurred. The combined federal state response is the most prevalent category, occurring at 62 sites. Of special note is the relatively limited (27 sites) occurrence of voluntary or negotiated responses by

Table 8.2
Disposition of the Original NPL Sites[a]

Response Category[b]	Number of NPL Sites
Voluntary or Negotiated (Private) Response	27
Federal and State Response	62
Federal Enforcement Response	42
State Enforcement Response	26
Actions to be Determined	16
Cleanup Status	Number of NPL Sites
Implementation activity underway, one or more operable units	9
One or more operable units completed, others may be underway	39
Implementation activity completed for all operable units	5

[a]The number of original sites has changed somewhat. Of the 110 sites originally included, 7 no longer appear on the NPL, while one comprehensive site in Florida labeled the Biscayne Aquifer has been split into three separate sites. The operable number of original sites is 105.

[b]With the exception of the "actions to be determined" category, the response categories are not discrete. It is quite common for a site to experience more than one type of response action. The numbers, therefore, should not be summed.

Source: Adapted by the author from data in U.S. Environmental Protection Agency, "National Priorities List Final and Proposed Sites through Update 4," (September 18), 1985, mimeo.

responsible parties. When that designation does exist, it is part of a joint governmental response. Only the Rose Park Sludge Pit in Salt Lake City, Utah, was subject to a solely private-party cleanup.

When the focus shifts to actual cleanup status, the image of action wanes. At only 5 of the original sites has implementation activity been completed. Thirty-nine sites (37%) were partially completed. Implementation activity was underway at an additional 9 sites; however, fully one-half of the original sites continued to lack cleanup activity. In other words, after four years on the NPL, cleanups had not begun at half of the original sites.

One of the reasons for the dearth of cleanups has to do with the structure of the first part of the cleanup process: the remedial investigation/feasibility study (RI/FS) stage. Once a site has been identified, assessed, inspected, and judged serious enough to warrant inclusion on the NPL, it becomes part of the annual update of the NPL. Assuming it survives the public comment period, the site then qualifies for remedial cleanup action. To the uninitiated, it may appear that salvation is at hand. Salvation turns out to be a slow process, however. As indicated in the 1984 GAO study of 538 sites, 80% of the sites scheduled for cleanup were in the RI/FS phase. This stage involves an investigation to gauge the type and extent of contamination at the site and the preparation of an action plan that analyzes available cleanup alternatives and assesses their cost-effectiveness. The process takes, on the average, one and one-half years, with an average cost of $800,000 for each RI/FS (Moorman, 1985). Once the alternatives are known, the EPA is charged with selecting a cost-effective remedy. In other words, the need for protecting public health, welfare, and the environment is balanced against the limited resources of the fund and the demands of other sites.

Cost-effectiveness became a real issue in remedial actions under Superfund. The first hint that it could be a contentious matter emerged from the *U.S. v. Vertac Chemical Corporation* case. A U.S. District Court judge in Arkansas ruled that Vertac's $2 million plan to isolate and contain dioxin-contaminated wastes at its site was preferable in both environmental protectionism and cost-effectiveness to the EPA's $22 million proposal that the wastes be excavated and reburied in a double-lined landfill at the site (Raffle, 1985). Technically, Vertac was not a Superfund case; however, it has value as a precedent. Because of the finite nature of Superfund resources, NPL sites compete against each other for cleanup dollars. Cost-effectiveness as a decisional criterion raises the difficult "How clean is clean?" question. The question becomes crucial as the EPA tackles the design the cleanup remedy. Until the remedy is designed, no cleanup can occur. This is precisely the reason that many of the original sites still languish in the "no cleanup" category.

The "clean" question is, in all likelihood, indeterminable. This does not mean that there are no attempts to address the issue of cleanup goals. In the U.S. Office of Technology Assessment's (1985) study, several variations on the "How clean is clean?" theme were examined. The OTA found two approaches for establishing cleanup levels to be either technically or economically impractical: restoring sites to pristine or background levels and using the best available technology. Another approach, using existing environmental standards or criteria for particular chemicals, was judged too limited in coverage to apply across the board. Two other alternatives, risk assessments and cost-benefit analyses, were deemed complicated but ultimately workable. The OTA's preferred approach for establishing clear cleanup goals involves the use of information and decisions about restoration, rehabitability, and reuse of the site. In other words, the future use of a site would determine the cleanup level. This way, high-cost techniques could be reserved for high-priority sites certain to be rehabitated and reused. Lower-cost, existing-standard approaches could be applied in situations where exposures are small and reuse is not an issue.

These considerations could assist the EPA in the final part of the cleanup process: the implementation of the remedy. However, as the data in Table 8.2 suggest, the process becomes even more complicated at this point. As noted earlier, the Mazmanian and Sabatier (1983) model may be useful in explaining why Superfund implementation has been so protracted.

APPLICATION OF THE MAZMANIAN AND SABATIER IMPLEMENTATION MODEL

The first of the Mazmanian and Sabatier components relates to *the level and extent of hierarchical integration within and among implementing institutions*. As they note, this can be a particularly difficult endeavor "in the case of federal statutes which rely on state and local agencies to carry out the details of program delivery in a very heterogeneous system" (Mazmanian and Sabatier, 1983: 27). With Superfund, the integration among participating organizations appears to be imperfectly hierarchical. The EPA cannot mount remedial actions without a formal agreement with the affected state government. The state is responsible for paying a percentage of the cleanup costs, for identifying available off-site disposal options, and for monitoring the site once remedial work is completed. As for the actual cleanup, either the EPA or the state may direct the work. When the EPA takes the lead, the state functions in an advisory capacity. The EPA contracts with private cleanup firms to undertake corrective measures. The U.S. Army Corps of Engineers eventually becomes involved in supervising the contractors. A state-run cleanup involves a cooperative agreement with the EPA. Superfund dollars are transferred to the state, and a work plan, schedule, and budget are developed before contractors are employed. The EPA serves as a monitor of state performance. Even under a cooperative agreement, state latitude is circumscribed by the EPA's internal management constraints, resource commitments, scheduling projections, and budget guidelines (Edelman, 1985).

Therefore, although the interplay of the governmental actors is supposed to be cooperative, states tend to occupy a subordinate position. Only loose integration is evident, and it is complicated by the EPA's headquarters-region structure. Headquarters directives can be a foil even when a harmonious relationship has been achieved between the EPA's regional officials and state actors. Some EPA regional officials have argued for a more aggressive Superfund program. This is in direct contradiction to EPA headquarters' pursuit of a more "limited" Superfund. Regional officials claim that $12 billion over the next five years is needed for Superfund. The headquarters figure is $5.5 billion (*Inside EPA*, 1985c). This headquarters-region divergence can cripple intra-agency integration.

Environmental agencies are not the only governmental organizations involved in Superfund. Both the Department of Health and Human Services and the Department of the Interior have Superfund responsibilities. Like the EPA, both of these agencies have been criticized for a snail-like implementation pace (Reisch, 1984). The Department of Justice plays a major role in Superfund. The design of Superfund requires that the EPA pursue responsible parties—generators, transporters, disposers, owners/ operators—connected to a site. If the EPA is unsuccessful in compelling their financial involvement in a cleanup, the agency turns to the Department of Justice for legal action against them. Involved also is the DOJ's state counterpart, the attorney general's office.

The decision rules of implementing agencies are another component of the model. From the outset, the EPA adopted decision rules that had the effect of impeding implementation. The EPA's director of emergency and remedial response noted that, "as a matter of policy, rather than law," the EPA required states to contribute 10% of the initial planning and design costs at a site in addition to the mandated 10% of cleanup costs. "That policy put a number of constraints on states. . . . 42 states either have no resources or very limited resources to come up with the 10% match" (Ward, 1983: 8). The EPA's decision rule meant that in most states cleanup could not begin because the prerequisite work in the cleanup process—the remedial investigation/feasibility study—had not been done. The rule, once its effect became clear, was replaced by 100% federal funding of the planning and design phases.

Another agency decision rule has proved troublesome to implement. The law requires the agency to attempt to compel responsible parties to clean up their site prior to governmental action. But the statute does not dictate how extensive the agency's efforts should be. Initially, the EPA delayed cleanup activity, preferring to involve responsible parties in negotiations over relative shares and extent of involvement. The EPA's efforts to foster a nonconfrontational spirit created a virtual impasse. Involving responsible parties before remedial investigation/feasibility studies were conducted led to unproductive posturing on both sides. Subsequently, the EPA has altered the process such that responsible parties are brought in to negotiate after a preferred cleanup option has been identified. At that point, responsible parties have three options: they can proceed with the selected course of action, they can let the EPA handle the cleanup and then settle for fund reimbursement, or they can withdraw and face a cost-recovery lawsuit. This new policy has not met with industry enthusiasm. In fact, some argue that this new decision rule and the problem of allocating costs among potentially responsible parties are two of the major barriers to voluntary industry cleanups (Moorman, 1985).

It appears that the EPA has become sensitive to charges of agency ineptitude from both environmentalists and regulated interests and is moving toward a more action-oriented style. For example, at the Chem-Dyne site, where approximately 200 firms were listed as "potentially responsible parties," the EPA and industry agreed to a settlement in which small generators bought their way out of joint and several liability (*Inside EPA*, 1985a). Generators that contributed large volumes of waste to the

Chem-Dyne site agreed to assume responsibility for any liability that exceeded the settlement sum. In addition, the EPA's 1985 settlement policy discards the decision rule that the agency would not negotiate a settlement representing less than 80% of the total cost of the cleanup. As one high-ranking EPA official noted, "the 80% threshold was, admittedly, an arbitrary rule, and it was misunderstood inside and outside the agency" (Mays, 1985: 8). The new rule states that the EPA will negotiate a settlement offer if it constitutes "a substantial proportion" of cleanup costs or remedial action.

The commitment and leadership skills of implementing officials are factors with direct causal links to implementation success. Mazmanian and Sabatier (1983: 34) suggest that the correspondence between a program's objectives and agency officials' priorities greatly affects the outcome. In addition, the officials' skill in converting priorities into realities directly influences a program's fate. With Superfund, this link became severely attentuated. Political appointees to the EPA made structural changes in the agency that, in Cohen's (1984) analysis, lowered morale and impaired organizational effectiveness. To the regulated community, this signaled a relaxation in enforcement. Agency leadership defended their nonconfrontational approach as cost-effective.

In 1982, there were congressional charges that the EPA used Superfund cleanup grants politically to influence the outcome of elections (Davis, 1984). This further fanned the flames of public discontent. The agency's political leadership, described as inexperienced, incompetent, and ideologically driven (Cohen, 1984), became estranged from careerists in the organization. No matter what the expertise and skills of the officials closest to the cleanup issue, their efforts were often compromised by the other-directed top leadership. Eventually Superfund implementation problems contributed to the replacement of the EPA's political management in early 1983.

Dissatisfaction with the pace of Superfund activity led to the creation of Clean Sites, Inc. Designed to serve as a buffer between government and responsible parties, the nonprofit organization was conceived by an uncommon alliance of the chemical industry and some environmental groups. Clean Sites' intent was to use collaborative efforts to structure an incentive system to spur settlement and cleanup (Reilly, 1984). In other words, Clean Sites was to assume the role of a "fixer." As such, it represents an organizational adjustment to conventional regulatory practice. Like other "third-sector" organizations, it brings private-sector flexibility to collective goods problems to forge what advocates claim will be more efficient solutions.

Despite its promise as a meshing organization (Rubin, 1984), Clean Sites faced an initial hurdle that has effectively hampered its performance. Because of the drying up of the private environmental liability insurance market (*Inside EPA,* 1985b), Clean Sites was unable to obtain insurance coverage. Due to the tremendous potential personal liabilities facing Clean Sites directors and personnel, the organization was virtually shut out of serious technical involvement in cleanups (*Environmental Forum,* 1985). Since the EPA's April 1985 agreement to indemnify Clean Sites for up to 15 million per NPL site that they work on, the organization has become involved in cleanup negotiations at nineteen sites. However, an additional obstacle confronts Clean Sites. Its financial support has rested, in large part, in the chemical industry. For a number of reasons, not the least of which is to bolster its independence, Clean Sites has been pursuing an expansion of that financial base.

Target group behavior (and more importantly, compliance) during implementation is another component of the Mazmanian and Sabatier model. The Superfund program would not have been necessary were involved parties behaving responsibly. As a result, the design of the statute, despite its vagueness, is adversarial. Relative levels of responsibility are apportioned. Involved parties are given the option of cleaning the site voluntarily (perhaps with a guarantee that no other legal actions will be taken against them) or face a governmental cleanup that will be followed by a settlement for reimbursement or a cost-recovery action. The experience thus far has been that some target groups will settle and others will not. The reasons underlying industry nonparticipation in a settlement range from economic to philosophical and legal. This disparate target group behavior complicates EPA's task. For example, at the precedent-setting Bluff Road site in South Carolina, the EPA identified twelve generators potentially responsible for waste that was stored at the site. Seven of the generators chose to settle and paid $1.95 million to clean up 75% of the site. The remaining portion was funded by the government while the five nonparticipating generators were sued.

Potentially responsible parties try to de-escalate the tensions that surround their case (Mott, 1983). For example, they may level counter-charges that the government was negligent in permitting or inspecting a site. These kinds of tactics suggest that target groups will likely be less than compliant and engage in delaying maneuvers. It is not clear whether renewed governmental activism in pursuing potentially responsible parties will be met with greater industry recalcitrance or gradual capitulation (Stanfield, 1984). The hazardous waste industry's position is that a settlement policy that contains incentives for voluntary industry cleanups will be beneficial to Superfund implementation. Moorman (1985) argues that there would be more responsible-party cleanups if the EPA's settlement policy built in significant cost savings for voluntary cleanups, offered litigation avoidance and contribution protection to settling parties, and granted releases to settling parties from further liability for the site and the wastes removed from it.

CONCLUSION

Governmental regulatory efforts that attempt to invoke cooperation among adversaries have inherent difficulties. The Superfund program demonstrates the consequences. As is evident with Superfund, poorly structured relationships among participating organizations, counterproductive decision rules, erratic commitments from implementers, and target group recalcitrance have functioned as drags on implementation. New sites are being added to the NPL faster than current sites can be remedied. And remedies are expensive. The EPA's baseline cleanup cost estimate is $8.1 million per site.

It appears that the lessons of the original Superfund program were not lost on the congressional designers of the new Superfund. The original act expired in October 1985, but the cleanup program was kept alive through a special appropriation. Congress sorted through the web of environmental and corporate interests to rewrite the law during 1986 (Weisskopf, 1986). The new Superfund law that was signed by the president in October 1986 represents a broad expansion of the original act (*Congressional Quarterly Weekly Report,* 1986). It increases the funding level to $8.5 billion, establishes on-site and off-site cleanup standards, and requires the EPA to begin investigating conditions at new sites and remedying those already investigated. The direction of these changes signifies a strengthened congressional commitment to hazardous waste cleanup. If Mazmanian and Sabatier (1983) are correct, this improved legislation provides a basis for improved bureaucratic performance.

REFERENCES

Bowman, Ann O'M., "Intergovernmental and Intersectoral Tensions in Environmental Policy Implementation: The Case of Hazardous Waste," *Policy Studies Review* 4 (November 1984): 230-244.

Carnes, Sam A., "Confronting Complexity and Uncertainty: Implementation of Hazardous Waste Management Policy," in Dean E. Mann, ed., *Environmental Policy Implementation* (Lexington, MA: D. C. Heath, 1982), 35-50.

Cohen, Steven, "Defusing the Toxic Time Bomb: Federal Hazardous Waste Programs," in Norman J. Vig and Michael E. Kraft, eds., *Environmental Policy in the 1980s* (Washington: CQ Press, 1984), 273-291.

Congressional Quarterly Weekly Report, "Congress Clears 'Superfund,' Awaits President's Decision," *Congressional Quarterly Weekly Report* 44 (October 11, 1986): 2532-2541.

Davis, Joseph A., "Superfund Contaminated by Partisan Politics," *Congressional Quarterly Weekly Report* 42 (March 17, 1984): 615-620.

Edelman, Larry, "Superfund and the States—Doing More," *Environmental Forum* 4 (October 1985): 39-41.

Environmental Forum, "Clean Sites at Age One: An Uneven Start," *Environmental Forum* 4 (July 1985): 27-31.

Freeman, George C., Jr. "Brief of Syntex Agribusiness, Inc.," filed in the U.S. Court of Appeals for the Eighth Circuit. N.d.

Inside EPA, "Chem-Dyne Liability, Buy-Out for Small Parties Harbinger of New EPA Approach," *Inside EPA* (June 21, 1985a): 7.

_____, "Pollution Insurance Rep Says Market Dismal, Calls for Channeled Liability," *Inside EPA* (June 21, 1985b): 7.

Inside EPA, "Sierra Club Study: EPA Regions See Funding Shortfall Big Superfund Problem," *Inside EPA* (June 28, 1985c):11.

Mays, Richard H., "EPA's Superfund Settlement Policy," *Environmental Forum* 3 (February 1985): 6-17.

Mazmanian, Daniel, and Paul A. Sabatier, *Implementation and Public Policy* (Glenview, Il: Scott, Foresman, 1983).

Melamud, Dennis, "Superfund: From Site Selection to Cleanup," *Environmental and Energy Study Conference Guide* (Washington, DC: Congressional Research Service, 1984).

Moorman, James W., "Superfund Settlement Policy—Will It Work," *Environmental Forum* 4 (June 1985): 8-16.

Mott, Randy, "Defense Tactics for the Hazardous Waste Responsible Party," *Environmental Forum* 1 (March 1983): 5-8.

Novick, Sheldon M., "What Is Wrong with Superfund?" *Environmental Forum* 2 (November 1983): 6-11.

Raffle, Bradley I., "Cost Effectiveness as a Criterion in Hazardous Waste Site Cleanups," *Environmental Forum* 3 (January 1985): 18-21.

Reilly, William K., "Cleaning Our Chemical Waste Backyard," *Wall Street Journal* (May 31, 1984): 30.

Reisch, Mark A. E., "Superfund: Hazardous Waste Cleanup," *Issue Brief* (Washington, DC): Congressional Research Service, 1984).

Rubin, Herbert J., "The Meshing Organization as a Catalyst for Municipal Coordination," *Administration & Society* 16 (August 1984): 215-238.

Stanfield, Rochelle, "Superfund Backers Push Big Expansion of Program to Clean Up Toxic Wastes," *National Journal* (September 22, 1984): 1762-1766.

U.S. General Accouting Office, *Hazardous Waste Sites Pose Investigation, Scientific, and Legal Problems* (Washington, DC: GAO, 1981a).

_____, *Environmental Protection Agency's Progress Implementing the Superfund Program* (Washington: GAO, 1981b).

_____. *EPA's Preliminary Estimates of Future Hazardous Waste Costs Are Uncertain* (Washington: GAO, 1984).

_____, *EPA's Inventory of Potential Hazardous Waste Sites Is Incomplete* (Washington: GAO, 1985a).

_____, "Status of EPA's Remedial Cleanup Efforts," Letter for Congressman James J. Florio (March 20, 1985b).

U.S. Office of Technology Assessment, *Superfund Strategy* (Washington, DC: OTA, 1985).

Ward, Bud, "A Conversation with Superfund Chief Bill Hedeman," *Environmental Forum* 2 (August 1983): 7-13.

Weisskopf, Michael, "New Standards Set for Superfund Work," *Washington Post* (August 1, 1986): A1, A10.

PART III

THE NATIONAL AND INTERGOVERNMENTAL LEVELS

9

Hazardous Wastes and the Politics of Policy Change

Richard Barke

In 1976 Congress passed the first legislation to provide for a significant federal role in the regulation of hazardous wastes. The Resource Conservation and Recovery Act (RCRA) required the Environmental Protection Agency (EPA) to identify hazardous wastes and to establish safety standards for hazardous waste production, transportation, storage, and disposal. After 1976 Congress had several opportunities to reauthorize and revise RCRA, culminating in the Hazardous and Solid Waste Amendments (HSWA) of 1984. During this short history of the federal role in hazardous waste regulation, significant changes occurred in this realm of public policy. The catastrophe of Love Canal introduced hazardous waste as an issue of national concern, the EPA's mismanagement of hazardous waste programs became headline news, and policymakers confronted their lack of understanding of hazardous wastes as it became clear that they had greatly underestimated the size, scope, and technological problems of implementing RCRA.

In a 1983 address at the University of North Carolina, EPA Administrator William Ruckelshaus observed that all environmental laws passed during the 1970s were based on assumptions about five crucial aspects of pollution control: (1) we knew what the bad pollutants were, (2) we knew what adverse effects they cause, (3) we knew how to measure the pollutants and their effects, (4) we knew how to regulate them to acceptable levels at reasonable costs, and (5) these environmental laws would be changed as new information brought these underlying assumptions into question (Miller, 1984). The first three assumptions are basically scientific and technological. The fourth assumption combines technological, economic, and political considerations, while the fifth is explicitly political. During the eight years between RCRA and HSWA each of these assumptions was put to an empirical test, and all were found to be weak or incorrect. As a result, it is particularly appropriate to study the evolution of hazardous waste policy as an example of policy change and policy learning.

POLICY LEARNING

Public policies develop and change in response to complex, inconstant, and often immeasurable sets of forces. The scientific study of the policy process has produced few general theories, but researchers have introduced some order to the numerous variables that shape policy. A framework of constraints has been applied to the evolution of hazardous waste policy, explaining policy changes in terms of legal limitations, coordination problems, scientific uncertainty, and political factors (Barke, 1986). Another approach was offered by Sabatier (1985), whose conceptual framework of policy evolution and learning can be applied to the case of hazardous waste policy (Figure 9.1). In this model, the unit of analysis is a policy subsystem consisting of those who are actively concerned with the particular issue and who are divided into advocacy coalitions that share similar normative and causal beliefs. Competition among these coalitions is mediated by policy brokers who seek consensus, or at least acquiescence in some formal decision. Policy evolution is shaped by two broad types of forces.

First, the advocacy coalitions are roughly defined by their belief systems. These may be divided into three types: deep core (normative) beliefs, which are very difficult to alter and thus the source of the most irresolvable conflicts; near core (policy) beliefs, which relate policy strategies to the achievement of deep core beliefs; and secondary beliefs, consisting of the tactics and information required to implement the policy beliefs. In the realm of hazardous waste policy, disputes over deep core beliefs would be revealed in debates over the inherent destructiveness of industrial society or the moral obligation of government to return man to (or save him from) a pristine natural state. Near core issues include the instruments of hazardous waste control (such as command-and-control regulation vs. increased legal liability for polluters), the allocation of authority between the federal and state governments, and the appropriate degree of public participation in decision making. Finally, secondary aspects of belief systems would include information about the success of prior programs, the scope of the hazardous waste problem, and the costs and benefits of various policy options.

In this framework policy evolution is also shaped by two types of variables that affect policy learning. The first category of variables consists of "a set of relatively stable (over several decades) constitutional, cultural, natural resource, and problem related parameters strongly resistant to

Figure 9.1
General Model of Policy Evolution Focusing on Competing Advocacy Coalitions within Policy Subsystems

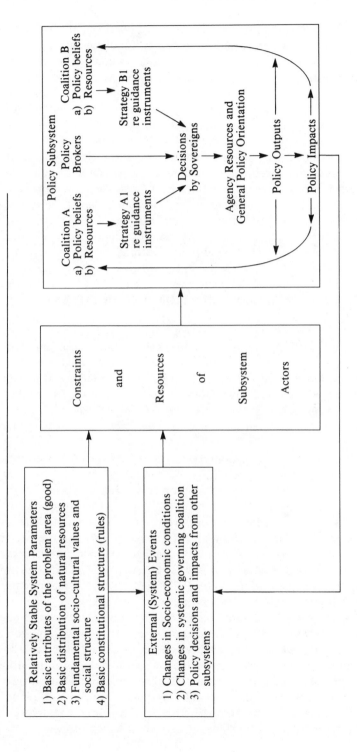

Source: Sabatier, 1985. Reprinted with permission.

change" (Sabatier, 1985: 8). These include basic attributes of the problem area, the distribution of natural resources, fundamental cultural values, and constitutional structure. The second category consists of factors that "can vary substantially over the course of a few years or a decade [thereby] altering the constraints and opportunities confronting subsystem actors" (Sabatier, 1985: 10). These include changes in socioeconomic conditions, changes in systemic governing coalitions, and impacts from other policy sectors and systems. According to Sabatier, analysis of the belief systems and external factors affecting a policy question should enable us to make general statements about the likelihood and direction of policy change and policy learning, which he defines as a "relatively enduring alteration of thought or behavioral intentions which result from experience and which are concerned with the attainment (or revision) of public policy" (Sabatier, 1985: 11). The evolution of hazardous waste policy from 1976 to 1984 is an example of policy change and policy learning.

THE RESOURCE CONSERVATION AND RECOVERY ACT OF 1976

Prior to 1976 there was no comprehensive public hazardous waste policy. Few states had their own regulatory programs, and federal environmental policies aimed at air and water quality had led to industrial practices which sometimes had actually increased the generation of solid hazardous wastes. For example, currently about 118 million dry metric tons of sludge (including toxic chemicals) are generated each year because of pollution control techniques—80% from air pollution controls alone.

In 1976 the Resource Conservation and Recovery Act was introduced as an amendment to the Solid Waste Disposal Act. The bill's Subtitle C, which focused upon hazardous waste problems, drew relatively little attention during hearings and floor debate, in large part because the scale of the hazardous waste problem was greatly underestimated. The record of congressional consideration of RCRA shows great optimism about the ability of the EPA to carry out the congressional mandate. It was intended to do for solid wastes what the Clean Air Act had tried to do for air pollution and the Federal Water Pollution Control Act had attempted to do for water: "cradle-to-grave" protection.

The 1976 RCRA required the EPA to establish (1) criteria for identifying hazardous wastes, (2) requirements for record keeping and for labeling, packing, and transporting such wastes, (3) standards for hazardous waste disposal facilities, and (4) a permit system for operators of hazardous waste facilities. Although there was a persistent perception that (in the words of one of the bill's sponsors) "RCRA was designed to encourage innovation in new technologies for waste disposal" (U.S. House of Representatives, 1982a), the EPA was forbidden to extend the hazardous waste provisions of

RCRA to wastes covered by several other statutes. Most of the EPA's new mandate was to be operative within eighteen months.

THE 1980 REAUTHORIZATION

In the short period before the scheduled reauthorization of RCRA the complexity of the hazardous waste problem began to be perceived. Partly because RCRA implementation was not a high priority at the EPA during the late 1970's, the agency missed its March 1978 deadline for issuing regulations under RCRA. The General Accounting Office (GAO) warned that "effective implementation" of RCRA would continue to be stymied by the EPA's inability to gather necessary data on such basics as the number of disposal sites, the effects of landfill disposal on groundwater quality, and alternative disposal technologies (Riley, 1983). The hazardous waste problem was becoming much more visible as a result of the Love Canal disaster and because of growing awareness that the number of dangerous landfills was much larger than originally estimated. At the same time industry was mobilizing to seek particular exemptions upon the renewal of RCRA.

After lengthy delays the Senate and House agreed on a reauthorization of RCRA in October 1980. Under the new law some industry-specific types of waste (such as drilling-rig muds) were exempted, but in general the legislation strengthened the enforcement powers of the EPA. This was hardly a congratulatory gesture: during hearings both chambers of Congress had severely criticized the EPA for its delays in promulgating regulations, for its inadequate allocation of resources to hazardous waste programs, and for its inability to reassure constituents that dumps had been identified and were being controlled. Nevertheless, no new regulatory strategies were urged upon the EPA.

In defense of the EPA it must be noted that it confronted an enormous and complex task. Like Congress, it has been unaware of how many waste sites there were; the EPA's early estimates of the number may have been short by a factor of one hundred. The technologies for disposal of hazardous wastes were also undeveloped. Landfill was the most common technique, but no one knew all of its side effects, and alternatives such as incineration, chemical stabilization, and high-temperature decomposition had received relatively little attention. In addition, RCRA had provided no authority or funds for the EPA to go beyond the task of managing current waste disposal; the Love Canal episode had shown that *past* disposal practices would require new legislation (the Comprehensive Environmental Response, Compensation, and Liability Act of 1980, or "Superfund"). Finally, RCRA was vague in its mandate to EPA officials, who could only wonder at exactly what Congress meant by the requirement that EPA regulations should "minimize the risk to public health and the environment." At any cost?

THE 1982 REAUTHORIZATION

In spite of the heightened public and congressional concern with the hazardous waste problem, implementation of RCRA slowed during the early years of the Reagan administration. In November 1980 David Stockman referred to RCRA in a planning memorandum as a "monument to mindless excess," and through subsequent actions the administration implemented this perception (Mosher, 1981). Referrals of hazardous waste actions to the EPA by regional offices dropped from eighty-six in 1980 to nine in 1981, and the federal government ended financial support to state governments for implementation of hazardous waste policies (U.S. House of Representatives, 1982a). EPA budget requests for hazardous waste programs in fiscal years 1983 and 1984 dropped considerably (Cook and Davidson, 1984).

After criticizing the administration's attitude during hearings on the scheduled 1982 reauthorization of RCRA, the Senate considered a bill that would have boosted funding for RCRA and authorized a study of the health risks of hazardous wastes by the National Academy of Sciences. The House of Representatives responded with a bill that would have (1) reduced the small-generator exemption from 1,000 to 100 kilograms per month, (2) recommended specific deadlines for the approval or closing of land disposal facilities, and (3) broadened the definition of hazardous substances to be covered by RCRA. No bill was produced, however, and the RCRA reauthorization died with the Ninety-seventh Congress.

At this stage of RCRA's history there was much new information about hazardous wastes available to congressional and regulatory policymakers. In particular, Congress had been given evidence during sixteen days of relevant hearings in 1982 that landfills—the most common (that is, the cheapest) method of hazardous waste disposal—were unreliable, even in the short term. In the February 5, 1981, *Federal Register* the EPA admitted that landfill leakage would "inevitably occur," and even the Chemical Manufacturers Association agreed that reliance on landfills should be minimized. Furthermore, preliminary studies by the congressional Office of Technology Assessment (OTA) were used to argue that "the regulatory structure that EPA has devised actually discourages any kind of commercial development of alternatives [to landfilling]" because the true costs of landfilling (such as maintaining and monitoring a secure landfill over thirty years or more) had not been internalized (U.S. House of Representatives, 1982a).

We can identify three general advocacy coalitions in the hazardous waste policy subsystem. By far the largest was composed of most members of Congress, state environmental officials, environmental activists, the hazardous waste disposal industry, and groups such as the League of Women Voters. This coalition shared perceptions not only over deep core and near core beliefs but also over secondary aspects such as past program performance and the seriousness of the hazardous waste problem. A second coalition consisted of the chemical industry, whose moderate position was that the hazardous waste problem was serious, that the EPA had done a poor job of resolving the regulatory and technological uncertainties about waste disposal, and that landfills, although the cheapest solution over the short term, should be minimized. The third coalition was dominated by the Reagan administration, which, under Anne Gorsuch's EPA, disputed not only the secondary beliefs of both the environmental and industry coalitions but also their near core beliefs concerning the proper scope of governmental activity in regulating hazardous wastes.

Ironically, policy change and policy learning had occurred by 1982, but in different institutions. Policy change could be seen at the level of implementation as the EPA tried to withdraw by cutting staff, research funds, and enforcement actions; this change was a result of the new systemic governing coalition of the Reagan administration. At the same time, some of what Sabatier identified as relatively stable variables were becoming better understood—particularly the basic attributes and distribution of the problem—which created pressure for policy change. Policy learning had occurred as possible improvements in hazardous waste regulation were brought to the attention of Congress, including better EPA coordination with state programs, stronger emphasis on recovery and recycling, and improvements in incineration techniques. This policy learning was still potential and unused, however. As late as December 1982, Rita Lavelle was testifying to Congress that "properly constructed, properly managed, and properly closed landfills" were a viable technology (U.S. House of Representatives, 1982b). The conflict that was emerging in 1982 was less over what needed to be done than over whether the EPA was willing to do it. The failure of Congress in 1982 to act on what it had learned set the stage for fundamental changes in 1983-1984.

HAZARDOUS WASTE REGULATION IN 1984

In the Ninety-eighth Congress advocates of stronger EPA action took hope in the naming of William Ruckelshaus as EPA administrator, but the agency continued to be accused of trying to further weaken its enforcement of RCRA standards (Stanfield, 1984). Given this growing dissatisfaction, arguments in favor of greater EPA flexibility (for example, permitting the EPA to define allowable levels of risk to be implemented via performance standards; see Buc and Haymore, 1983) had become even more politically infeasible.

The EPA's regulatory strategies came under intense scrutiny in two comprehensive studies requested by Congress. In early 1983 OTA released the results of a three-year study which found significant flaws in hazardous waste control, including

1. inconsistent federal and state programs for data collection, risk assessment, and waste management;
2. inadequate data on the scope and complexity of hazardous waste problems;
3. significant federal exemptions of small-quantity waste generators and of particular types of hazardous wastes; and
4. federal programs that provided stronger incentives for land disposal than for resource recovery or treatment (U.S. Congress, Office of Technology Assessment, 1983).

OTA also found that RCRA regulations were inadequate to prevent RCRA-regulated sites from becoming Superfund sites, and that there were some enormous discrepancies between RCRA and Superfund rules. It criticized the EPA's allocation of research and development funds, since only about 10% of its hazardous waste R&D budget was devoted to alternatives to land disposal. At about the same time the National Academy of Sciences NAS) published a report focusing on control technologies rather than regulatory strategies. The NAS strongly recommended "in-plant options," or industrial process modifications, and pointed to the need for research on the conversion of hazardous waste into nonhazardous waste (National Research Council, 1983).

These two reports revealed a fundamental problem that Congress and the EPA had failed to address and solve. Industrial technology and short-term market forces, operating compatibly, created the hazardous waste problem as industries avoided internalizing the full costs of hazardous waste production. Cleanup costs were geographically shifted or postponed since there were no marketplace incentives to invest in the technology required to effectively recover, recycle, or dispose of hazardous wastes. By 1983 it had become inescapably clear that market forces alone would play a minimal role in a solution to the hazardous waste problem, and current regulatory schemes were demonstrably inadequate as inducements to include the costs of hazardous waste control in the decisions of private firms. The OTA report was particularly thorough in its presentation of the policy options (and the implementation problems each would entail) for consistent and effective hazardous waste control.

After the failure of Congress to pass reauthorizing legislation in 1982, the House and Senate began anew in 1983. Nearly forty days of hearings related to hazardous waste policy revealed the breadth of support for policy change, the ever-increasing magnitude of the problem, and the inadequacy of RCRA as a mandate for effective EPA action. In May 1983, noting that hazardous waste legislation confronted a task of "unparalleled scope and complexity," the House Committee on Energy and Commerce reported HR 2867, the "Hazardous Waste Control and Enforcement Act." This bill extended regulation to small-quantity (100-1,000 kg/month) waste generators, required the EPA to actively discourage land disposal, and expanded regulatory enforcement powers. The bill reflected congressional displeasure with the EPA's implementation of RCRA by severely restricting the agency's discretion. The bill was supported by environmental groups, while some business groups objected to the reduction in the EPA's flexibility. HR 2867 passed the House on November 3, 1983.

The Senate version of the RCRA reauthorization (S 757) was reported by its Environment Committee in July 1983, but floor passage took nearly a year. The Reagan administration gave the bill only lukewarm support, objecting to its "inflexible and unnecessary regulatory mandates which could impose from $10 billion to $20 billion per year in added costs on the economy" (*Congressional Quarterly Weekly Report,* 1984). Floor consideration was delayed by proposed changes and specific exemptions, but on July 25, 1984, the Senate voted 93-0 for its version of hazardous waste legislation. Senator Jennings Randolph (D-WV) labeled the bill as part of a "refinement process as experience in implementing the program outline[d] deficiencies and oversights in existing law," while George Mitchell (D-ME) called S 757 a "strong congressional expression of disapproval of EPA's slow and timid implementation of the existing law" (*Congressional Record,* July 25, 1984: S 9151). Disagreements with House Democrats (primarily about Superfund-related amendments to S 757) were settled in conference committee, and a compromise bill was produced and signed by President Reagan on November 9, 1984.

THE HAZARDOUS AND SOLID WASTE AMENDMENTS OF 1984

Three aspects of HSWA stand out: its treatment of landfills, its mandate to the EPA, and increased regulation of small waste generators and underground storage tanks. The conferees bluntly stated that they intended "to convey a clear and unambiguous message to the regulated community and the Environmental Protection Agency; reliance on land disposal of hazardous waste has resulted in an unacceptable risk to human health and the environment," and "land disposal should be used only as a last resort" (*Congressional Record,* October 3, 1984: H 11126). To that end, the act prohibited the disposal of noncontainerized or bulk liquid hazardous waste in landfills and required the EPA to produce regulations minimizing the disposal of particular substances on the "California list" of specific hazardous wastes (e.g., substances containing high concentrations of arsenic, cadmium, chromium, lead, mercury, and other metals or polychlorinated biphenyls). Land disposal of "dioxin-containing hazardous wastes" would be banned within twenty-four months.

Reflecting complaints about the EPA's impermeability to public demands and requests, Congress authorized the administrator to appoint an ombudsman "of sufficient stature within the Agency that citizens will be able to secure meaningful assistance as quickly as possible." The law also expanded the rights of citizens to bring legal actions in situations involving an "imminent and substantial" endangerment caused by the management or disposal of solid or hazardous waste, although limitations on citizens' suits were included in order to avoid delays in Superfund cleanups or interference with current RCRA enforcement actions.

Other specific requirements of HSWA included guidance for the EPA in developing a schedule for land disposal of hazardous wastes. The House-Senate conferees pointedly observed that they "do not expect EPA to undertake a rigorous assessment of risk for purposes of developing the schedule" because such assessments would lead to lengthy delays and the intent of Congress clearly was to speed up the regulatory process. Furthermore, while past EPA policies restricted the scope of corrective action to the boundaries of a polluting facility, Congress found that "such a restriction has no basis in logic" (given the tendency of contaminated groundwater to flow), and the EPA was ordered to require corrective action wherever necessary. In order to eliminate ambiguities about the intent of Congress, the act also included detailed specifications regarding the permeability of liners (0.0000001 cm/sec), the resistivity of soils in which underground storage tanks would be used (less than 12,000 ohms), particular substances to be included on EPA lists of hazardous wastes (e.g., halogenated dibenzofurans), and so on.

Regarding the scope of hazardous waste regulation, the act extended the EPA's jurisdiction over waste generators to those producing from 100 to 1,000 kg/month. (Some states such as Rhode Island had eliminated all small-generator exemptions.) Estimates of the amount of hazardous waste escaping through the previous 1,000 kg/month loophole ranged from 10% of that produced by large-quantity generators to "approximately an equal amount." In addition, the act required the regulation of underground tanks for the storage of petroleum and other hazardous substances.

Most significantly, Congress established automatic deadlines for EPA action. Explicit instructions were included to ensure that provisions written into the act would become operative should the EPA not issue regulations (e.g., on small-quantity generators) by the statutorily required date. This congressional "hammer" represented a radical shift in congressional delegation of regulatory authority to an agency. Representative James Florio (D-NJ) wrote that "Congress itself has had to assume the role of regulator, making some of the detailed and administrative determinations typically left to the implementing agency" (1986: 351). In limiting the EPA's discretion in delaying promulgation of regulations, Congress recognized that the agency could make distinctions based on "waste characteristics, waste management practices, and locational criteria."

THE EVOLUTION OF HAZARDOUS WASTE POLICY

In April 1984 EPA Administrator Ruckelshaus described environmental protection as

an enormously complicated technical process; that it now shares the aura of Motherhood and the Flag makes it less, rather than more, likely that we will do a good job of it. This is because we encourage public officials to strike extreme postures as defenders of the environment, while we shy away from requiring the hard decisions implied by such decisions. . . . This passes the buck to the executive agency.

The public appears to be demanding immediate but not very painful solutions to long-standing problems that we don't know how to fix. Congress appears to believe that the way to satisfy this public demand is to load the statutes with specific constraints and directives. Motion is its own reward, whether or not it is in the right direction. (*Congressional Record*, April 25, 1984: S4766)

Did Congress pass the buck, moving for the sake of moving on the subject of hazardous waste, or was Ruckelshaus's fifth assumption (cited at the beginning of this article) in fact correct: that environmental laws would be changed in response to new information? Change certainly occurred, but was it a rational change based on policy learning?

Policy Learning

Whatever learning occurred in Congress was not imposed from the outside. Congress had set in motion a sequence of actions that resulted in increased knowledge—if the legislators chose to pay attention. This knowledge included (1) vastly improved understanding of the scope and seriousness of the problem, (2) awareness of the flawed attempts by the EPA to formulate and implement a complex policy based on a simple mandate granting broad authorities, (3) evidence of the failure to coordinate RCRA with Superfund and state laws, and (4) information about progress in developing and implementing new treatment and disposal technologies.

Knowledge is not politically neutral, and therefore neither is its application. As Ruckelshaus suggested, publicly salient issues offer political incentives for action that may overwhelm technological or economic realities. Yet technical details can be a diversion from political trade-offs, so technological questions may be gratefully embraced by lawmakers facing intense issues (Barke, 1986: 174-175). In the case of hazardous waste policy, there was both political and scientific logic behind passage of HSWA.

The evolution of hazardous waste policy cannot be attributed to shifts in the political power of competing groups with different core belief systems. The central disputes were over near core beliefs, with only one major actor—the Reagan administration—outside the emerging consensus on the need for a change in the EPA's mandate. All other parts of the policy subsystem had begun to recognize the causal relationships between past regulatory strategies and policy failure. Moreover, as the definition of the problem shifted from environmental to public health (with evidence of the migration of toxic chemicals from landfills) the near-core-belief disputes among the prochange advocacy coalitions dissolved and the willingness to impose costs on hazardous waste producers grew. This finding is consistent with Sabatier's hypothesis: "policy-oriented learning across belief systems is most likely when there is an intermediate level of informed conflict between the two. This requires that: (a) each have the technical resources to engage in such a debate; and that (b) the conflict be between secondary aspects of one belief system and core elements of the other, or, alternatively, between important secondary aspects of the two belief systems" (Sabatier, 1985:21).

The role of professional forums for policy learning on hazardous wastes was also significant. Sabatier hypothesized that "policy-oriented learning across belief systems is most likely when there exists a forum which is: (a) prestigious enough to force professionals from different coalitions to participate; and (b) dominated by professional norms" (also see Jenkins-Smith, 1985). The bases for agreement in Congress were strengthened when the forum for much of the analysis on hazardous waste management policies shifted to the more "neutral" arenas of OTA and NAS, rather than the discredited Reagan EPA. After all, while EPA research funding had increased during the early 1980s, it had been largely against the wishes of the agency's officials, and there had been a shift in research priorities "from emphasis on long-term health effects and new technology development to short-term programs to support the direct promulgation of regulations" (Congressional Budget Office, 1985: 91; also see Andrews, 1984).

Changes in Policy System Parameters

Several of the factors that Sabatier identified as relatively stable varied substantially over the eight-year history of RCRA. A large amount of information about the *basic attributes* of the problem area was discovered and applied to policy options (for example, the physical characteristics of liquid wastes and the technologies of landfilling and incinerating). Although the fundamental nature of hazardous wastes did not change, what was known about them did. Similarly, the ability of policymakers to quantify and measure aspects of the problem (e.g., monitoring of leachates from landfills) progressed, as did the sophistication of causal models of the many factors affecting hazardous waste disposal; the legitimacy of the OTA and NAS studies was never seriously questioned. Second, what was known about the *basic distribution* of hazardous wastes grew enormously during 1976-1984. Hazardous wastes progressed from being a rather scarce "resource" to a much-too-common one, with clear implications for the salience of the policy area; for example, there were not distinct regional coalitions opposing the strengthening of RCRA. The third stable external factor discussed by Sabatier—*constitutional structure*—was unchanged. However, while the fourth variable—*fundamental cultural values*—also was largely static, that very stability played a vital role in the changes from RCRA to HSWA. Not only were public values regarding environmental protection largely unchanged during the period (Mitchell, 1984), but the espisodes of James Watt and Anne Gorsuch had rekindled some of the old environmental activism that underwrote congressional attempts to strengthen the hazardous waste laws (and thereby block the Reagan policy changes).

The case of change in hazardous waste policy can also be applied to Sabatier's "external event factors." *Socioeconomic conditions* remained relatively stable over this period. No externally imposed shocks on the environmental policy system occurred, with the possible exception of the Love Canal and Times Beach incidents (but these were not "perturbations in social and economic conditions"). On the other hand, there was a significant change in the *systemic governing coalition.* Although there had been criticism of delays under Carter's EPA, these were supplemented with allegations of actual malfeasance under the Reagan administration. Many Republicans in Congress may have been sympathetic to enforcement slowdowns in 1982, but by 1984 few Reagan supporters could avoid criticizing the EPA's implementation of RCRA, and the White House largely acquiesced in the final consideration of HSWA. Finally, the *impacts from other policy subsystems* upon hazardous waste policy were significant. Many of the details of HSWA were drawn from the experiences of state-level programs such as the "California list" of substances completely banned from landfills, and the vigor of state officials (who had often been blocked by EPA inaction) in pressing Congress to strengthen federal laws was evident at most hazardous waste hearings. Furthermore, the hazardous waste problem was becoming more obviously connected to other policy subsystems, especially groundwater contamination.

CONCLUSION

The degree to which the 1984 Hazardous and Solid Waste Amendments constituted "rational" policy learning depends on the consistency between the law's provisions and its efficiency at attaining the desired goals. The EPA did begin to move faster and more forcefully. For example, the agency's Final Rule on Hazardous Waste Management Systems, published in the *Federal Register* on July 15, 1985, announced "profound changes in the way that this country manages hazardous wastes" and acknowledged that to a large degree it "simply codified into the regulations the statutory language associated with each provision" (pp. 28702, 28703). As required by HSWA, the EPA published the first of a series of regulations restricting land disposal of hazardous wastes on November 7, 1986. Despite estimates that the new rules could increase the cost of disposing of some wastes such as solvent sludges as much as tenfold, the EPA had little choice given the statutory provisions that would have automatically banned all land disposal of solvent- and dioxin-containing wastes in the absence of agency action.

Some analyses of the 1984 amendments reveal that Congress may have failed to adequately require the necessary changes to achieve its stated goals. A study by the Congressional Budget Office indicated that additional enforcement mechanisms, such as a variable unit tax on waste disposal methods, would greatly increase the effects of HSWA (see Table 9.1). In a report issued in September 1986, OTA found many problems with RCRA to have been inadequately addressed by the 1984 amendments (U.S. Congress, OTA, 1986: 15). Action at the state level also continued, most noticeably in California, where in November 1986 voters approved by nearly 2 to 1 an initiative called Proposition 65, prohibiting the discharge of chemicals known to cause cancer or birth defects in any place where they could enter domestic drinking water supplies.

Regardless of additional changes in hazardous waste legislation and strategies, the first eight years of federal efforts in this policy arena offer a vivid example of policy change. Through the application of general approaches to inquiry such as the constraint and policy learning frameworks, analysts can gain insights into the forces that affect the likelihood not only that policy change will occur but also that it will be based on improved understanding of policy problems and the utility of proposed solutions.

REFERENCES

Andrews, Richard N. L., "Deregulation: The Failure at EPA," in Norman J. Vig and Michael E. Kraft, eds., *Environmental Policy in the 1980s: Reagan's New Agenda* (Washington, DC: CQ Press, 1984).

Barke, Richard, *Science, Technology, and Public Policy* (Washington, DC: CQ Press, 1986).

Buc, Lawrence G., and Curtis Haymore, "Regulating Hazardous Waste Incinerators under the Resource Conservation and Recovery Act," *Natural Resources Journal* 23 (July 1983) 3:549-564.

Congressional Budget Office, *Hazardous Waste Management: Recent Changes and Policy Alternatives* (Washington, DC: Government Printing Office, 1985).

Congressional Quarterly Weekly Report, "Senate Votes to Toughen Toxic Waste Law" (July 28, 1984): 1817.

Table 9.1
Effects of RCRA, HSWA, and Alternative Policies

Alternative	Annual Cost to Industry (In billions 1983 dollars)	Annual Cost to Federal Government (In millions of 1983 dollars)	Effect on Waste Reduction	Effect on Management Practices
1983 Baseline (1976 RCRA)	5.8	175	Negligible incentives for waste reduction; 266 million metric tons (MMT) generated in 1983; could increase to 280 MMT by 1990.	Encourages land disposal.
1984 HSWA	8.4–11.2	235	Limited incentives because of regulatory uncertainty; 1990 waste generation of 229 MMT–280 MMT.	Discourages or bans land disposal of high priority wastes. Increases incineration and pretreatment of wastes before land disposal.
1984 HSWA plus Waste-End Taxes	9.0–13.9	235	Strong incentives from increased cost of waste disposal; 1990 waste estimated at 229 MMT.	Encourages waste recycle, recovery and resale first; waste destruction second; waste hazard reduction third.
1984 HSWA, plus Waste-End Taxes, and other improvements such as Accelerated R&D, Capital Formation Assistance, Increased Enforcement Efforts, and Deposit/Refund System for Certain Wastes	9.0–13.9	0–335	Strong incentives from increased cost of waste disposal, information transfer, and enhanced enforcement; 1990 waste generation estimated at 210 MMT.	Encourages waste handling; encourages waste management; hierarchy as above.

Source: Congressional Budget Office, *Hazardous Waste Management: Recent Changes and Policy Alternatives,* May 1985; p. xvii.

Cook, Mary Etta, and Roger H. Davidson, "Deferral Politics: Congressional Decision Making on Environmental Issues in the 1980s," Paper presented at Annual Meeting of American Political Science Association, Washington, DC, 1984.

Florio, James J., "Congress as Reluctant Regulator: Hazardous Waste Policy in the 1980's," *Yale Journal on Regulation* 3 (Spring 1986) 2:351-382.

Jenkins-Smith, Hank, "Analytical Debates and Policy Learning," Paper presented at Annual Meeting of Western Political Science Association, Las Vegas, 1985.

Miller, Stanton, "Whither Environmental Progress?" *Environmental Science and Technology* 18 (January 1984) 1:10A.

Mitchell, Robert Cameron, "Public Opinion and Environmental Politics in the 1970s and 1980s," in Norman J. Vig and Michael E. Kraft, eds., *Environmental Policy in the 1980s: Reagan's New Agenda* (Washington, DC: CQ Press, 1984).

Mosher, L., "Reaganites, with OMB's List in Hand, Take Dead Aim at EPA's Regulations," *National Journal* (February, 14, 1981): 256-259.

National Research Council, *Management of Hazardous Industrial Wastes: Research and Development Needs* (Washington, DC: National Academy Press, 1983).

Riley, Richard, "Toxic Substances, Hazardous Wastes, and Public Policy: Problems in Implementation," in James P. Lester and Ann O'M. Bowman, eds., *The Politics of Hazardous Waste Management* (Durham, NC: Duke University Press, 1983).

Sabatier, Paul A., "An Advocacy Coalition Framework of Policy Change within Subsystems: The Effects of Exogenous Events, Strategic Interaction, and Policy-Oriented Learning over Time," Paper presented at Annual Meeting of the Western Political Science Association, Las Vegas, 1985.

Stanfield, Rochelle L., "Superfund Backers Push Big Expansion of Program to Clean Up Toxic Wastes," *National Journal* (September 22, 1984): 1764.

U.S. Congress, Office of Technology Assessment, *Technologies and Management Strategies for Hazardous Waste Control* (Washington, DC: Government Printing Office, 1983).

_____, *Serious Reduction of Hazardous Waste* (Washington, DC: Government Printing Office, 1986).

U.S. House of Representatives, Subcommittee on Commerce, Transportation, and Tourism, Resource Conservastion and Recovery Act Reauthorization, Hearings, March 31 and April 21, 1982a.

_____, Subcommittee on Natural Resources, Agriculture Research and Environment, EPAs Regulations for Land Disposal of Hazardous Wastes, Hearings, November 30, December 8 and 16, 1982b.

10

Judicial Enforcement of Hazardous Waste Liability Law

Werner F. Grunbaum

The courts have played a major role in formalizing environmental policy within our political process. Beginning with the *Scenic Hudson*[1] case in 1971, the courts allowed environmental groups access to the judicial process (Grunbaum, 1976). Early suits pursuant to the National Environmental Policy Act (NEPA) of 1969 focused primarily on environmental impact statements required before government projects could be constructed.

Today, some 2,000 environmental cases later, the courts have begun to deal primarily with substantive issues while earlier cases had dealt more with procedural problems. Although the courts have turned to substantive environmental concerns, they continue to formulate broad judicial policies (Hill, 1967). This chapter examines the courts' interpretation of the Comprehensive Environmental Response, Compensation, and Liability Act's hazardous waste liability provisions as an example of judicial policymaking directed toward a substantive environmental problem.

HAZARDOUS WASTE ENFORCEMENT PROBLEMS

Improper disposal of hazardous wastes has resulted in one of the nation's most serious problems (Lester, 1983). Waste sites have been blamed for contaminating drinking water for thousands, have resulted in fires and explosions, and have been linked to the increased incidence for surrounding populations of birth defects, leukemia, and other forms of cancer. According to Richard K. Willard, chief of the Justice Department's civil enforcement division, toxic waste claims against the federal government may exceed $200 billion for the next ten years.

Originally, the federal government's power was limited to enforcing statutes only against businesses that directly discharged pollutants into the air and water. However, as 30,000 to 50,000 improperly managed waste sites were identified, it became clear that existing environmental statutes were insufficient to solve the nation's hazardous waste problems.

The Federal Water Pollution Control Act[2] (FWPCA) proved ineffective against improperly managed waste sites because it imposes liability only on present discharges. Thus, it is effective in stopping illegal dumping that poses an immediate threat to the environment, but it cannot be used to clean up hazardous waste sites already in existence. FWPCA, under Section 311, prohibits only actual or potential hazardous wastes from being discharged into navigable waters.

The Resource Conservation and Recovery Act[3] (RCRA) passed by Congress in 1976 was specifically directed at unregulated land disposal of discarded material and hazardous waste. RCRA authorized the EPA to set standards for dealing with hazardous waste. The EPA then set standards for waste permits, transport permits, container regulations, and treatment, storage, and disposal facilities. While RCRA was effective in upgrading some waste sites, it did not provide a practical solution for the cleanup of thousands of potentially dangerous dormant waste sites.

Even RCRA's limited purpose of upgrading operating waste sites was flawed because in practice, RCRA encourages waste generators to contract for off-site waste disposal with independent contractors and thereby avoid RCRA regulations applicable to on-site disposal. As a result, some waste generators were able to shift liability to waste haulers and waste disposal site operators in spite of the fact that RCRA applied strict liability standards for transporters, generators, and operators. In the end, many transporters and disposal site operators either disappeared or did not have sufficient financial resources to pay for damages for which they were responsible.

RCRA's framers did not place primary liability on waste generators because they felt that enforcement could be achieved through EPA regulations and extensive record keeping. In addition, RCRA did not impose retroactive liability for damages caused by improper waste disposal that took place prior to the time of its enactment by Congress.

Although the EPA pursued litigation against waste generators under RCRA, the courts interpreted RCRA's enforcement provisions quite narrowly. Under Section 7003, RCRA limits enforcement to waste sites posing an "imminent hazard." Therefore, the courts held that "RCRA does not apply to the thousands of dormant sites that are not currently posing an imminent hazard."[4]

In 1980 Congress passed the Comprehensive Environmental Response, Compensation, and Liability Act[5] (CERCLA—also known as the Super-fund Act) to overcome RCRA's serious gaps. First, Congress intended to provide a comprehensive solution for the thousands of dormant waste sites identified in the United States. Second, Congress was concerned about the difficulty in locating financially responsible operators of waste disposal sites.

CERCLA established a $1.6 billion Superfund that the EPA could use to clean up dormant hazardous waste sites. These funds would be generated by a tax placed on the chemical industry (Note, 1983). In addition, CERCLA authorizes the government to sue generators and transporters of hazardous waste to recover cleanup costs. While the act left little doubt concerning its intent, Congress unfortunately did not state specifically who is liable under the act (Brenner, 1981).

JOINT AND SEVERAL LIABILITY UNDER CERCLA

Waste site liability problems may involve dozens and even hundreds of potentially liable parties. The issue of joint and several liability becomes a central one because of the characteristics of typical waste sites. Due to commingling and chemical reactions of wastes that are stored at disposal sites, it becomes difficult, if not impossible in some cases, to prove which generator is responsible for environmental damage. The doctrine of joint and several liability allows the government to recover its cleanup costs, including costs for unknown or financially insolvent waste generators. Without joint and several liability, the government could prove liability only in limited situations and could under such circumstances recover few, if any, of its cleanup costs.

Initially, two different CERCLA bills proceeded simultaneously through the House and Senate. The original versions contained the terms *strict liability* and *joint and several liability* (Eckardt, 1981). Unfortunately, the Senate deleted both the strict liability and the joint and several liability provisions from CERCLA on November 24, 1980, in the last days of the Ninety-sixth Congress.[6] The Senate compromise was fashioned as a response to Senator Jesse Helms, who had threatened to filibuster against the bill. Since the threatened filibuster occurred close to the end of the session and since Senators Robert Stafford and Jennings Randolph, the bill's floor leaders, felt that federal common law would effectively fill the void left by the deletions, the compromise was accepted and passed by the Senate. On December 3, 1980, the House accommodated its version of CERCLA to correspond with the Senate version.[7] The final bill was enacted in that form.

CERCLA addresses the tremendous potential cost[8] of cleaning the many dormant hazardous waste sites in the nation by authorizing the government to recoup as much of the costs as possible that are incurred in cleaning up hazardous waste sites. However, numerous defendants often were involved at a single waste site. CERCLA's statutory language offers no guidance to

Table 10.1
Table of Cases: Hazardous Waste Disposal Generator Liability

United States v. Outboard Marine
  No. 78-C-1004 (N.D. Ill. Oct. 8, 1982)
  12 ELR 21153   556 F.Supp. 54   18 ERC 1087

United States v. Reilly Tar & Chemical Corp.
  No. 4-80-469 (D. Minn. Aug. 20, 1982)
  12 ELR 20954   546 F.Supp. 1100   17 ERC 2110

United States v. Reilly Tar & Chemical Corp.
  No. 4-80-469 (D. Minn. June 23, 1983)
  13 ELR 20897   20 ERC 1052

United States v. Reilly Tar & Chemical Corp.
  No. 3-85-473 & No. 4-80-469 (D. Minn. Apr. 5, 1985)
  15 ELR 20348   606 F.Supp. 412   22 ERC 1753

Velsicol v. Reilly Tar & Chemical Corp.
  No. CV-1-81-389 (E.D. Tenn. Aug. 16, 1984)
  15 ELR 20103   21 ERC 2118

United States v. Price [Price I]
  No. 80-4104 (D. N.J. Sept. 23, 1981)
  11 ELR 21047   523 F.Supp. 1055   17 ERC 1994

United States v. Price [Price II]
  No. 82-5030 (3d Cir. Sept. 14, 1982)
  12 ELR 21020   688 F.2d 204   17 ERC 2155

United States v. Price [Price III]
  No. 80-4104 (D. N.J. July 28, 1983)
  13 ELR 20843   523 F.Supp. 1055   19 ERC 1638

United States v. Chem-Dyne Corp.
  No. C-1-82-840 (S.D. Ohio Oct. 11, 1983)
  13 ELR 20986   572 F.Supp. 802   19 ERC 1953

United States v. Wade [Wade I]
  No. 79-1426 (E.D. Pa. Sept. 7, 1982)
  12 ELR 21051   564 F.Supp. 785   17 ERC 2138

United States v. Wade [Wade II]
  No. 82-1715 (3d Cir. Pa. Aug. 5, 1983)
  13 ELR 20815   713 F.2d 49   19 ERC 1561

United States v. Wade [Wade III]
  No. 79-1426 (E.D. Pa. Dec. 20, 1983)
  14 ELR 20096   577 F.Supp. 1326   20 ERC 1277

United States v. Wade [Wade IV]
  No. 79-1426 (E.D. Pa. Feb. 2, 1984)
  14 ELR 20435   30 ERC 1657

United States v. Wade [Wade V]
  No. 79-1426 (E.D. Pa. Mar. 8, 1984)
  14 ELR 20436   21 ERC 1346

United States v. Wade [Wade VI]
  No. 79-1426 (E.D. Pa. Mar. 23, 1984)
  14 ELR 20437   20 ERC 1849

United States v. Wade [Wade VII]
  No. 79-1426 (E.D. Pa. Apr. 27, 1984)
  14 ELR 20439   21 ERC 1348

Table 10.1 *(continued)*

United States v. Wade [Wade VIII]		
No. 79-1426 (E.D. Pa. Apr. 27, 1984)		
14 ELR 20440		21 ERC 1352
United States v. Wade [Wade IX]		
No. 79-1426 (E.D. Pa. Apr. 27, 1984)		
14 ELR 20441		21 ERC 1352
United States v. A & F Materials Co. [A&F I]		
No. 83-3123 (S.D. Ill. Jan. 20, 1984)		
14 ELR 20105	578 F.Supp 1249	20 ERC 1353
United States v. A & F Materials Co. [A&F II]		
No. 83-3123 (S.D. Ill. Mar. 30, 1984)		
14 ELR 20432		20 ERC 1957
U.S. v. Northeastern Pharmaceutical & Chem. Co. [NEPACCO I]		
No. 80-5066-CV-S-4 (W.D. Mo. Sept. 30, 1983)		
13 ELR 20992		19 ERC 2187
U.S. v. Northeastern Pharmaceutical & Chem. Co. [NEPACCO II]		
No. 80-5066-CV-S-4 (W.D. Mo. Jan. 31, 1984)		
14 ELR 20212	579 F.Supp. 823	20 ERC 1401
United States v. Conservation Chemical Co.		
No. 80-0885-CV-W-J (W.D. Mo. Aug. 19, 1981)		
12 ELR 20238	523 F.Supp. 125	16 ERC 1630
United States v. Conservation Chemical Co.		
No. 82-0983-CV-W-5 (W.D. Mo. Feb. 3, 1984)		
14 ELR 20207		20 ERC 1427
United States v. South Carolina Recycling and Disposal, Inc.		
No. 80-1274-6 (D. S.C. Feb. 23, 1984)		
14 ELR 20272		20 ERC 1753
United States v. Stringfellow [Stringfellow I]		
No. CV-83-2501-MML (C.D. Cal. Feb. 17, 1984)		
14 ELR 20381		20 ERC 1659
United States v. Stringfellow [Stringfellow II]		
No. CV-83-2501-MML (C.D. Cal. Apr. 5, 1984)		
14 ELR 20385		20 ERC 1905
United States v. Stringfellow [Stringfellow III]		
No. CV-83-2501-MML (C.D. Cal. Apr. 9, 1984)		
14 ELR 20388		20 ERC 1912
United States v. Stringfellow [Concerned Neighbors in Action and Penny Newman, Intervenors-Appellants]		
No. 84-5682 (9th Cir. Feb. 18, 1986)		
16 ELR 20458		23 ERC ____
J.V. Peters & Co. v. Ruckelshaus		
No. C 83-4436 (N.D. Ohio, Feb. 17, 1984)		
14 ELR 20277	584 F.Supp. 1005	20 ERC 2222
J.V. Peters & Co. v. Ruckelshaus		
No. 84-3229 (6th Cir. July 3, 1985)		
14 ELR 20646	767 F.2d 263	22 ERC 2073
United States v. Westinghouse Electric Corp.		
No. IP 83-9-C (S.D. Ind. June 29, 1983)		
14 ELR 20483		22 ERC 1230
United States v. Johnson & Towers, Inc.		
No. Crim. 83-83 (D. N.J. Sept. 6, 1983)		
14 ELR 20883		20 ERC 2073

Table 10.1 *(continued)*

Jones v. Inmont Corp.		
No. C-1-83-1202 (S.D. Ohio, Apr. 26, 1984)		
14 ELR 20485		20 ERC 2251
Colorado v. ASARCO, Inc.		
No. 83-C-2388 (D.C. Colo. May 13, 1985)		
15 ELR 20253	608 F.Supp. 1484	22 ERC 1926
Colorado v. ASARCO, Inc.		
No. 83-C-2383 (D.C. Colo. Aug. 29, 1985)		
16 ELR 20046	616 F.Supp. 822	23 ERC _____
United States v. Ward		
No. 83-63-CIV-5 (E.D. N.C. May 14, 1984)		
14 ELR 20804		22 ERC 1235
United States v. Ward		
No. 83-63-CIV-5 (E.D. N.C. Sept. 9, 1985)		
16 ELR 20127	618 F.Supp. 884	23 ERC _____
Fishel v. Westinghouse Electric Corp.		
No. 85-0216 (M.D. Pa. Oct. 1, 1985)		
16 ELR 20001		23 ERC _____

the courts how to apportion liability among large groups of cited defendants at single waste sites. CERCLA contains no guidelines (1) how to solve the liability problem inherent in commingling toxic wastes, (2) whether liability should be apportioned on the basis of volume or toxicity, or (3) how the liability should be apportioned between site owners, operators, transporters, and waste generators. In order to fill this void, the courts have formulated broad policy to implement a torts approach that allows the government to collect cleanup costs effectively from large groups of diverse defendants associated with a single hazardous waste site.

Since CERCLA did little more than to specify who was liable[9] under the act, the courts examined CERCLA's legislative history to determine congressional intent for liability guidelines. Moreover, the statute was hastily and inadequately drafted because the final bill was a compromise drafted by an ad hoc committee of senators. However, the courts held that the congressional intent to solve the hazardous waste problem was beyond dispute.

Senator Helms, who voted against the CERCLA compromise bill, did his best during floor debate to discredit CERCLA's liability provisions. Senator Helms argued that CERCLA would impose financial responsibility for massive costs on defendants who had contributed only minimally to a release or injury. He felt that an industry-based fund coupled with joint and several liability constituted a type of double indemnity. He concluded that the compromise was quite clear in eliminating joint and several liability for generators.

Chief Judge Alvin Rubin in the *Chem-Dyne*[10] decision (for background of settlement in this case, see Bernstein, 1983) held that under Supreme Court guidelines used for statutory construction, very little weight is accorded to opponents of bills when courts ascertain statutory intent. Therefore, Judge Rubin held that the courts should give little attention to Senator Helms's interpretation that Congress did not intend for courts to apply joint and several liability. Judge James Foreman, in the *United States v. A & F Materials Co., II* case, added that Senator Helms's CERCLA interpretation was not shared by any other legislator in the debates.

Senator Randolph, one of the bill's sponsors, explained that CERCLA's reference to Section 311 of the Clean Water Act specified the application of strict liability standards and principles of federal common law. He added that the changes made by the ad hoc committee reflected the difficulty of equitably applying statutory standards under different circumstances and in no way reflected a rejection of the joint and several liability standards in the earlier version of the act.

Representative James Florio, sponsor of the bill, explained that despite the deletion of the terms *strict* and *joint and several liability* in the compromise version, the strict liability standard approved earlier by the House was still preserved in the compromise bill. He further explained that the liability of joint tortfeasors will be determined by transitional and evolving principles of common law. He stressed that a uniform federal rule of law was necessary to prevent waste operators from locating in those states with the most lenient laws.

Judge Rubin held that in the CERCLA bill Congress was clear in specifying joint and several liability. He relied on established federal rules used by judges to determine statutory interpretation. These guidelines give substantial weight to the statements of sponsors of legislation, although the remarks of single legislators are given little weight.

The imposition of joint and several liability in effect puts the burden of proof on the defendants. Without the joint and several liability doctrine it would be difficult if not impossible for the government to prove which waste generator was responsible for a given leakage due to commingling of wastes and due to chemical reactions that take place between wastes supplied by different generators. Thus, joint and several liability allows the government to recover its entire costs, including costs actually caused by unknown or insolvent generators.

FEDERAL COMMON LAW

The landmark *Erie*[11] doctrine, proclaimed by the Supreme Court in 1938, took away from the federal courts the power to create federal common law (Hart, 1954). However, Judge Rubin in *Chem-Dyne* ruled that Congress's intent for the courts to formulate a uniform federal common law under CERCLA constituted an exception to the *Erie* doctrine. He cited Supreme

Court precedent upholding exceptions to the *Erie* doctrine that allow federal common law of a specialized rather than general nature when it is "necessary to protect uniquely federal interests." Judge Rubin stressed that the United States had a significant monetary interest in the $1.6 billion Superfund collected from industry taxes and from general revenues and that such an interest could be protected only through implementation of a uniform federal policy.

Judge Foreman, in *A & F Materials Co. I*, summarized four compelling reasons for the development of a uniform common law under CERCLA: (1) Congress linked RCRA and CERCLA to protect the entire nation in the abatement of toxic waste hazards. (2) CERCLA provided for federal enforcement of hazardous waste standards, and it is only appropriate to carry such standards out by applying federal common law. (3) A federal common law would prevent disposal operators from seeking out those states with more lenient waste laws. (4) The United States must be able to protect its fiscal interests in carrying out cleanup with federal funds.

The courts held that no compelling state interest exists in the hazardous waste area that must be protected by the federal government. The joint and several doctrine is necessary to protect federal interests in this area. Such a common law approach is supported by CERCLA's reference to FWPCA enforcement provisions, by the *Restatement (Second) of Torts,*[12] or by both.

The common law holds that when two or more persons acting independently cause a distinct or single harm for which there is a reasonable division of harm according to the contribution of each, each person is liable only for the share of the total harm that he himself has caused.[13] However, when two or more persons cause a single and indivisible harm, each person is liable for the entire harm. When persons who are subject to liability under CERCLA and who have violated the statute seek to limit their liability on the ground that the entire harm is capable of apportionment, the burden of proof as to apportionment is upon each defendant.

Relying on statements made by CERCLA's sponsors in Congress, Judge Rubin held that the deletion of a statutory mandate governing joint and several liability was indeed fortuitous in furthering equitable settlements under torts law:

A reading of the entire legislative history in context reveals that the scope of liability and term joint and several liability were deleted to avoid a mandatory legislative standard applicable in all situations which might produce inequitable results in some cases.[14]

Judge Rubin held that the deletions were made to give judges greater latitude in determining the scope of liability for generator defendants. Thus, courts can perform a case-by-case evaluation of complex factual situations involved in multiple-generator sites to assess the propriety of applying joint and several liability (Reed, 1984).

Generator defendants have unsuccessfully argued that Congress could not have intended to impose such a heavy burden of liability without a clear and precise statutory expression of intent. They have pursued their arguments in extensive litigation in various parts of the country. However, their arguments have been rejected by seven district courts to date.[15] The government has won all seven cases on joint and several liability applied under uniform federal common law principles.

SCOPE AND NATURE OF CERCLA LIABILITY

Liability for Waste Generators

In their effort to enforce CERCLA, federal judges have exercised broad policymaking powers. First, they have interpreted CERCLA as a strict liability statute in accordance with Section 311 of FWPCA. Secondly, the courts have held that CERCLA creates a joint and several liability for responsible parties.

Although joint and several liability was deleted from the CERCLA comprise, the courts have implemented a federal uniform common law under FWPCA, the *Restatement (Second) of Torts*, or both. The CERCLA common law application was held to be an exception to the *ERIE* doctrine. The joint and several liability doctrine applied according to federal common law is significant. Without such an interpretation, it would be difficult if not impossible for the government to prove generator liability and recover vast sums required for waste site cleanup.

Landowner Liability

Section 107(a) includes four categories of persons with potential liability under CERCLA: (1) operators of waste facilities, (2) past operators, (3) hazardous waste generators, and (4) waste transporters. As mentioned above, the first group of CERCLA cases focused on the liability of waste generators. Recently, litigation has shifted to landowners.

The definition of *person* includes owners as well as operators of waste facilities, all types of business units, and state and local governmental units. Because of the huge potential liability, owners have tried to dispose of their property (Reed, 1985). However, owners cannot dispose of their liability by selling dump sites. In fact, their liability may carry over to new owners. The courts have not relaxed liability provisions, not even for governmental units.

WHO CLEANS UP?

The EPA has the authority under CERCLA to clean up hazardous waste disposal sites itself or to require those responsible to do so in accordance with an EPA-approved plan. Section 106 of CERCLA gives the federal government the authority to force those parties responsible for "imminent" hazards to public health or to the environment to clean up or remedy environmental contamination. Section 104 empowers the EPA itself to remedy or contract to remove environmental pollution.

Under CERCLA, the EPA has implemented a National Contingency Plan (NCP). According to NCP guidelines, the EPA must first attempt to negotiate a satisfactory cleanup plan with responsible parties before it conducts its own cleanup. However, such negotiations are often unsuccessful. In one case the EPA took control over an industry-directed cleanup before the industry could complete the job. If the EPA does a poor job of cleaning a site or if unanticipated problems arise, responsible parties still have a continuing liability for such problems. As a result, even responsible parties who have sufficient financial resources have had numerous disputes with the EPA over cleanup costs and cleanup methods. If the EPA does the job, these parties have no control over cleanup costs and are still liable for both past and future environmental hazards.

Whenever the EPA cleans a waste disposal site itself, it may sue to recover its costs because Section 107 makes "responsible parties" liable for cleanup costs. In practice, the courts have held that the combination of Sections 104 and 107 gives the EPA authority to clean up a dump site and to recover the costs from the responsible parties. (If the responsible parties cannot be identified, cannot be found, or have no financial resources, the EPA can pay for cleanups from the "Superfund.")

Since there is widespread scientific disagreement over antipollution methods, there are no generally accepted solutions for cleanups (Reed, 1985). As a result, responsible parties have tried to litigate to get greater control over cleanup procedures.

Every court that has dealt with the issue of EPA preenforcement efforts under Section 104 has refused to exercise judicial review over the remedies selected by the EPA for its response actions. In *J. V. Peters & Co. v. Administrator*,[16] the Sixth Circuit held that EPA's cleanup decisions cannot be reviewed by the courts *until* the EPA brings a Section 107 action to recover its costs from responsible parties. The court held that the Administrative Procedures Act did not apply because CERCLA did not explicitly provide for that type of agency review. Also, since CERCLA did not expressly authorize judicial review of preenforcement action by the EPA, the court felt that to impute such meaning to CERCLA would frustrate CERCLA's legislative purpose, which is to clean up imminent hazards speedily. The court finally argued that due process was not violated because responsible parties could still challenge EPA cleanup costs at such time as the EPA sued to recover its costs.

While the litigants in early CERCLA cases tried to avoid their liability altogether, the litigants in later cases have attempted to minimize their liability. This shift in defendants' legal strategy resulted from an almost total legal victory by the government in establishing joint and several liability standards.

While recent cleanup cases still favor the government, there are signs that the government may not be as successful as it was in earlier liability litigation. The provisions of CERCLA governing cleanup disputes are ambiguous because the cleanup process is complex and scientific knowledge about removing toxic substances from the environment is limited. In addition, the continuing high volume of litigation, in itself, is a threat to the cleanup program. While amendments to CERCLA appear imminent and will aid in the abatement process, erratic enforcement procedures by the EPA, as well as anticipated federal budget cuts, are likely to hinder the process.

CONCLUSION

Initially, the federal courts established their jurisdiction over environmental disputes. In this phase, the courts allowed environmental groups to use the courts as a forum to pursue their concerns by expanding existing doctrine governing standing to sue. The second phase represented mostly procedural issues, such as disputes involving the issuance of environmental impact statements by government agencies. The third phase involves substantive problems, represented by the present cases that set standards for hazardous waste liability. The hazardous waste cases typify a trend common to all three phases of environmental litigation. The federal courts, especially the lower federal courts, continue to exercise significant policymaking functions in our political process. In fact, the courts have played a greater role in interpreting CERCLA than any previous federal pollution control statute.

NOTES

1. *Scenic Hudson Preservation Conference v. Federal Power Commission*, 453 F. 2d. 463 (2d Cir. 1971).

2. 33 U.S.C. Sections 1251-1376 (1976 & Supp. III 1979).

3. 42 U.S.C. Sections 6901-6987 (1976 & Supp. III 1979), as amended by Solid Waste Disposal Act Ams. of 1980, 94 Stat. 2334.

4. *U.S. v. A & F Materials Co.* (*A & F Materials* I), No. 83-3123 (S.D. Ill. Jan. 20, 1984), 14 ELR 20105, 20106; 579 F.Supp. 1249; 20 ERC 1353; and *U.S. v. Price* (*Price* III), No. 80-4104 (D. N.J. Jul. 28, 1983), 13 ELR 20843; 523 F.Supp. 1055; 19 ERC 1638.

5. 42 U.S.C. Sections 6901-6987.

6. 126 *Cong. Record*, Pt. 23, 30956-30987, 96th Cong., 2d Sess. (Senate, Nov. 24, 1980).

7. 126 *Cong. Record*, Pt. 24, 31967-31980, 96th Cong., 2d Sess. (House, Dec. 3, 1980).

8. CERCLA (the Superfund bill) is charged with collecting and spending $1.6 billion over its five-year authorization period. Most of Superfund's revenue (87.5%) comes from a tax on heavy metals, toxic chemicals, and petrochemical feedstocks. More than 750,000 businesses generate some hazardous wastes. The EPA estimates (1979) that 30,000 to 50,000 sites contain hazardous waste and that 90% of hazardous waste management does not meet new EPA standards. The cleanup of the 1,200 to 2,000 most significant problem sites would cost between $26 billion and $44 billion, according to Thomas C. Jorling, Assistant Administrator, Water and Waste Management, EPA (1979). See n. 2-8 "Liability for Generators of Hazardous Waste: The Failure of Existing Enforcement Mechanisms," *Georgetown L. J.,* 69: 1047.

9. CERCLA, Section 9607(a) provides:

Notwithstanding any other provision or rule of law, and subject only to the defenses set forth in subsection (b) of this section—

(1) the owner and operator of a vessel (otherwise subject to the jurisdiction of the United States) or a facility,

(2) any person who at the time of disposal of any hazardous substance owned or operated any facility at which such hazardous substances were disposed of,

(3) any person who by contract, agreement, or other wise arranged for disposal or treatment, or arranged with a transporter for transport for disposal or treatment, of hazardous substances owned or possessed by such person, by any other party or entity, at any facility owned or operated by another party or entity and containing such hazardous substances, and

(4) any person who accepts or accepted any hazardous substances for transport to disposal or treatment facilities or sites selected by such person, from which there is a release, or a threatened release which causes the incurrence of response costs, of a hazardous substance, shall be liable for—

(A) all costs of removal or remedial action incurred by the United States Government or a State not inconsistent with the national contingency plan;

(B) any other necessary costs of response incurred by any other person consistent with the national contingency plan; and

(C) damages for injury to, destruction of, or loss of natural resources, including the reasonable costs of assessing such injury, destruction, or loss resulting from such a release. (42 USC Section 9607 [a].)

10. *U.S. v. Chem-Dyne Corp.,* No. C-1-82-840 (S.D. Ohio Oct. 11, 1983), 572 F.Supp. 802, at 806; 13 ELR 20986; 19 ERC 1638.

11. *Erie R.R. v. Tompkins* 304 U.S. 64 (1938).

12. *Restatement (Second) of Torts,* Sections 443A, 881 [1976].

13. Ibid.

14. Supra, n. 8, 572 F.Supp. 802, at 808.

15. *Chem-Dyne,* n. 8; *A & F Materials Co.* I & II, n. 4; *U.S. v. Wade,* No. 79-1426 (E.D. Pa. 1982-1984), *Wade* I–*Wade* IX, 12 ELR 21051, 13 ELR 20815, 14 ELR 20096, 14 ELR 20435, 20436, 20437, 20439, 20440, 20441; *U.S. v. NE Pharmaceutical & Chem Co.* No. 80-5066-CV-S-4 (W.D. Mo. Sept. 30, 1983 & Jan. 31, 1984), 13 ELR 20992, 14 ELR 20212; *U.S. v. Conservation Chem. Co.* No. 80-0885-CV-W-J (W.D. Mo. Sept. 30, 1983 & Feb. 3, 1984), 12 ELR 20238, 14 ELR 20207; *U.S. v. South Carolina Recycling and Disposal, Inc.* No. 80-1274-6 (D. S.C. Feb. 23, 1984), 14 ELR 20272; *U.S. v. Stringfellow* (*Stringfellow* I, II, III), No. CV-83-2501-MML (C.D. Cal. Apr. 1984), 14 ELR 20381, 20385, 20388.

16. *J. V. Peters & Co. v. Ruckelshaus,* No. 84-3229 (6th Cir. July 3, 1985), 767 F.2d 263, 14 ELR 20646, 22 ERC 1230.

REFERENCES

Bernstein, Norman W. "The *Enviro-Chem* Settlement: Superfund Problem Solving," *Environmental Law Reporter* 13 (1983): 10402-10405. [Mr. Bernstein was co-chairman of the seventeen-member industry steering committee that allocated generator liability among themselves.]

Brenner, Joseph K., "Liability for Generators of Hazardous Waste: The Failure of Existing Enforcement Mechanisms," *Georgetown Law Journal* 69 (1981): 1047-1081.

Eckardt, Robert C., "The Unfinished Business of Hazardous Waste Control," *Baylor Law Review* 33 (1981): 253-265. [Rep. Eckardt (member 1964-1980) participated in the CERCLA debates.]

Grunbaum, Werner F., *Judicial Policymaking: The Supreme Court and Environmental Quality* (Morristown, NJ: General Learning Press, 1976).

Hart, Henry M., "The Relations between State and Federal Law," *Columbia Law Review* 54 (1954): 489-542.

Hill, Alfred, "The Law-Making Power of the Federal Courts: Constitutional Pre-emption," *Columbia Law Review* 67 (1967): 1024-1081.

Lester, James P., "The Process of Hazardous Waste Regulation: Severity, Complexity, and Uncertainty," in James P. Lester and Ann O'M. Bowman, eds., *The Politics of Hazardous Waste Management* (Durham, NC: Duke University Press, 1983), 3-22.

Note. "Generator Liability under Superfund for Clean-up of Abandoned Hazardous Waste Dumpsites," *University of Pennsylvania Law Review* 130 (1983): 1229-1280.

Reed, Phillip D. "Comment. CERCLA Litigation Update: The Emerging Law of Generator Liability," *Environmental Law Reporter* 14 (1984): 10224-10236.

_____, "CERCLA 1985: A Litigation Update," *Environmental Law Reporter* 15 (1985): 10395-10406.

11

Federal-State Hazardous Waste Management Policy Implementation in the Context of Risk Uncertainties

Rae Zimmerman

INTRODUCTION

Hazardous waste policies are often formulated and implemented in the context of scientific and political uncertainty.[1] It is argued here that if these uncertainties are not explicitly confronted at the outset of policy implementation, they can drive the implementation process in unexpected and unintended directions. That is, decisions become ineffective or are controversial to the point of delaying action indefinitely.[2]

This contention is examined in light of some hazardous waste contamination cases where the removal of hazardous wastes from waterways by dredging was considered. These cases are listed and briefly described in Table 11.1. In order to relate decision outcomes to uncertainty, the following approach is taken:[3]

1. Decision outcomes and the environmental conditions (location, environmental setting, etc.) under which cases occurred are identified.

2. Variability in the outcomes is demonstrated within the group of cases.

3. It is further shown that cases occurred under generally similar conditions in spite of the differences in outcomes.

4. The existence of scientific and political uncertainty is established across several steps in decision making.

5. Finally, when differences in environmental conditions are eliminated as explanations for differences and inconsistencies in outcomes, a major factor explaining the differences that remains is the existence of a large number of scientific and political uncertainties that arose during policy implementation and the absence of strategies tailored to confront these new uncertainties.

Table 11.1
Summary of Hazardous Waste Cases Involving Dredging for Waste Removal

Case	Hazard	Source	Population	Outcome of Dredging (By Location)
Foundry Cove, NY	Cadmium	Industrial wastewater	2,000	Dredge, plus on-site entombment of wastes
Berry's Creek, NJ	Mercury	Industrial wastewater	15,000	Decision pending for dredging and on-site entombment of wastes
Ticonderoga Bay, NY	Mercury	Industrial wastewater		No dredging
Hudson River, NY	PCBs	Industrial wastewater	44,000	Decision pending for selected dredging and off-site land disposal
College Point, NY	PCBs	Industrial waste disposal	19,774	Dredging, plus off-site disposal by commercial disposal operation
Love Canal, NY	Miscellaneous Organics	Industrial waste disposal	1,000*	Dredging, plus treatment and off-site disposal
James River, VA	Kepone	Industrial wastewater	25,000	No dredging

*This population estimate includes only homeowners immediately in the vicinity of the landfill, not those that attended the school on it that migrated from the area.

Source: R. Zimmerman, 1982a, "The Management of Risk," Executive Summary, Final report to the National Science Foundation, Table 1.

There are many approaches to decision making under uncertainty. Mathematical and probabilistic approaches to uncertainty have been common for more than two centuries.[4] Economists have approached the problem using expected utility theory.[5] Behavioral psychologists have explored the heuristics and biases that are the foundations of human judgment in the face of uncertainty.[6] Bargaining and negotiation models of choice processes focus upon the institutions and decision-making procedures for dealing with uncertainty.[7] Thus, there is no shortage of theories to explain how decisions can be made under uncertainty. These theories are generally deductive and explore what decision options exist given different kinds and levels of uncertainty. Here a more empirical focus is adopted, which looks at how different decision makers seem to be responding to uncertainty when faced with similar situations.

GENERAL UNCERTAINTIES IN WASTE REMOVAL DECISIONS BY DREDGING

Before discussing the details of the cases, general uncertainties common to all of the decisions are analyzed. The single decision that all of the cases shared was the removal by dredging of contaminants from waterways and adjacent land areas. The decision to dredge contaminants or leave them in place is a common problem nowadays. In the past, contaminants have accumulated in areas now defined in legislation as environmentally sensitive (for example, floodplains, wetlands, recharge areas for water supplies). Such a practice is not considered acceptable by current standards. Two major sources of contamination are past industrial wastewater discharges to natural waterways and waste disposal. Two areas of uncertainty that have contributed to the buildup of wastes from these sources include poor state-of-the-art knowledge for detecting hazardous substances and their health effects and the legal uncertainties surrounding governmental jurisdiction controlling their disposal.

Uncertainties in Detection of Contaminants

Dredging has been used for more than a century as a means of removing sediments from waterways for navigation, flood control, and waterfront and offshore construction. The controversy with respect to dredging arises when contaminants in the dredged material enter natural waterways. The amount of dredged material that remains in the water is an indirect measure of contamination. This is estimated to be 2% to 4% of the material dredged.[8] Toxicity, which is a more important indicator of contamination in dredged material than the amount of suspended material generated, includes heavy metals and complex organic substances. Estimates of toxicity are less precise. The number of parameters that are used to characterize toxicity has been debated, and revisions aimed at expanding the list were proposed in mid-1986.[9] The scientific basis for establishing toxicity limits for dredged material has also been debated. There are scientific uncertainties in some analytical procedures used to evaluate the quality of dredged material for removal and disposal. Many procedures were developed in 1977, and their effectiveness is currently being reevaluated.[10]

Legal Uncertainties

Many dredging decisions are centralized at the federal level under the U.S. Army Corps of Engineers (COE) in the Department of Defense. The COE has two conflicting responsibilities in dredging. First, the COE conducts dredging to maintain federal navigation channels and to meet the needs of other governmental agencies and private parties.[11] Second, the COE regulates dredging under several statutes, each with its own requirements. The COE issues permits for the disposal of dredged material in U.S. waters and wetlands under Section 404 of the Clean Water Act, and formerly under the Rivers and Harbors Act of 1899. It has joint authority with the U.S. EPA to issue permits to transport dredged material for ocean disposal and to certify ocean disposal sites under Section 103 of the Marine

Protection, Research, and Sanctuaries Act of 1972. Finally, the COE issues construction permits in navigable waters under Section 10 of the Rivers and Harbors Act of 1899. Many of these decisions are made in conjunction with the U.S. EPA, other federal agencies (such as the Fish and Wildlife Service), and appropriate state environmental and health departments under whose jurisdiction the activity falls.

In the course of carrying out these two responsibilities, the COE has to deal with many uncertainties in the laws that define its jurisdiction. Past legislation, under which many of the cases discussed below were first identified, presented a large number of uncertainties. While regulations gradually reduced some of these problems, the emergence of new laws affecting the management of dredged material have created new ones. These new laws are the Resource Conservation and Recovery Act (RCRA), as amended by the Hazardous and Solid Waste Amendments (HSWA) of 1984, and the Comprehensive Environmental Responsibility Compensation and Liability Act of 1980 (CERCLA). RCRA/HSWA specifies criteria for designating certain components of dredged material as hazardous waste.[12] CERCLA lists uncontrolled waste sites on the National Priorities List and prescribes ways of determining whether dredging will be required as part of cleanup and removal actions. The specifications for dredging in these laws often differ from one another and from the laws under which the COE operates, namely, the Marine Protection Research and Sanctuaries Act (MPRSA), the Clean Water Act (CWA), and the Rivers and Harbors Act (RHA). Furthermore, CERCLA and RCRA are administered exclusively by the U.S. EPA, not the COE.

SIMILAR CONDITIONS AND DIFFERENT DECISION OUTCOMES AND POLICIES TOWARD DREDGING

Table 11.1 summarizes, for some dredging cases, the origin and extent of hazardous waste accumulation and the outcome or ultimate decision on the disposition of the waste material. While the cases are similar to one another in many respects, their outcomes often differ. These differences in outcomes can be related to the existence and treatment of scientific, technical, and institutional uncertainties rather than to differences in initial circumstances or conditions.

Similar Conditions

The cases occurred under similar conditions, in spite of differences in the chemicals of concern and numbers of people potentially at risk. First, they involved industrial waste discharges from manufacturing that accumulated in sediments or soil near the site of manufacture. Second, the cases occurred in the same legislative context. Waste buildup began prior to the passage of the environmental laws of the early 1970s and continued for over a decade thereafter. The cases were almost exclusively brought under early versions of the Clean Water Act and the Rivers and Harbors Act, though in the late 1970s new laws, such as RCRA and CERCLA, began to prevail. Third, while cases differed in the amounts and types of contaminants generated (see Table 11.1), they shared a human hazard potential regarded as significant under prevailing laws[13] and a significantly large population estimated to be at risk. Finally, the cases all occurred in older urban areas along the eastern seaboard, many in the New York area alone, and affected the quality of major natural water bodies or adjacent environmentally sensitive lands.[14]

Different Outcomes

Table 11.1 shows that while the cases occurred under similar conditions, their outcomes differed in significant ways: (1) the decision to dredge or not—two decisions were clearly made against dredging (James River, Ticonderoga Bay), three advocated and ultimately implemented dredging (Love Canal, College Point, Foundry Cove), and two decisions were delayed or suspended pending further study (Hudson River, Berry's Creek);[15] (2) the decision regarding the place of disposal, that is, on the site of the manufacturing activity or off-site—four involved (or were planning) disposal on-site (Foundry Cove, Berry's Creek, Ticonderoga Bay, James River), and three involved (or were planning) off-site disposal (Love Canal, College Point, Hudson River).[16] As discussed above, these differences in decision outcomes, especially with regard to the decision to dredge or not, occur in spite of similarities in sources of contaminants, legal context, the potential for a human health hazard, and geographic location. It can be shown that in part these different outcomes reflect uncertainties in the legal and scientific settings in which the decisions were made and uneven responses to these uncertainties, rather than being a result of a deliberate choice process on the part of government or the private sector.

CLASSIFICATION SYSTEM FOR UNCERTAINTY

Uncertainty occurs in decision making in many places and in many forms. A classification system for types of uncertainty is therefore useful as a basis for understanding how and where uncertainties emerged in each of the cases. Table 11.2 categorizes uncertainty in each case according to steps commonly used to characterize decision making. These steps are problem identification, the basis for control in standards and other criteria, the method of control or management strategies, and finally, the technological means to reduce risks. The manner in which uncertainties can arise during each of these steps is described briefly in the list following Table 11.2.

Table 11.2.
Nature of Uncertainty in Hazardous Waste Management Decision Making

	Identification of the Problem	Basis for Control: Environment and Health Standards
Foundry Cove, NY	• Extent of problem: Uncertainty about depth of cadmium contamination; federal and industry measurement methods and sampling results differ for Cd concentration in sediments; exposure and food chain data highly uncertain	Standards used to identify and characterize the problem (1971): • Significance of cadmium levels in exposed fish vs. normal levels in fish (e.g., 1,000 times natural levels found) • Comparison of levels in exposed organisms with lab data levels shown to cause harm — uncertain analogies between test species, data and environmental conditions Standards used to control the problem: • International standards (Japanese level of 1.0 ppm) — supporting information is circumstantial only • Effluent standard: 1.1 lbs/week (1971), 0.44 lbs/day (1973), 0.12 lbs/day (1976) — uncertain relationship between discharge limits and hazard • Ambient standard: 0.32 ppm for estuaries (EPA), 0.3 ppm (NYS) (1974) — uncertain relationship to exposure and hazard levels • Dredging threshold: 900 or 1,000 ppm in sediments
Berry's Creek, NJ	• Extent of problem: Uncertainty about depth and extent of mercury and accumulation in biota, and extent of spread to the Hackensack Meadowlands	• Effluent standards and limits: Not clearly linked to exposure and hazard • Ambient standards: Not initially specified directly in standards (i.e, under the general category of toxins)
Ticonderoga Bay, NY	• Extent of problem: Uncertainty about spread of mercury in the Bay and into aquatic organisms	See Berry's Creek above
Hudson River, NY	• Source: Whether PCB or PCB associated contaminants, Dioxin or Dibenzofurans, were the cause of potential hazards • Extent of problem: Uncertainty about PCB contamination in fish and uptake by plants; migration downstream, volatilization and dispersal via air	Standards used to control the problem: • Exposure standards: FDA uncertainty regarding 5 ppm vs. 2 ppm limit for fish • Effluent standards not well linked to exposure and effects; ultimately they go to zero when PCB manufacture was banned • Ambient standards non-existent in water quality

Table 11.2 (continued)

	Identification of the Problem	Basis for Control: Environment and Health Standards
Hudson River, NY		standards until 1980 criteria issued at 10 µg/l • 50 ppm as dredging guideline has uncertain scientific backing • OSHA 1 µg/m³ in air had an uncertain relationship to environmental standards
College Point, NY	• Nature of problem: Initially identified as a waste oil problem, the discovery of PCBs emerged several years later when attention was drawn to PCBs statewide and nationwide	Standards used to control the problem not well justified: • Limits placed on concentration of PCB in oil (10 ppm) and in wastewater allowed into NYC sewage treatment plants (30 ppm) • Federal threshold of 50 ppm for dredging not well justified
Love Canal, NY	• Nature of problem: The initial cause of the chemical contamination was not known at first: the types of contaminants were not known until a gas chromatographic technique was developed by the Health Department of certain chemicals in 1978 • Nature of problem: Extent and implications of exposure were highly uncertain, along with data and methodologies to establish exposure effects	A lack of standards for organics, other than for drinking water, made problem identification and control prevail in a highly uncertain environment; subsequently, such standards were passed
James River, VA	• Extent of problem: Uncertainty as to the extent of contamination from unchecked waste discharges	Standards to identify problem: • Uncertainty in lab animal test data for kepone • Uncertainty in action levels for aquatic organisms: 0.1 ppm (finfish) and 0.4 ppm (crabs) proposed (1977) after problem well underway Standards used to control the problem: • Effluent limits: 3 ppm (1973) reduced to 0.5 ppb (1975) • OSHA worker exposure limits

1. *Identification of the Problem:* The origin, location, and extent of an environmental problem can be uncertain because of unidentified errors in measurement technology. *Measurement uncertainty* refers to the limits of detectability of substances with existing instrumentation and the reliability of and consensus on the measures used.

2. *Basis for Control—Standards:* Standards are a major framework for the control of hazardous substances. A standard is broadly construed here as any numerically defined or generally described limit placed upon or prescribed for an activity. Uncertainties arise in the availability and existence of clear, consistent standards based on reliable information and methodologies and the degree of consensus surrounding the standards.

3. *Method of Control—Management Strategies:* Uncertainties surround the existence, reliability, clarity, and consistency of regulatory requirements or nonregulatory incentives and programs to control a problem. Uncertainties also occur in the availability and applicability of financial and human resources for the implementation of mitigation measures (such as engineering controls).

4. *Mitigation or Abatement Measures—Technology:* The existence, availability, performance or effectiveness, reliability, and political acceptability of technologies to reduce or eliminate the problem are often unknown, imprecise, or undemonstrated.

APPLICATION OF TYPES OF UNCERTAINTY TO THE CASES

Two aspects of uncertainty arise in looking at each of the cases. First, each of the four types of uncertainty occurred in each case as shown in Table 11.2. Second, decision makers reacted to these uncertainties during policy implementation in a way that ignored or minimized the importance of the uncertainties.

Problem Identification

Uncertainties in the early stages of decision making—during problem identification—often determine the direction of decision making, and lock decisions irreversibly into certain options and resource expenditures by screening out problems that appear to be inconsequential or simply failing to uncover certain problems. The importance of problem identification has been underscored in a discussion of decision making about societal risks:

The problem definition establishes the universe of discourse for the decision-making process. It determines the options and consequences to be considered and the kinds of information and uncertainty to be taken into account. In many cases, the decision has effectively been made once the definition is set. (Fischhoff et al., 1981: 9)

1. Existence of Uncertainties of Problem Identification

The points at which uncertainty can occur in problem identification are in defining origins of a problem (in terms of a particular activity or type of substance), geographic extent of a problem, and number of persons exposed. The way in which sources of uncertainty arose in the cases is discussed below.

Origin of the Problem. The activity, namely an industrial establishment, that produced the environmental problem was usually known with certainty. For example, at Foundry Cove cadmium originated from the Marathon Battery plant, at Berry's Creek the source of mercury was the Velsicol plant, at Ticonderoga Bay the source of mercury was from an Allied Chemical plant, and the PCBs in the Hudson River originated from two General Electric plants.

The origin of the problem in terms of which chemicals in the wastes presented a hazard, however, was not entirely known with certainty. In some cases, governmental agencies focused on one substance, only to discover later that a different substance with greater risks was present in waste material. For example, dibenzofurans, a chemical often found in association with PCBs (polychlorinated biphenyls), were found in association with PCBs in sediments in the Hudson River case. This shifted the focus of investigations from PCBs to dibenzofurans. At College Point, Queens, the original focus was on a generic waste—waste oil. When PCBs became a nationwide issue, the PCBs found in the oil became the focus of attention. This is an example of changing public policies toward environmental risks influencing which sources of risks are emphasized.

Geographic Extent of the Problem: In the cases reviewed the extent of contamination could not be measured with certainty, and, in most cases, mathematical models were unable to accurately simulate transport of substances from sources to humans.

1. *Measurement uncertainty.* In the 1970s environmental concerns focused on the human health effects of low concentrations of substances. Measurement techniques to detect these low levels were largely unavailable in the early 1970s (Lisk, 1974). Uncertainties in measurement techniques and protocol created discrepancies in measurements for cadmium in Foundry Cove. Inadequate data prevented accurate measurements for kepone contamination below one foot of sediment. A breakthrough in measurement technology, a new type of gas chromatograph, allowed numerous organic contaminants to be identified at Love Canal in the mid-1970s.

2. *Model uncertainty.* Models were often used to estimate and predict environmental fate and transport of toxic substances and their health effects at low doses. Uncertainties in the models originated from simplifying assumptions and the absence of data sets with which to calibrate and validate them, with the exception of the modeling of kepone transport in the James River (O'Connor, Mueller, and Farley, 1983). The more common models were developed around parameters such as dissolved oxygen, relevant to environmental protection but not human health. Transport routes mainly emphasized physical and chemical transport

mechanisms, rather than transport via biological systems (e.g., fish migration). Models did not incorporate extreme events like storms or floods. Deficiencies in the state of the art of pollutant transport and ecological modeling produced considerable uncertainties in several of the cases. For example, PCB migration in the Hudson River could not easily be modeled. Scientific studies concentrated on localized studies of chemical uptake by organisms or empirical studies of uptake under laboratory conditions.

The structure of many highly quantitative models requires precise inputs. Uncertainties expressed as value ranges and error terms were often not reflected in the final results. This gave model results the appearance of certainty, when in fact uncertainties were being camouflaged. This characteristic of complex models has been recognized many times. According to Fischhoff et al. (1981: 18), modeling is characterized by "counterintuitive or politically awkward" results, results that can be interpreted in a variety of ways, the absence of test situations for model calibration, and the unavailability of high-quality data for model runs. Fairley, Meyer, and Chernick (1985: 404) point out further that

the results of complex quantitative models, such as Probabilistic Risk Assessments (PRAs) for nuclear power plants, are generally reported without reference to such uncertainties as the quality of the data, the analyst's degree of confidence in the model, or the analyst's prior beliefs about the relevant probabilities.

Number of People Exposed: Estimate of number of people exposed is a direct outcome of the location of contaminants. Uncertainty in estimating the magnitude of the population exposed originates from a lack of information on population location relative to the location of contaminants. It is often uncertain whether contamination has moved toward people or whether people have moved into areas of contamination. In some of the cases population exposure increased as contamination spread. For example, at Love Canal migration of contaminants to other populated areas occurred when canal materials were removed for use in construction elsewhere (Kim, et al., 1981; New York State Department of Health, 1981). In the Hudson River, PCBs migrated downstream to populated areas along the river when the dam at Fort Edwards was removed, releasing PCBs trapped in a pool behind the dam. The 100-year flood in 1976 moved PCBs even further downstream.

In other cases, population exposure increased because people moved into contaminated areas. Population expanded adjacent to Love Canal during the 1960s after the waste site had been well established. Existing land-use, health, and environmental controls did not prevent such growth. In Berry's Creek proposed developments in the Meadowlands could potentially increase the exposure of future populations to mercury vapor. In Foundry Cove, New York, people's eating habits increased their exposure: the consumption of blue crabs from the river (which concentrated the cadmium) with tomato sauce (which leached the cadmium out) created a health hazard of such proportions that a state health warning was issued (Hazen, 1982).

In addition to numbers of persons exposed, types of people exposed often shifted over the course of a given case. For example, in the Hudson River PCB case, the original focus was on consumers of PCB-laden fish. Later, the focus was on consumers of PCB-contaminated water supplies. When mitigation efforts were planned, the problem shifted once again to an occupational health problem related to airborne PCBs potentially affecting dredging operators and landfill workers.

In summary, during problem identification, relatively little uncertainty existed with regard to the origins of problems. The geographic extent of the problem and the extent of the population at risk, in contrast, were the subject of considerable uncertainties.

2. Reaction to Uncertainties

In reaction to uncertainties in the geographic extent of the risk and the size of the population at risk, government agencies emphasized strategies to control contaminants in areas where they knew they were located, rather than continuing extensive sampling programs in adjacent areas to refine the location and extent of contamination. Uncertainty regarding extent of contamination was thus set aside rather than directly confronted. This occasionally resulted in new areas of concern appearing later on. In some of the later cases, such as Love Canal, this was not entirely the case. Over $8 million was spent for sampling efforts to determine the fate and transport of environmental contaminants in the immediate vicinity of the canal, but this effort primarily emphasized nearby areas covered under the federal emergency declaration order.[18] In the James River case, extensive sampling of the Chesapeake Bay was conducted to identify the spread of contamination there, but relatively little was done to determine the depth of contamination in the river itself.

One way to directly examine health effects among exposed populations is via health assessment studies. Such studies were either not conducted systematically or not conducted at all at the sites reviewed here. One exception was at Love Canal, where some blood sampling, health questionnaires, and genetic studies were carried out. The results were so controversial that they were set aside. Subsequent to Love Canal, health studies have rarely been conducted at hazardous waste sites, and when they have, the results have generally been inconclusive.[19]

Basis for Control: Standards

1. Existence of Uncertainties in Standards

In many cases, agencies and the companies responsible for the contaminants looked for guidance to definitive criteria, standards, guidelines, and other norms as a framework to control the substances in the environment. One purpose of developing standards was to encourage a debate over uncertainty at an earlier state in the decision-making process outside of the context of a specific case.

Uncertainty in the design of standards or guidelines often stems from uncertainties in the scientific data bases, research designs, judgments of experts with regard to appropriate test systems, and the interpretation of test results. These uncertainties have been well documented (see Whittemore, 1983; Fischhoff et al., 1981).[20] As in problem identification, the development of standards depends on models, and these models can produce highly uncertain results, which carry forward into the standards themselves.

Table 11.2 itemizes uncertainties in the development of standards. The absence of human health effects studies in practically all of the cases precluded the establishment of a linkage between levels of exposure and effect for the chemicals of concern. Numerous animal studies existed; however, results from species to species were not consistent, analogies between laboratory conditions and the actual environmental conditions in the cases could not always be drawn, and thus, standards often simply did not exist before decision makers had to come up with answers. This was true in the use of standards in a number of the cases. In the Foundry Cover case, cadmium levels in exposed fish were 1,000 times the normal level in fish, but it was unclear how this comparison related to FDA standards ("action levels") for cadmium concentrations in fish. In the James River case, FDA standards for finfish and crabs were first proposed in 1977, well after the problem had to be dealt with by regulatory agencies, forcing these agencies to act in an environment of uncertainty. At the time the Berry's Creek problem first arose, numerical limits for mercury existed only for drinking water (not easily related to sediment concentrations in the creek). The Clean Water Act standards for the ambient water environment and the state standards developed under similar legislation only referred to general toxic levels that could affect lower organisms and did not comprehensively cover all chemicals. This created a high degree of uncertainty in the regulatory arena. The concentrations of mercury in sediments (for which there were no standards) could not be related to water standards that existed except through the use of highly complex models, whose problems were discussed above. Similarly, in the Hudson River case, PCB concentrations in sediments could not be clearly related to effects in fish or people via water or fish consumption.

2. Reaction to Uncertainties

One common response to scientific and political uncertainties in standards is to modify tolerance limits for hazardous substances over time and to tailor standards to a particular circumstance. In the cases reviewed, both tendencies were observed. Permissible levels for hazardous substances in wastewater discharges were modified and tailored to the situation at hand by shifting limits from less stringent to more stringent levels:[21]

- Effluent limits developed in the Foundry Cove case for cadmium from the industrial plant fell from .44 pounds per day to .12 pounds per day.

- Effluent limits developed in the James River case for kepone were reduced from 3 ppm to 0.5 ppb.

- PCB standards in fish (action levels) set by the U.S. Food and Drug Administration at the time the Hudson River case was occurring fell from 5 ppm to 2 ppm.

Thus, when the effects of adhering to certain levels for contaminants were not known with certainty, a conservative stance was taken—adhere to the more stringent levels.

Uncertainties also led to the assignment of variable concentrations for the same substance in different environments, namely, air, water, and food. That is, concentrations set for each environment often translated into different human exposure levels. Furthermore, variations existed for different public groups. Derr et al. (1985: 260) have shown that different EPA and OSHA standards for the same substance often result in variable protection of workers versus the general public. These uncertainties originate in part from differences in the approach to environmental health risk assessment taken by different governmental agencies. The National Research Council (1983: 62-68) pointed out that such agency variations can be explained in terms of differences in the comprehensiveness of risk assessment guidelines from agency to agency (often for the same substance), the degree of detail of the risk assessment steps, the type of evidence that is accepted, and the degree of discretion exercised in using the guidelines. In the cases reviewed this was clearly seen. In the Hudson River case the threshold of 50 ppm used to define areas for dredging bore no relationship to the standards set for fish and for humans in an occupational setting.

Method of Control: Management Strategies

Management strategies for hazardous substances include regulation and, less frequently, quasi-regulatory strategies, such as financial incentives and disincentives for pollution.[22] These strategies are aimed at reducing either risk sources or the magnitude of the exposed population. The way in which uncertainties in regulatory and one nonregulatory strategy—financing—surfaced in these cases and shaped their outcomes is discussed below.

Table 11.3
Nature of Uncertainty in Hazardous Waste Management Decision Making

	Method of Control: Implementation Mechanisms (Regulatory)	Mitigation or Abatement Measures
Foundry Cove, NY	• EPA vs. New York State authority in the matter • Legal uncertainties involving federal liability, since U.S. Army Corps of Engineers was once an owner of the site	• Disposal: Uncertainty regarding the effectiveness of on-site entombment against leaching — initial system does break down resulting in cadmium migration and re-entry into the Cove's ecosystem
Berry's Creek, NJ	• Wastewater Discharge Permit (RAPP/NPDES): Uncertainty regarding validity of limits imposed on plant; uncertainty as to the viability of pre-treatment and subsequent discharge into local treatment plant • Resources for control: Uncertainty surrounding applicability of NJ Spill Compensation Fund and Superfund • Liability: Complex uncertainties regarding extent and nature of corporate liability, ultimately resolved in a lengthy court case	• Disposal: Uncertainty regarding effectiveness of containment methods, and potential effects on proposed development in Berry's Creek
Ticonderoga Bay, NY	• Rivers and Harbors Act: Difficulties establishing casual linkages and irreparable harm for mercury levels	• Dredging: Uncertainty surrounded whether or not mercury would become resuspended during dredging, and make contamination potential worse
Hudson River, NY	• Wastewater Discharge Permit (NPDES): Limits not coincident with effect levels for PCB • Resources for control: Applicability of various funding programs under P.L. 92-500 and Super-fund uncertain, prompting Congressional authorization; federal government never able to supply R&D funds to explore treatment technologies	• Dredging: Relative effectiveness of Pneuma vs. Hydraulic Dredges; uncertainty regarding dredging strategy — hot spots vs. cold spots • Treatment: Technologies for breakdown of PCBs not well developed, though some identified — Wright-Malta, Nichols, Franklin Institute processes • Disposal: Problems of volatilization and leaching at land disposal sites not well resolved
College Point, NY	• NYS Dredge and Fill Permits were not oriented specifically to toxics until after the incident • 6 NYCRR Parts 360 and 364 permits for hazardous waste disposal and transport —	• Treatment: Uncertainty regarding method and extent of removal of PCBs once they are found in sediments

Table 11.3 *(continued)*

	Method of Control: Implementation Mechanisms (Regulatory)	Mitigation or Abatement Measures
College Point, NY	effectiveness of control limited by resource constraints and the large number of entities to which laws were applicable • Resources for control: Inability of Coast Guard to use Clean Water Act monies for cleanup under Section 311	
Love Canal, NY	• Emergency powers: New authority had to be passed to declare an emergency • Superfund emerged as a result of Love Canal, demonstrating the need for mechanisms to deal with situation	• Dredging/removal operations: Uncertainty as to whether sufficient areas dredged • Treatment: Chemical waste treatment system meets with community opposition because of uncertain side effects
James River, VA	• Pesticide registration: Early laws not sufficiently stringent to control adverse effects from the use or manufacture of kepone • NPDES program: Dischargers are able to avoid more stringent requirements by filing a "short form" under the assumption of connecting to a wastewater treatment plant • Liability: Considerable uncertainties regarding corporate liability of parent company, resolved in a lengthy court case	• Dredging: Decision not to dredge fraught with considerable uncertainty, especially regarding the possibility of a 100-year storm occurring that would dislodge kepone

1. Existence of Uncertainties in Management Strategies

Regulatory Strategies. The regulatory context in which the cases occurred was characterized by considerable uncertainty, especially in the early 1970s. This resulted in part from constantly changing laws,[23] laws that were vague and had loopholes (Sabatier and Mazmanian, 1979), and laws that provided an incomplete and often inconsistent coverage of types of chemicals or routes by which they moved in the environment.

Uncertainties that prevailed in the legal environment were reflected in the fact that court cases were numerous,[24] highly complex, and unique. This showed up in a number of the cases reviewed. For example, the thousands of pages of legal documents generated in the Berry's Creek court case were indicative of its compexity. In addition, some cases were complex by virtue of reliance upon extensive proofs to demonstrate harm. In the James River case a demonstration of corporate conspiracy and negligence was required.[25] The Berry's Creek case took a unique turn: The state was brought in as a guilty party and was required to institute corrective action at its own expense.[26] New laws and modifications of existing statutes enacted after many of these cases were active have removed some of the legal and enforcement problems that were encountered prior to the 1970s.

Some Nonregulatory Alternatives—Finance

Financial incentives and disincentives are used to prevent contamination from occuring and to encourage cleanups after the fact. Funding sources for cleanup efforts were often uncertain, prior to the passage of CERCLA. Even under CERCLA, problems with federal appropriations periodically halted the cleanup program. In addition, the financing structure for Superfund was the subject of considerable debate prior to the passage of CERCLA (White, 1981: 149), and this has continued in the course of designing its amendments. Applicability of funding mechanisms and availability of funds within potentially applicable programs were unclear. Resources were often generated case by case. Funds under Section 201 of the Clean Water Act (normally reserved for waste water treatment facilities) and under Section 311 (reserved for oil and hazardous materials cleanup) were not easily adaptable to the after-the-fact waste cleanup cases dealt with here. State cleanup funds were similarly difficult to apply, because money was earmarked for specific purposes. For example, the use of the state of New Jersey's spill compensation fund (for oil spills) for the cleanup of mercury in Berry's Creek was challenged in court.[27] Research and development funds to develop and apply new technologies for cleanups were also hard to obtain. A number of benchmark technologies for PCB removal could not be applied to the Hudson River PCB problem, since no funding was available to refine them and increase their reliability. The applicability of Superfund to the cleanup of cadmium in Foundry Cove was uncertain, since a federal agency, the Corps of Engineers, had originally constructed the plant and was ineligible for cleanup funds.

2. Reactions to Uncertainty

Regulation. In order to reduce these regulatory uncertainties, decision makers chose managerial systems for regulation that emphasized clear-cut and certain procedures. Uncertainties were thus ignored or set aside (Zimmerman, 1984; O'Brien, Clarke, and Kamieniecki, 1984). Two examples of such managerial systems are permit programs and advisory committees.

Permit systems and other approval or certification processes are considered closed systems because they rely upon well-defined limits and conditions. There is little opportunity for negotiation once limits and conditions are set at the beginning of the process. The uncertainties underlying the limits are normally not considered by the regulator issuing a permit. Newer permit programs have structures and degrees of prescription similar to older ones, though they allow a little more latitude in addressing uncertainties.

Many contaminants escaped these older permit programs. In spite of the fact that the industrial dischargers held permits, mercury still accumulated in Berry's Creek, and PCBs still accumulated in the Hudson River. Manufacturers of kepone filed wastewater discharge permits but have neglected to reveal the presence of certain discharges (Goldfarb, 1980: 132). Kepone escaped from the manufacturing establishment, before more stringent limits were invoked. In the Love Canal case, the potential risks eluded federal and state solid waste management procedures, water quality and health laws, and local land-use controls over several decades.

A second common management mechanism to reduce or circumscribe scientific uncertainty in governmental regulation has been the creation of expert panels or advisory committees. These entities are often created to achieve consensus on scientific debates. Jasonoff (1985: 237) points out that these are far more prevalent in Europe than in the United States. Zimmerman (1982: Table 5) observed that advisory committees set up in the cases reviewed here were confined to discrete tasks and a single decision. In the case of Love Canal, numerous committees were set up to exercise discrete functions. A blue ribbon panel was set up to examine health effects, in particular, to evaluate a genetic study. Another, comprised of several federal agencies, was set up to comment on the results of the EPA's monitoring program. Still another one, the revitalization task force, was set up to study how the area could be revitalized after the incident. In the Hudson River case the advisory committees included the PCB Settlement Advisory Committee, which evaluated technical information on PCB reclamation and disposal, and the PCB Reclamation Project Task Force, which prepared an environmental assessment of options. In the James River case, a federal-state advisory committee was recommended by the EPA in 1978 to continue surveillance of kepone in the river.

Mitigation and Abatement Measures—Technology

Mazmanian and Sabatier's (1983) framework for policy implementation identified technology as an important input into defining and solving problems and developing standards. The dredging, treatment, and disposal cases have raised serious questions concerning the reliability of technology in eliminating potential chemical hazards. For example, some dispersion of chemicals occurs during dredging in spite of the use of sophisticated dredging equipment and proper scheduling of dredging operations to avoid dispersion. Variations in site conditions make it difficult to predict the exact amount of dispersion in any given situation. Many technological uncertainties cannot be resolved because government has not invested in new technologies.

1. Existence of Uncertainties in Abatement Technologies

In a number of contamination cases, uncertainties arose when a technology was applied that either did not perform as predicted or resulted in unpredictable operational failure. At Love Canal, scientific uncertainties regarding the effectiveness of the waste treatment program were the basis of doubts about allowing rehabitation of the area once it was cleaned up. The Office of Technology Assessment's (OTA) conclusions with regard to this issue strongly emphasize this uncertainty:

With available information it is not possible to conclude either that unsafe levels of toxic contamination exist or that they do not exist in the Emergency Declaration Area (EDA). The OTA analysis does not support an interpretation of the DHHS decision that would lead to the immediate and complete rehabitation of the EDA. There remains a need to demonstrate more unequivocally that the EDA is safe immediately and over the long term for human habitation. If that cannot be done, it may be necessary to accept the original presumption that the area is not habitable. (Office of Technology Assessment, 1983: 3)

In the Hudson River case, the viability of various state-of-the-art treatment technologies such as biodegradation and thermal destruction were very uncertain. Problems of how PCBs would react in landfills, if that disposal option was exercised, were also uncertain.

A major area of uncertainty in the dredging cases was whether contaminants would become dislodged during dredging, resulting in widespread dispersal of the contaminants. This was particularly identified as a problem area in the case of mercury in both Berry's Creek and

Ticonderoga Bay, PCBs in the Hudson River, and cadmium in Foundry Cove.

2. Reactions to Uncertainty

Government responded to technological uncertainty by placing greater emphasis upon conventional, tested methods as opposed to investing in new, state-of-the-art technologies. Conventional technologies had a track record, and their uncertainties in reducing water contaminants were considered relatively low. Thus, decisions were aimed at reducing technological uncertainty.

In the cadmium case, the mitigation measure used (entombment of sediments on site) was considered technologically sound in terms of currently acceptable waste treatment techniques. The system was endorsed by federal and state officials. It became defective a few years later, sending cadmium back into Foundry Cove. The site ultimately became listed as a Superfund site under CERCLA. In the James River case, a Kepone Mitigation Feasibility Study recommended against dredging the river altogether because of resuspension and disposal problems, in spite of the existence of dredges that minimized resuspension. Only very recently in one case has a relatively advanced technology been actively considered. At Love Canal, a plasma arc process for decomposing wastes, which has had limited applicability before this, has been evaluated.

SUMMARY AND CONCLUSION: IMPACT OF THE LACK OF FOCUS UPON UNCERTAINTIES IN POLICYMAKING

In the cases reviewed, uncertainty appeared in all of the cases along the four different dimensions defined above. The desicion-making system reacted to these uncertainties by discounting them or ignoring them. In *problem identification*, uncertainties in quantitative models to estimate pollutant transport were often dropped because the framework of the models could not accommodate them. In *control via standards*, a similar problem with model uncertainty occurred. In addition, uncertainties in standards led to the adoption of policies that lowered permissible limits. In choosing *methods for control*, government often adhered to circumscribed regulatory systems, such as permits and advisory committees with very restricted and well-defined roles. Financial investments were restricted to known technologies. As a result, many problems and their solutions, not easily categorized under existing regulatory and funding programs, were ignored. Finally, even where uncertainties appeared in the *technologies* to control contamination, they were considered for implementation.

In summary, implementation of hazardous waste policy emphasized uncertainty reduction or a dependency upon precision and circumscribed procedures. Federal and state governmental responses were conservative or conventional: standards were lowered, only known technologies were approved, and existing regulatory devices were used that reflected a dominance of existing programs such as permitting.

The failure to develop new management strategies to address uncertainty during implementation drove the implementation process toward ineffective action, actions provoking irresolvable and often costly controversy, and inaction:

- Cases resulting in ineffective action: In the Foundry Cove case, adherence to an "assured" technology and avoidance of uncertainties in new approaches led to the choice of a technology that performed poorly. This resulted in continued contamination of Foundry Cove by cadmium for almost a decade after implementation. In a number of cases, government adhered to preexisting regulatory devices that did not prevent an environmental problem from escalating.
- Cases resulting in heightened and costly controversy: In the case of Love Canal, uncertainty about human health effects and the legal framework for cleanup dominated the public debate and generated a high degree of controversy about the effectiveness of dredging the canal. These uncertainties had ramifications for the evacuation and rehabitation decisions.
- Cases resulting in no action or postponed action: In the Berry's Creek case, legal and liability uncertainties took so long to resolve that little action was taken for almost two decades. In the Hudson River case, uncertainty about appropriate levels of contamination, transport mechanisms, and financing mechanisms for cleanup suspended cleanup action for close to a decade. In the James River and Ticonderoga Bay cases, uncertainties about transport mechanisms for contaminants in disturbed sediments turned decision making away from dredging, even though there was no assurance that a flood or storm would not dislodge the contaminants in the future or attempt to assess the acceptability of such a risk.

Thus, scientific and political uncertainties had major effects on outcomes. The absence of a clear strategy directed toward these uncertainties contributed under similar environmental conditions.[28] Different solutions to different problems may be warranted, since environmental conditions and chemicals vary, but this implies a more conscious choice situation than actually existed in the cases reviewed.

One way to avoid the adverse effects of uncertainty on decision making is to devise ways to address uncertainty at the outset, during problem identification, and to continue evaluating it through subsequent stages of decision making. In this way, uncertainty can constructively shape the analysis of the problem and the choice and implementation of solutions. Otherwise, uncertainties will drive the decisions to unpredictable and inconsistent solutions.

Such a procedure can be established for cases that have in common similar decisions, like dredging. More specifically, this process can be developed as follows: (1) identify the types of uncertainty likely to occur at the outset, using various screening techniques (Walker, 1986), such as hazard identification or qualitative risk assessment; (2) locate where uncertainties might occur at the different stages of policy implementation; (3) weigh the quality, significance, and importance of uncertainties to focus management policy; (4) conduct a sensitivity analysis on the uncertainties to determine whether resolving a given uncertainty makes a difference in the choice of solutions to the problem, and focus only on those uncertainties that appear to make a difference; and (5) for significant uncertainties, concentrate on procedures for uncertainty reduction.

NOTES

1. This work was supported in part from a National Science Foundation grant to R. Zimmerman entitled "The Management of Risk" (Grant No. PRA 8209795).

2. This argument was explored in a critique of the risk assessment performed for a hazardous waste site cleanup in New Hampshire. That study found that ignoring the uncertainties during the site assessment led to per capita cost estimates that could vary by four orders of magnitude. The authors concluded that, first, the site investigation should have incorporated these uncertainties, and second, such a range of values severely limited the usefulness of the analysis for public policy (Evans, Petito, and Gravallese, 1986).

3. The approach taken here uses the cases illustratively, for the purpose of examining in a qualitative way the validity of the hypothesis as a basis for deciding whether to examine it further in greater depth.

4. Cox and Bayhutt (1981) summarize many of the statistical approaches to conducting uncertainty analysis. Raiffa (1968: 104) argues that subjective judgments about uncertainties should be translated into probabilities, which can then be evaluated mathematically.

5. The application of this theory to hazardous waste issues is discussed briefly in Evans, Petito, and Gravallese (1986: 24).

6. Kahneman, Slovic, and Tversky, 1982).

7. Pressman and Wildavsky (1984: 222), for example, discuss the utility of the negotiation approach in the context of conventional pollution problems. Leblebici and Salancik (1981: 580) similarly argue for a process framework and describe uncertainty as being a property of decision situations, that is, decision-makers and their political environments.

8. Maximum concentrations of sediment at the dredging site can be as high as 500 mg/1, and the dredging plume can extend anywhere from 300 to 500 yards downstream (Malcolm Pirnie, Inc., 1983a).

9. See 51 *Federal Register,* June 22, 1986).

10. The analytical techniques for dredged material slated for ocean disposal were first outlined in U.S. EPA/COE, "Ecological Evaluation of Proposed Discharge of Dredged Material into Ocean Waters" (Vicksburg, MI: U.S. Army Engineer Waterways Experiment Station, 1977) as revised by "Guidance for Performing Tests on Dredged Material to Be Disposed of in Ocean Waters" (New York: COE, April 18, 1982). One of the major techniques for determining the leachability or migration

of toxic contaminants in dredge material is the "EP toxicity test." These procedures are outlined in 40 CFR Part 261, Appendix II. While these procedures were a considerable advance over those in the previous decade, the Hazardous and Solid Waste Amendments to the Resource Conservation and Recovery Act of 1984 mandated an evaluation of the effectiveness of some of these tests largely because of uncertainties arising in test procedures.

11. In the COE's New York District alone, the rate of dredging has been 10-20 million cubic yards a year. Private dredging accounts for another 2 million cubic yards a year (U.S. Army COE, 1983; Malcolm Pirnie, Inc., 1983b).

12. Under RCRA/HSWA, hazardous wastes and hazardous waste constituents are defined under 40 Code of Federal Regulations Part 261.24 and 261.3. Dredged material is not specifically listed as a hazardous waste source, nor is it explicitly exempted under 40 CFR 261.4. However, many constituents of contaminated dredged material are listed as hazardous wastes. These listings occurred after 1980, long after many of the substances covered in the cases reviewed here had been discharged to sediments.

13. The hazard potentials of these substances were refined after 1980 under RCRA regulations (kepone was assigned code U142, cadmium D006, and mercury D009, and the various contaminants at Love Canal had various codes depending on the particular substance), and TSCA (for PCBs). Prior to that, they were recognized in legislation such as Clean Water Act toxic water standards passed as a result of the 1976 federal consent decree (*Natural Resources Defense Council* [*NRDC*] *v. Train*, No. 75-172, 8 ERC 21 20 [D.D.C. June 8, 1976]) and pesticide legislation dating as far back as the 1940s (for kepone). Water quality criteria published during the 1960s and 1970s also identified the substances as hazardous to lower organisms.

14. The chemicals involved in the contamination incidents differed in terms of characteristics that affect their fate in the environment, and the areas of contamination may have differed in terms of local hydrologic regimes. It is unlikely that the decisions, at the time they were made, were sensitive to these differences.

15. The decision to treat the dredge material in order to concentrate or reduce toxins prior to disposal differed only in one case—treatment was undertaken only at Love Canal.

16. While action had been pending in the Hudson River and Berry's Creek cases at the time of this writing, disposal options had been extensively analyzed, and preliminary decisions had been made in the event that dredging might go forward.

17. The framework outlined below and several of the components, particularly problem identification, the development of standards and criteria, and mitigation measures, are similar to those outlined in decision analysis and frameworks for the planning process.

18. U.S. EPA, *Environmental Monitoring at Love Canal,* vol. 1 (May 1982).

19. See J. W. Grisham, *Health Aspects of the Disposal of Waste Chemicals* (New York: Pergamon, 1986), chapter 8: "Disposal Site Health Studies." The amendments to CERCLA, the Superfund Amendments, and the Reauthorization Act of 1986 (P.L. 99-962) require health assessment studies as part of hazard identification and analysis of hazardous waste disposal sites, strengthening this aspect of CERCLA.

20. These uncertainties include the extent to which empirical studies relating exposure to health effects using animals and lower organisms can be extrapolated to

humans, the extent to which models used to estimate responses at low doses of substances are accurate, and effect of the variability in human susceptibility to and tolerances for toxic substances on response estimates.

21. Though not among the cases reviewed here, the vinyl chloride standard also showed a clear progression downward over the years (Doniger, 1978; Zimmerman, 1984).

22. For a discussion of nonregulatory options see Baram (1982) and Breyer (1982).

23. An example of changing laws was the fact that there were three major amendments to the Clean Water Act during the 1970s alone. Additionally, a number of key court cases altered agency decision making (e.g., *NRDC v. Train*). Finally, new laws emerged, such as RCRA, TSCA, and CERCLA, controlling many of the same substances that had been previously under the jurisdiction of the Clean Water Act.

24. For example, Wenner (1984) points to a general rise in the number of environmental cases brought between 1970 and 1982, especially those brought by government and industry.

25. For an extensive discussion of this, see Goldfarb (1980).

26. In the case of mercury in Berry's Creek, the state of New Jersey was required by the court to initiate some corrective actions that were within its existing powers. *State of NJ Dept. of Environmental Protection v. Ventron Corporation*, Nos. C-2996-75, C-1954-77, C-110078 (NJ Super. Ch. Div., Decided August 27, 1979); for a discussion of the issue of government liability, see Tasher (1981): 212-214.

27. *Mobil Oil Corp. et al. v. State of NJ DEP and State of NJ Dept. of the Treasury, Spill Compensation Fund*. Docket C-1110-78.

28. Consistency is not necessarily required or even desirable in policymaking. One expects consistency, however, when conditions are so similar.

REFERENCES

Baram, M. S., *Alternatives to Regulation* (Lexington, MA: Lexington Books, 1982).

Breyer, S., *Regulation and Its Reform* (Cambridge, MA: Harvard University Press, 1982).

Cox, D. C., and P. Bayhutt, "Methods for Uncertainty Analysis: A Comparative Survey," *J. of Risk Analysis* 1 (December 1981) 4: 251-258.

Derr, P., et al., "Protecting Workers, Protecting Publics: The Ethics of Differential Protection," in *Risk Analysis in the Private Sector,* edited by C. Whipple and V. T. Covello (New York: Plenum, 1985), 257-269.

Doniger, D. *The Law and Policy of Toxic Substances Control* (Baltimore, MD: The Johns Hopkins University Press, 1978).

Evans, J. S., C. T. Petito, and D. M. Gravallese. "Cleaning Up the Gilson Road Hazardous Waste Site: A Case Study" (Cambridge, MA: Harvard University, JFK School of Government, February 1986).

Fairley, W. B., M. B. Meyer, P. L. Chernick, "Insurance Market Assessment of Technological Risks," in *Risk Analysis in the Private Sector,* edited by C. Whipple and V. T. Covello (New York: Plenum, 1985), 401-416.

Fischhoff, B., S. Lichtenstein, P. Slovic, S. L. Derby, and R. L. Keeney, *Acceptable Risk* (Cambridge: Cambridge University Press, 1981).

Goldfarb, W., "Kepone: A Case Study," in *Water Quality Administration*, edited by B. Lamb (Ann Arbor, MI: Ann Arbor Science, 1980).

Grisham, J. W. *Health Aspects of the Disposal of Waste Chemicals* (New York: Pergamon, 1986).

Hazen, R. E. "Cadmium in an Aquatic Ecosystem." Ph.D. Thesis, New York University, Department of Environmental Medicine, 1982.

Jasonoff, S. "Legitimating Private Sector Risk Analysis: A U.S.-European Comparison" in *Risk Analysis in the Private Sector*, edited by C. Whipple and V. T. Covello (New York: Plenum, 1985).

Kahneman, D., P. Slovic, and A. Tversky. *Judgment under Uncertainty: Heuristics and Biases* (New York: Cambridge University Press, 1982).

Kim, C. S., et al., "Love Canal: Chemical Contamination and Migration," Unpublished paper (Albany, NY: NYS Department of Health, 1981).

Leblebici, H., and G. R. Salancik. "Effects of Environmental Uncertainty on Information and Decision Processes in Banks," *Administrative Science Quarterly* 26 (December 1981): 578-596.

Lisk, D. J. "Recent Developments in the Analysis of Toxic Elements." *Science* (June 14, 1974): 1137-1141.

Malcolm Pirnie, Inc. Hudson River Federal Channel Maintenance Dredging. Final EIS and Appendices. For the New York District Corps of Engineers. (White Plains, NY: Malcolm Pirnie, January 1983a).

_____, Feasibility Study for Use of Dredged Material from NY/NJ Harbor as Sanitary Landfill Cover. For the New York District Corps of Engineers. (White Plains, NY: Malcolm Pirnie, May 1983b).

Mazmanian, D. A., and P. A. Sabatier, *Implementation and Public Policy* (Glenview, IL: Scott, Foresman and Company, 1983).

National Research Council, *Risk Assessment in the Federal Government: Managing the Process* (Washington, DC: National Academy Press, 1983).

New York State Department of Health, *Love Canal: A Special Report to the Governor and Legislature* (Albany, NY: NYS DOH, April 1981).

O'Brien, R. M., M. Clarke, and S. Kamieniecki, "Open and Closed Systems of Decision Making: The Case of Toxic Waste Management," *Public Administration Review* 44 (1984): 334-340.

O'Connor, D. J., J. A. Mueller, and K. J. Farley, "Distribution of Kepone in the James River Estuary," *J. of Env. Eng.* 109 (April 1983): 396-413.

Office of Technology Assessment, "Habitability of the Love Canal Area" (Washington, DC: OTA, June 1983).

Pressman, J. L., and A. Wildavsky, *Implementation* (Berkeley, CA: University of California Press, 1984).

Raiffa, H. *Decision Analysis* (Reading, MA: Addison-Wesley, 1968).

Sabatier, P., and D. Mazmanian, "The Conditions of Effective Implementation: A Guide to Accomplishing Policy Objectives, *Policy Analysis* (1979) 5: 481-504.

Tasher, S. A., "Technical Elements of the Government's Case," In *Hazardous Waste Litigation,* edited by R. M. Mott (Washington, DC: Practicing Law Institute, 1981).

U.S. Army Corps of Engineers, New York District. March 1983. *Final Environ-*

mental *Impact Statement Disposal of Dredged Material from the Port of NY and NJ* (New York, NY: COE, March 1983).

U.S. Army Corps of Engineers, "Regulatory Programs of the Corps of Engineers; Final Rule," *Federal Register* 51 (November 13, 1986). 219: 41206-41260.

Walker, W. E., "The Use of Screening in Policy Analysis," *Management Science,* 32 (April 1986): 389-402.

Wenner, L. M., "Judicial Oversight of Environment Deregulation," in *Environmental Policy in the 1980s*, edited by Norman Vig and Michael Kraft (Washington, DC: Congressional Quarterly, 1984).

White, L. J. *Reforming Regulation* (Englewood Cliffs, NJ: Prentice-Hall, 1981).

Whittemore, A., "Facts and Values in Risk Analysis for Environmental Toxicants," *J. of Risk Analysis* 3 (March 1983) 1: 23-34.

Zimmerman, R. *The Management of Risk.* Final Report of the National Science Foundation. New York: New York University, Graduate School of Public Administration. 2 volumes and executive summary. 1982a.

———, "Formation of New Organizations to Manage Risk," *Policy Studies Review,* vol. 1, no. 4: 736-747, 1982b.

———. "Management Systems of Low-Probability/High-Consequence Events," in *Low-Probability High-Consequence Risk Analysis*, edited by R. A. Waller and V. T. Covello (New York, NY: Plenum, 1984).

———, "The Management of Risk," in *Risk Evaluation and Management*, edited by V. T. Covello, J. Menkes, and J. Mumpower (New York: Plenum, 1986).

PART IV

THE COMPARATIVE AND INTERNATIONAL LEVELS

12

A Comparative Analysis of Hazardous Waste Management Policy in Western Europe

William R. Mangun

INTRODUCTION

The purpose of this article is to (a) examine the policy formulation and implementation responses of several Western European countries to the problem of hazardous waste management and (b) evaluate the utility of several indicators that appear to be related to policy formulation. Comparative state policy researchers (Dye, 1968; Walker, 1969; Hofferbert, 1970; Lester et al., 1983) have suggested a number of socioeconomic indicators that could be used to explain the presence of different policy patterns. In particular, the variables used by Lester et al. in their comparative study of American state hazardous waste policies provide applicable models to explain the different processes by which public policies are formulated and particular results are produced. Models encompassing similar elements of their "technological pressures," "resources," and "administrative-organizational factors" are examined in this article to determine their utility for comparing the policy responses of Western European countries. Although the quality of the data in Europe may not be the same due to cross-national variation in reporting and availability of information, an attempt will be made to approximate the basic intent of the Lester et al. study, that is, to determine whether certain independent variables appear to contribute to the formulation of hazardous waste management policies more than others.

A review of the hazardous waste management literature concerning Western Europe (Butlin, 1983; Crawford, 1981; Defregger, 1983; Jerabek, 1981; NATO/CCMS, 1977-1981; Piasecki, 1984; Piasecki and Davis, 1984; Whitehead, 1985; Wolbeck, 1983) demonstrates that the approaches to the handling of hazardous waste in these countries are gaining widespread attention and are being compared and contrasted with management efforts throughout the world. Some of the Western European countries are substantially ahead of the United States in developing regulatory procedures for the control of hazardous wastes. In an assessment of the missing links in hazardous waste controls in the United States, Piasecki and Gravander (1985) observed that several Western European countries had evolved regulatory and managerial systems for hazardous waste problems some fifteen years before such problems gained public recognition in the United States.

Whitehead (1985) suggests that the success experienced by the Western Europeans is related to the consistency in public policy due to the fact that the people who propose environmental laws are likely to be the same people who administer them. The reason for this is that the better university graduates tend to seek employment in the public sector in European countries and remain there, and this leads to higher levels of trust between government, industry, and the public, based on tradition and familiarity.

PROBLEMS INVOLVED IN TRANSBOUNDARY
HAZARDOUS WASTE MANAGEMENT

The case of the missing dioxin chemicals from Seveso, Italy, clearly illustrates the complexity which the issue of hazardous waste management can attain when multiple political jurisdictions across national boundaries are involved. In 1983, a Hoffman-LaRoche chemcial manufacturing plant exploded, leaving forty-one drums of dioxin to be disposed of. The drums were collected and sent to the firm's headquarters in Switzerland for destruction, but during their transport, the chemicals mysteriously disappeared at the Swiss-Italian border. The chemicals remained missing for several months. After a great deal of international concern and a five-country search, the chemicals were found eventually in France. Subsequently the chemicals were shipped to Basel in June of 1983 and stored underground but were not destroyed until mid-1984. The employees of the Ciba-Geigy hazardous waste disposal furnace had to be fully aware of the pollution possibilities of the materials in order to ensure their proper disposal (*International Environmental Law Reporter,* 1984a).

Another incident that further illustrates the complexity of the transboundary pollution problem of hazardous waste disposal occurred when a West German aluminum company dumped industrial waste illegally in Belgium. Possibly due to less stringent disposal regulations in Belgium than in West Germany, the Petrans company was able to achieve a comparative economic advantage by discharging the waste in a quarry near Brussels throughout 1983, according to the *International Environment Law*

Reporter (1984b). Supposedly, 26,900 metric tons of toxic wastes were dumped in the quarry at a cost of about $15 per ton (including transportation), which compares quite favorably with a rate of $30-35 per ton in West Germany or $20 per ton in France ($200 per ton if chemically treated)—roughly a savings of over a half million dollars. The individuals responsible circumvented a recent Belgian law prohibiting the importation of dangerous wastes, allegedly by changing license plates near the border and declaring the substance to be industrial material and not waste.

In 1986 two major toxic chemical spills occurred in Switzerland, resulting in a great deal of damage in West Germany. On November 1 a fire at the Sandoz chemical company released toxic chemicals into the Rhine River. A short time later, the chemical group of Ciba-Geigy released a substantial amount of weedkiller into the Rhine. Together, these incidents resulted in potentially long-term damage along the Rhine River and over a half million dead fish. Partially as a result of the divergent national legal and regulatory systems, West German officials are experiencing difficulty in settling legal claims (Marsh, 1987). Switzerland is outside of the European Community (EEC), and there are problems of proving actual economic damage. The severe pollution damage to the Rhine River made *chemicals* a dirty word in West Germany with subsequent implications for the January 1987 parliamentary election (Hunter, 1987). For example, the environmentalist Green party took more than 8% of the vote and increased its representation in the Parliament from twenty-seven to forty-two seats. Furthermore, the Green party and the conservative coalition in power in the Parliament pressed for more environmental controls for chemicals.

The above scenarios highlight the complex coordination problems across sovereign political jurisdictions. The scenarios also illustrate that the success of any hazardous waste control policy will be determined in large part by the level of organizational and financial resources made available for its implementation and by the willingness to comply of those subject to the regulations. For example, since the Seveso incident only four European Economic Community (EEC) countries have adopted tighter rules for handling and storing chemical waste (Marsh, 1987).

LEGAL REQUIREMENTS FOR HAZARDOUS WASTE MANAGEMENT

From 1973 to 1980, the North Atlantic Treaty Organization's Committee on the Challenges to Modern Society (NATO/CCMS) conducted the most comprehensive assessment of hazardous waste management practices ever made. In an evaluation of hazardous waste management legislation and organization requirements, the NATO/CCMS working group determined that the necessary legal requirements are as follows:

1. definition of hazardous waste
2. provision of binding hazardous waste management principles
3. provisions for the distribution of responsibility
4. regulations on financing, including provisions for abandoned sites and long-term care and maintenance
5. planning regulations
6. legislation on control mechanisms regulating
   a) waste generation
   b) waste transportation
   c) import of wastes
   d) waste disposal facilities including facilities for storage, and
   e) waste stream control. (Szelinski, 1983)

The first step of defining what constitutes "hazardous waste" is a difficult problem and one that complicates matters when making any comparison across countries. A recent Organization for Economic Cooperation and Development study (1984) revealed that regulations vary considerably across countries, with such terms as *hazardous waste, toxic waste, chemical waste, special waste,* and *pollution-generating waste* being used to describe similar materials. Also, there is often considerable variance between countries as to when and where a situation would dictate that the waste in question was indeed hazardous. For example, in the United Kingdom, "special waste" is a substance that is dangerous to life (i.e., presents serious hazards for a dose of 5 cm^3 ingested by a child weighing 20 kg or in inhalation or contact with the skin or eyes for a period of 15 minutes) or is flammable at least at 21° or is a prescription medicine or is a radioactive substance with dangerous properties other than radioactivity (Control of Pollution Act 1974; 1980 Regulations No. 1709).

EUROPEAN COMMUNITIES AS A POLITICAL FORCE IN POLICY FORMULATION

Western European countries exhibit differing pressures and demands resulting in different institutional responses leading to different levels of effectiveness in hazardous waste management. Acknowledging such variation in political and economic pressures, the Commission of European Communities (EEC) has been attempting to harmonize standards for hazardous waste management across all of its member countries with differing levels of success. The EEC approach is somewhat similar to the U.S. Environmental Protection Agency's effort to get the American states to develop standardized programs under the 1976 Resource Conservation and Recovery Act (RCRA). Greater harmonization of hazardous waste management standards and policies has been fostered through Commission of European Communities' Programmes for Action on the Environment for 1973, 1977, and 1983 and a series of directives promoting the development of actions by member states for the classification, handling, and transport of hazardous wastes. The directive of March 20, 1978, on toxic and dangerous waste (78/319/EEC), for example, requires member countries to take the necessary steps to dispose of toxic and dangerous waste without endangering human health and without harming the environment. Problems attributable to the unavailability of local facilities and a desire to avoid more stringent national regulations led to the establishment of another EEC directive on December 6, 1984, for the surveillance and control of cross-frontier hazardous waste transfers. The individual country responses to these directives have varied substantially. By 1983, only six out of the ten member states had developed their basic legal framework in compliance with the spirit of the 1978 directive (Butlin, 1983). An EEC evaluation of the policy implementation effort, furthermore, found significant discrepancies between the reality and the spirit of the regulations that were implemented (Commission of European Communities, 1982b). In 1981 alone, Italy and Belgium were taken before the European Court of Justice for failing to adopt environmental directives on hazardous waste within prescribed time limits (Butlin, 1983). Other member nations have exhibited a greater willingness to cooperate. According to Crawford (1981), Denmark, France, the United Kingdom, Belgium, and Luxembourg had applied some of the rules, while only West Germany and the Netherlands were in substantial compliance with EEC directives. Crawford observed that there was a big difference between the legal situation and actual practice. For example, he found that Dutch chemical companies were dumping illegally or exporting their wastes without adequate controls, and English chemical companies were mixing their chemical waste with domestic waste in landfills or dumping it into the sea. One of the goals for the Year of the Environment, which the European Community designated 1987, is to get local authorities in the different countries in the EEC to develop cooperative efforts toward harmonization of hazardous waste management practices and laws (Rich, 1986). The March 20, 1978, directive required the development of hazardous waste management programs in the member countries. However, the directive permits the individual countries to specify the quantities or concentrations that constitute a risk to health or the environment, which in actuality results in substantially different policies in each of the member countries.

Also, according to Louis Jourdan of the European Council of Chemical Manufacturers' Federations (Rich, 1986), the different countries allow chemical companies to choose waste disposal methods themselves. The Organization for Economic Cooperation and Development partially addressed this problem by narrowing the definition of what constitutes a hazardous waste through six criteria covering conditions of disposal, destination, generic type, constituents, origin, and characteristics. A further complication identified by Laurie Rich in a discussion of the need for a global accord on hazardous waste is the variation from one country to another in their fundamental approaches to waste management. For example, some countries like the United Kingdom rely primarily on land disposal while others such as Denmark and Sweden prefer thermal destruction of wastes.

Despite the rather uneven record of compliance with international environmental standards, organizations such as the Commission of European Communities and the Organization for Economic Cooperation and Development provide important means to overcome the differences in the institutional and legal systems of individual countries that can hinder the developement of effective hazardous waste management programs. Bernd Wolbeck (1983) has noted that such supranational assistance helps countries overcome the institutional barriers that have evolved over time. In addition, the existence of hazardous waste control regulations or guidelines imposed from above may relieve the individual governments from a certain amount of political accountability for those regulations. In short, the cross-institutional and intergovernmental nature of hazardous waste problems may have helped to shape the structure and organization of government efforts to control hazardous waste.

POLICY FORMULATION PATTERNS

Western Europeans give a high priority to environmental protection policy. In a 1982 survey of representative national samples in the member states of the Commission of the European Communities, citizens indicated that environmental protection was to be given priority treatment even in the face of price instability and economic growth (Commission of European Communities, 1982a). An examination of specific policy areas revealed that hazardous waste disposal was one of the more salient issues. Only damage to sea life and beaches from oil tanker spills or discharges were ranked higher than the disposal of industrial chemicals. The disposal of nuclear waste was a close third. This high level of concern may account for the ambitious hazardous waste management policies that have been initiated and implemented in selected Western European countries over the past several years. In those countries willing to invest the necessary resources, bold and innovative steps have been taken toward the development of policies for the proper handling of hazardous waste from its inception to ultimate disposal. On the basis of a tour of Europe's hazardous waste facilities, Bruce Piasecki and Gary Davis (1984) concluded that Denmark and West Germany were the leading Western European countries in the development of innovative hazardous waste management systems with

Sweden, Finland, Austria, Norway, and the Netherlands following their lead. Table 12.1 lists the hazardous waste management laws established in several Western European countries.

The general management patterns across these countries include subsidies tied to strict regulations, strict control of hazardous wastes, central collection via multiple collection sites, standards for on-site handling, transportation controls, strict monitoring, government ownership in those countries with the more successful programs, and a general emphasis on technological approaches as opposed to landfill operations. One pattern that has emerged on the negative side, however, is that some countries with lax regulations have become havens for hazardous wastes, resulting in the need for tightened transboundary transportation regulations. A prime example of this behavior can be found in East Germany, where they charge

Table 12.1
Hazardous Waste Laws in Selected Western European Countries

Country	Formal Hazardous Waste Law	Date
Belgium	Law on Toxic Waste	1974 (July 22)
Denmark	Law on Disposal of Waste Oils and Chemicals	1972 (May 24)
	Order No. 121 on Chemical Waste	1976 (March 7)
Finland	Waste Management Act	1978 (August 31)
France	Law on Waste Disposal and Recovery of Materials	1975 (July 15)
	Decree on Special Waste	1977 (October 12)
Greece	None	
Ireland	Regulation No. 33 on Toxic and Hazardous Waste	1982
Italy	Waste Disposal Act	1982 (September 10)
Luxembourg	Regulation on Toxic and Hazardous Waste	1982 (June 18)
Netherlands	Chemical Waste Act	1976 (February 11)
Norway	Pollution Control Act	1983 (October 1)
Spain	None	
Sweden	Ordinance No. 346 on Environmentally Hazardous Waste	1975 (May 22)
Switzerland	Law on Environmental Protection	1983 (October 7)
	Ordinance on Trade in Toxic Substances	1983 (September 19)
United Kingdom	Deposit of Poisonous Waste Act	1972 (March 30)
	Control of Pollution Act Regulation No. 1709 on Special Waste	1980 (October 30)
West Germany	Waste Disposal Act	1972 (June 7)
	Administrative Order on Special Waste	1977 (May 24)
	Administrative Order on Notification of Waste	1974 (July 29)
	Administrative Order on Waste Transport	1983 (August 24)

Source: Organization for Economic Cooperation and Development 1984; European Environmental Bureau 1981; and personal communication with the respective national environmental agencies.

less for disposals. In 1983, 300,000 tons were sent from West Germany and 40,000 tons from the Netherlands to East Germany for disposal (Smets, 1985). Some West Germans are particularly irritated with this situation because of the threats associated with the increased traffic in hazardous wastes across their borders en route to East Germany and potential groundwater flow problems back toward West Germany. The OECD estimates that a shipment of toxic wastes crosses a European border an average of once every five minutes (Marsh, 1987).

POLICY IMPLEMENTATION PATTERNS

There appears to be considerable variance across Western European countries with regard to their ability to attain statutory objectives related to hazardous waste control. On paper, several of the countries appear to possess the necessary political mechanisms to achieve the goals and objectives of a good hazardous waste management policy. As noted above, Denmark, France, the Netherlands, and the United Kingdom have developed highly significant legislation, while other countries like Belgium, Italy, and Portugal are significantly behind in efforts to deal with this critical ecological management issue. But even the more advanced countries often find it difficult to meet stated policy objectives. Although the French have established one of the more comprehensive collections of laws and regulations for the control of hazardous waste, their success in controlling hazardous waste has been somewhat constrained by a relatively poor implementation of both their own laws and the regulations of the EEC. The principal difficulty may lie in the reluctance of key French officials in the central government to acknowledge the severity of the hazardous waste management problem. Since support from high-level officials is one of the key elements of a successful policy implementation effort, this attitude may affect the implementation efforts at the local level, especially in a highly centralized government such as France. In contrast, the West German approach is characterized by a combination of federal guidelines and local initiatives that shape hazardous waste control policies. The key elements in this approach are the Waste Disposal Law (*Abfallbeseitigungsgesetz*) of 1977, a public-private cooperative management effort, and government subsidies. The Waste Disposal Law assigns all waste management responsibility to the federal government, which then delegates implementation authority to the various state governments. By 1980, five out of ten of the state governments of West Germany had used their authority to establish "joint-venture companies" for the processing of hazardous waste (Jerabek, 1981). The state governments provide extensive subsidies to ensure proper handling of wastes. Bavaria, for example, funds approximately 50% of the waste treatment and recycling activities. As the work of Mazmanian and Sabatier (1983) on policy implementation clearly illustrates, the key to successful implementation lies in the way in which a particular statute structures implementation to maximize the probability of compliance from implementing officials and target groups. The *Abfallbeseitigungsgesetz* accomplishes this successfully by (1) assigning authority to a sympathetic agency—the Environmental Division of the Ministry of the Interior; (2) establishing a hierarchically integrated system—general guidance from the federal level with specific authority delegated to the state governments (*Länder*), which delegate that authority where appropriate to local governments; (3) delegating specific authority to the state governments, which provides additional power to their decision rules of these primary implementing agencies; and (4) providing financial resources through a "polluter-pays-principle" tax on hazardous waste generators which is supplemented by state government resources. Through these specific features the statute itself facilitates the implementation of policies for the control of hazardous wastes in West Germany. The most successful example of hazardous waste management policy implementation appears to be the policies established by the government of Denmark. Denmark has developed a nationwide hazardous waste management control system emphasizing national standards which are implemented by local governments. Two key elements in Denmark's control system are a major fiscal subsidy and an extensive network of collection sites combined with a centrally located processing facility (Piasecki and Davis, 1984). The focal point of the Danish network of collection sites is a quasi-public corporation that was initiated by the national government but is now somewhat self-supporting through fees charged to industrial firms that do not choose to (or cannot) process hazardous waste on-site at their plant locations. Kommunekemi A/S provides a central processing plant in Nyborg to process the waste funneled to it from various satellite collection sites strategically located around the country. The national regulations require all firms to either use the Kommunekemi system or process waste on-site at their plants in order to minimize the distance hazardous waste must be transported. For those firms that are given permission to process their wastes on-site, the Danish government provides up to a 15% subsidy to support those efforts (Piasecki and Davis, 1984). An evaluation of the Danish system of hazardous waste management demonstrates that it also does particularly well in meeting the conditions for effective policy implementation as described by Mazmanian and Sabatier. The Danish laws identify and provide jurisdiction over sufficient policy factors to establish ample potential for the attainment of objectives. The Kommunekemi A/S, which is owned by the Association of Danish Cities, is a quasi-public agency that is both sympathetic and supportive. The nodal collection system that provides input into the central collection facility establishes a highly integrated hierarchical system that also provides adequate financial incentives for participants, with the central government establishing the overall policy guidelines and each participating municipality owning the nodal collection site. Through this organization the country is provided with a cadre of implementing officials who are highly skilled in hazardous waste management techniques. Due to the public-private interaction and economic subsidies that facilitate participation by the private sector, support for the Kommunekemi system tends to exist across constituency groups as well as the sovereign government. Further support is derived from the decentralization principle of Danish environmental legislation, whereby local authorities are usually given approval authority over local environmental standards (Kampmann, 1984). Collectively, all of these features have made the Danish system one of the best in the world. In November 1985 the Swedish government followed the Danish lead by enacting a law that requires all hazardous waste to be sent for destruction to a central processing facility by the name of SAKAB or another state-approved facility (Rich, 1986).

In spite of the concerted efforts of the leading countries, the disposal of hazardous waste continues to remain a major difficulty for all Western European countries. Part of the problem is the tremendous volume of hazardous wastes in relation to the number and capacity of facilities available for their treatment. By 1981, there were 170 hazardous waste incinerator units located throughout Western Europe with a total capacity rated at 6 million tons per year (Crawford, 1981). This capacity is simply not enough in light of the production of an estimated 20 million tons of toxic and dangerous waste each year in the European Community.

ANALYSIS

Table 12.1 indicates that there has been a varied response to the hazardous waste pollution problem in selected Western European countries. As a dependent variable, the presence of a formal hazardous waste law poses an interesting policy question. What are some of the independent variables that contribute to an explanation for the presence or absence of a legally established hazardous waste management control program in any particular country? Ten independent variables were examined in an attempt to develop some measures of association with the dependent variable in the form of a formal hazardous waste management law. A resource measure (Table 12.2) was obtained by examining the per capita gross national product, population size, and level of environmental concern (the latter for EEC countries, based on a 1982 survey) for each country. A technological measure (Table 12.2) was obtained by examining the extent of the contribution of industry to the gross domestic product, and for selected OECD countries, the annual total and per capita hazardous waste generation was used. Finally, an administrative-organizational support measure (Table 12.3) was derived by determining whether each country had an environmen-

Table 12.2

Resource and Technological Characteristics of Selected Western European Countries

Country	Resource Characteristics			Technological Characteristics		
	Population (mid-1981)[a] (thousands)	GNP (US $)[b] Per Capita	Environmental[c] Concern	Percent Industrial[d] Activity in Gross Domestic Product	Annual Hazardous[e] Waste Generation (Million Tonnes)	Annual[e] Kg Per Capita Hazardous Waste
Belgium	9,861	11,920	81	29%	na	na
Denmark	5,122	13,210	92	18%	.060	12
Finland	4,801	10,680	na	29%	.087	18
France	53,963	12,190	93	29%	2.000	38
Greece	9,707	4,420	88	20%	na	na
Ireland	3,440	5,230	85	26%	na	na
Italy	56,223	6,960	92	35%	na	na
Luxembourg	364	15,910	96	33%	na	na
Netherlands	14,246	11,790	98	26%	.280	20
Norway	4,100	14,060	na	34%	.120	30
Spain	37,973	5,640	na	29%	na	na
Sweden	8,324	14,870	na	25%	.520	63
Switzerland	6,473	17,430	na	na	.093	15
United Kingdom	56,005	9,110	95	29%	1.500	27
West Germany	61,666	13,450	96	36%	4.5-5.0	80

Source: a) World Bank, 1984; b) World Bank, 1984; c) Commission of European Communities, 1982; d) United Nations, 1983, e) Organization for Economic Cooperation and Development, 1984.

Table 12.3
Administrative-Organizational Characteristics of Selected Western
European Countries

Country	Formal National Environmental Agency[a]	Environmental Assessment Procedure[b]	General Environmental Law (pre-1979)[c]
Belgium	None	Informal	No
Denmark	Ministry of Environmental Affairs	Informal	1973
Finland	Department of Environmental Protection	No	No
France	Ministry of Environmental Protection	Informal	1976
Greece	None	No	1976
Ireland	Department of the Environment	Informal	1976
Italy	Ministry of Culture and Environmental Quality	No	No
Luxembourg	Ministry of the Environment	Informal	No
Netherlands	Ministry of Health and Environment	Formal	No
Norway	Ministry of the Environment	No	No
Spain	Ministry of Public Works and Urbanism	No	No
Sweden	National Environmental Protection Agency	Informal	1969
Switzerland	Department of the Environment	Informal	No
United Kingdom	Department of the Environment	Informal	1974
West Germany	Division of Environmental Protection	Informal	No

Source: a) Andrews and Natkin (World Environment Center), 1983; and correspondence with the respective national environmental agencies; b) Burton, 1983; and correspondence with the respective national environmental agencies; c) Organization of Economic Cooperation and Development, 1979.

tal impact assessment procedure, a formal national environmental agency, a pre-1979 general environmental law, and a pre-1979 waste law. The pre-1979 laws were examined in an attempt to insert a time dimension to the strength of the environmental concerns in each country. A simplified analytical procedure was used in an attempt to ascertain the general extent to which the various independent variables may have contributed to the dependent variable (Table 12.4). A mean value for each variable was determined, and each country was assigned a plus or minus for that item on

Table 12.4
Country/Variable Matrix

Country	1	2	3	F1	4	5	6	7	F2	8	9	10	F3	T	D
Belgium	+	−	−	−1	+	−	−	+	0	+	na	na	1	0	Yes
Denmark	+	−	+	1	+	+	+	+	4	−	−	−	−3	2	Yes
Finland	−	−	na	−2	−	+	−	+	0	+	−	−	−1	−3	Yes
France	+	+	+	3	+	+	+	+	4	+	+	+	3	10	Yes
Greece	−	−	−	−3	−	−	+	−	−2	−	na	na	−1	−6	No
Ireland	−	−	−	−3	+	+	+	+	4	−	na	na	−1	0	Yes
Italy	−	+	+	1	−	−	−	−	−4	+	na	na	1	−2	Yes
Luxembourg	+	na	+	2	+	+	−	−	0	+	na	na	1	3	Yes
Netherlands	+	−	+	1	+	+	−	+	2	−	−	−	−3	0	Yes
Norway	+	−	na	0	−	+	−	−	−2	+	−	−	−1	−3	Yes
Spain	−	+	na	0	−	−	−	+	−2	−	na	na	−1	−3	No*
Sweden	+	−	na	0	+	+	+	+	4	−	−	+	−1	3	Yes
Switzerland	+	−	+	1	+	+	−	−	0	na	−	−	−2	−1	Yes
United Kingdom	−	+	+	1	+	+	+	+	4	+	+	−	1	3	Yes
West Germany	+	+	+	3	+	+	−	+	2	+	+	+	3	7	Yes

Explanation of column headings:

F1 = Resource factor total;
F2 = Administrative-Organizational factor total;
F3 = Technological factor total;
T = factor total;
D = dependent variable (i.e., presence of hazardous waste law);
 1 = GNP per capita (World Bank, 1983);
 2 = Population mid-1981 (World Bank, 1983);
 3 = Environmental Concern (based on Commission of European Communities 1982 survey);
 4 = Environmental Impact Assessment Procedure (Burton, 1983; Organization for Economic Cooperation and Development, 1979; and personal communication with the respective national environmental agencies;
 5 = Formal National Environmental Agency (Andrews and Natkin (World Environment Center), 1983; and personal communication with the respective national environmental agencies;
 6 = Pre-1979 General Environmental Law (Organization for Economic Cooperation and Development, 1979);
 7 = Pre-1979 Waste Law (Organization for Economic Cooperation and Development, 1979);
 8 = Percent of Industrial Activity in Gross Domestic Product (United Nations, 1983);
 9 = Annual Total Hazardous Waste Generation (Organization for Economic Cooperation and Development, 1984);
10 = Per Capita Hazardous Waste Generation (Organization for Economic Cooperation and Development, 1984).

Key:
+ = greater than mean value for variable;
− = less than mean value for variable;
na = not available and not applicable for Luxembourg due to small population size;
* = Catalonia enacted an Industrial Waste Act in 1983 (OECD 1984).

the basis of whether the mean value was exceeded or not. Analysis of the data for specific patterns revealed few consistent relationships between the variables. However, some associations appear to exist between certain variables for the countries that have been reputed to have the more promising hazardous waste management programs. For example, those countries with a higher combined score for the resource and administrative-organizational variables (France, Denmark, West Germany, United Kingdom, the Netherlands, and Sweden) seem to have the more advanced management policies based on their legislative and regulatory initiatives. Furthermore, those countries with the greatest reported per capital volume of hazardous waste (West Germany, France, and Sweden) have enacted some of the stronger hazardous waste management laws. One could interpret these limited findings to indicate that those countries that have greater individual wealth may tend to be better organized and, hence, more likely to produce advanced policy approaches. Furthermore, those countries with the greatest volume of hazardous waste may also be more inclined, out of necessity, to adopt formal mechanisms to deal with the problems. Some of the less economically well-off countries like Greece and Italy are low on most of the variables, and this is reflected in the lack of a formal hazardous waste management law. Fortunately, as mentioned earlier, some of the variance between policy approaches adopted by individual countries is being reduced through the concerted efforts of supranational organizations like the Commission of European Communities and the Organization for Economic Cooperation and Development via the development of uniform hazardous waste management policy approaches.

SUMMARY AND CONCLUSION

Why do some countries appear to be more successful in dealing with hazardous waste management problems than other countries? The answer to this question seems to be related to the technological, resource, and administrative-organizational pressures placed upon the policy formulation and implementation processes in respective countries. Those countries that are noted for their strong records in formulating environmental legislation appear to be more successful in implementing effective policies, for example, Denmark, the Netherlands, and West Germany. This would tend to support the Mazmanian and Sabatier (1983) contention that statutes structure the implementation process and that implementation success is closely related. However, the formulation of strong laws and regulations is not sufficient to guarantee successful policy implementation. There is considerable variation among economic and social conditions and organizational structures to confound the best plans conceivable. In a recent assessment of the political implications of hazardous waste management, Bernd Wolbeck (1983) ascertained that "after having introduced strong regulatory control mechanisms for proper hazardous waste disposal, most of the industrialized countries experience serious difficulties in offering waste generators sufficient technical and practical options (facilities) for them to treat their waste in the way required by laws and regulation." Of all of the countries reviewed in the foregoing analysis, Denmark appears to be the only possible exception to this glaring weakness. No other country has such a complete system of hazardous waste management firmly predicated upon laws and regulations. The Danish system provides for collection of hazardous waste close to its origin in households, farms, and industries; storage in nodal collection sites, and transportation to a centrally located collection facility for final processing in a timely and efficient manner. On a subnational level, the West German state of Bavaria appears to offer a similarly efficient system. In both examples, there is a presence of strong regulations, extensive handling and processing facilities, and economic incentives to industries to facilitate their participation in the approved waste disposal systems. In sum, both of these systems reflect a commitment to the objective of effective hazardous waste management from public officials throughout all levels of government, a necessary prerequisite for successful policy implementation.

REFERENCES

Andrews, S., and M. Natkin, *World Environment Handbook: A Directory of Government Natural Resource Management Agencies in 144 Countries* (New York: World Environment Center, 1983).

Burton, I., "Environmental Impact Assessment: National Approaches and International Needs," *Environmental Monitoring and Assessment* 3 (1983): 133-150.

Butlin, J., *A Study of the Hazardous Waste Activities in NATO Member Countries Following Completion of the Pilot Study: Final Report Prepared for the Ministry of the Interior, Federal Republic of Germany* (Bonn: Ministry of the Interior, 1983).

Commission of European Communities. *The European and the Environment* (Brussels: Directorate General for the Environment, 1982a).

_____, *Present Situation Concerning the Disposal of Toxic and Dangerous Wastes in the Community, Implementation of Directive 78/319 and Future Actions, XI/338/82-EN* (Brussels: Directorate General for the Environment, 1982b).

Cope, C. B., W. H. Fuller, and S. L. Willets, *The Scientific Management of Hazardous Wastes* (Cambridge: Cambridge University Press, 1983).

Crawford, P. J., "The OECD Approach to Chemicals Control," in European Environmental Bureau, *Report of an International Workshop on Toxic Substances, Bonn, September 6-8, 1981* (Brussels).

Defregger, F. "European Experiences on Disposal of Industrial Hazardous Wastes," In S. K. Subramanian, ed., (Tokyo: Asian Productivity Organization, 1983).

Dye, T., *Politics, Economics, and the Public* (Chicago, IL: Rand McNally, 1968).

European Environmental Bureau, *Report of an International Workshop on Toxic Substances, Bonn, September 6-8, 1981* (Brussels).

Hofferbert, R., "Elite Influences in State Policy Formation: A Model for Comparative Inquiry," *Polity 2* (1970):316-326.

Hunter, D., "A Dirty Word in West Germany," *Chemical Week* 140 (1987):14.

International Environmental Law Reporter, 1984a, 7, 8.

_____, 1984b, 7, 104.

Jerabek, S., *An American Appraisal of Hazardous Waste Management in Europe, Report to the German Marshall Fund and Institute for European Environmental Policy* (Washington, DC: German Marshall Fund, 1981).

Jones, C. O., *An Introduction to the Study of Public Policy*, 3rd ed. (Monterey, CA: Brooks/Cole, 1984).

Kampmann, J., "Benefits from and Problems Experienced with the Danish Hazardous Waste Management System," in Chemcontrol A/S, *2nd International Symposium on Operating European Centralized Hazardous (Chemical) Waste Management Facilities, Odense, Denmark* (Copenhagen: National Agency of Environmental Protection, 1984).

Lester, J. P., J. L. Franke, A. O. Bowman, and K. W. Kramer, "A Comparative Perspective on State Hazardous Waste Regulation," in J. P. Lester and A. O. Bowman, eds., *The Politics of Hazardous Waste Management* (Durham, NC: Duke University Press, 1983).

Marsh, D., "Beyond the Spill on the Rhine," *World Press Review* 34 (1987) 1:50.

Mazmanian, D. A., and P. A. Sabatier, *Implementation and Public Policy* (Glenview, IL: Scott, Foresman and Company, 1983).

North Atlantic Treaty Organization, Committee on the Challenges of Modern Society, *Disposal of Hazardous Wastes: Recommended Procedures for Hazardous Waste Management, Report No. 62* (Brussels, 1977).

Organization for Economic Cooperation and Development, *The State of the Environment in OECD Member Countries* (Paris, 1979).

_____, *Identification of Responsibilities in Hazardous Waste Management*, ENV/WMP/83.11 (Paris, 1984).

Piasecki, B., "Europe's Detoxification Arsenals: Lessons in Waste Recovery and Exchange," in B. Piasecki, ed., *Beyond Dumping* (Westport, CT: Greenwood Press, 1984).

_____. and G. A. Davis, "A Grand Tour of Europe's Hazardous-Waste Facilities," *Technology Review* 26 (1984) 7:20-29.

_____, and J. Gravander, "The Missing Links: Restructuring Hazardous Waste Controls in America," *Technology Review* 88 (1985) 7:43-52.

Rich, L., "Waste Regulators Seek Global Accord," *Chemical Week* 139 (1986) 10:20-24.

Risch, B., "Toxic and Dangerous Waste in the European Community," in *European Conference on Waste Management, 17-19 June, 1980* (London, 1980).

Smets, H., "Transfrontier Movements of Hazardous Wastes—An Examination of the Council Decision and Recommendation," *Environmental Policy and Law* 14 (1985):16-21.

Szelinski, B. A., "Hazardous Waste Legislation/Organization," in P. Lehman, ed., *Hazardous Waste Disposal* (New York: Plenum Press, 1983).

United Nations, *United Nations Yearbook of National Accounts Statistics* (New York, 1983).

Walker, J. L., "The Diffusion of Innovations Among the American States," *American Political Science Review* 63 (1969):860-899.

Whitehead, C. E. C., "Environmental Policy Is Model for Other Nations: Many Are Studying European Toxic-Waste Management Programs," *Europe* 251 (1985):30-31.

Wolbeck, B., "Political Dimensions and Implications of Hazardous Waste Disposal," in J. P. Lehman, ed., *Hazardous Waste Disposal* (New York: Plenum Press, 1983).

World Bank, *1983 World Bank Atlas: Gross National Product, Population, and Growth Rates* (Washington, DC: World Bank, 1983).

13

Complex Interdependence and Hazardous Waste Management along the U.S.-Mexico Border

Stephen P. Mumme

INTRODUCTION

Hazardous waste management is usually approached from an intranational rather than an international perspective. Hazardous wastes, however, are fugitive resources by nature and not easily confined by national boundaries. Where borders meet, hazardous waste managers must negotiate dissimilar social, economic, political, and administrative systems. This is the case along the U.S.-Mexico border, stretching nearly 2,000 miles from the Pacific coast to the Gulf of Mexico. Here, rapid growth in the last twenty years and stark differences in economic development combine to generate a vast range of actual and potential hazardous waste problems.

It is common to analyze issues in U.S.-Mexican relations through the optic of dependency theory. In this view, Mexico is bound to the United States by a web of economic, social, and strategic relationships that limit its capacity to exert leverage in binational affairs. According to Mario Ojeda, "the structure of the relationship prevents Mexico from negotiating problems with the United States on an equal footing and frequently obliges Mexico to accept unilateral decisions from Washington without alternative" (Ojeda, 1983: 318). Such an assessment of the United States' capacity to exert leverage might lead one to assume that increased interest in hazardous waste regulation in the United States would translate into increased binational attention to these matters along the U.S.-Mexico border.

As the rest of this paper demonstrates, that conclusion is hardly justified. Instead of a dependency relationship defining relations in this sphere, efforts at binational cooperation have been shaped by what Robert O.

Keohane and Joseph S. Nye label mutual dependence, or "complex interdependence" (Keohane and Nye, 1977: 8-9). Under conditions of complex interdependence, nation-states, particularly powerful nation-states, are likely to find themselves strategically constrained in relation to other, less powerful nations due to the proliferation and diversity of relations maintained with these states. As a variant of political realism in international relations, a dependency model stresses the primacy of economic and military power in structuring international relations among states. Complex interdependence, in contrast, emphasizes goal diversity, the specificity of power to discrete issue areas as instruments of state policy, agenda formation shaped by sets of factors operating within discrete issue areas, the diminished efficacy of issue linkage across unlike issue areas, and greater subnational or supranational involvement in foreign-policy making (Table 13.1).

Several of the conditions said to characterize relations of complex interdependence apply rather well to the case of hazardous waste management along the U.S.-Mexico border. First, while there is little doubt of Mexico's economic and strategic dependency on the United States as a global generalization, it is also true that geographic continuity and the pattern of border development make the United States heavily dependent on Mexico for environmental quality along the border. Mexico's very economic dependence, in fact, has reinforced a system of domestic policy priorities favoring economic growth at the expense of environmental quality, with spillover effects on U.S. border communities. Attaining the goal of environmental improvement, therefore, is not a function of global economic or security relations between Mexico and the United States. In fact, these goals may be directly in conflict.

Second, because this is so, a solution must be approached discretely, tailoring the means employed to address the unique requirements of this issue area. Both the agenda and the means, in short, are shaped by conditions largely internal to the issue area and only loosely related to the dominant priorities of binational relations.

Third, it follows that issue linkage is not likely to prove effective for eliciting Mexico's cooperation in addressing these problems. In this issue area the record shows that Mexico has been able to resist direct U.S. pressures to step up domestic regulation of hazardous wastes and continues to pursue its own national priorities in border development. While this is not to say some linkages may not be conducive to cooperative behavior, the efficacy of these linkages cannot be assumed without careful examination of the options and means most appropriate to the case at hand. Such linkages are apt to be most effective if they tie together very similar types of problems within an issue area.

Finally, within this issue area it is clear that nonstate actors, in this case border states and communities, have played a significant role in prodding

Table 13.1*

Dependence and Complex Interdependence Political Process Assumptions Compared

	Dependence	Complex Interdependence
Goals:	Economic hegemony and military superiority are overriding goals of states.	Goals are diverse and vary by issue area.
Means:	Military force undergirds security relations; economic power employed to attain and maintain hegemony over other states.	Means of state policy vary as appropriate to specific issue areas.
Agenda:	Potential shifts in the balance of power, and security threats (including threats to economic security), set the agenda in high politics and strongly influence other agendas.	Agenda is shaped by conditions internal to the issue areas under consideration.
Issue Links:	Inter-issue linkages reduce differences in outcomes and reinforce international hierarchy.	Linking unlike issues may exaggerate outcome differences and prove ineffective as means of goal attainment.
Non-State Actors Roles:	Little role for non-state actors.	Non-state actors may play significant role in foreign policy depending on the issue.

*Table adapted from Robert O. Keohane and Joseph S. Nye, *Power and Interdependence: World Politics in Transition* (Boston: Little, Brown, 1977), 37.

national governments to act on transboundary hazards problems and have helped shape the outcomes of agreements in force.

This chapter profiles this interdependent relationship and some of its implications for bilateral diplomacy and cooperation in hazardous waste management. It begins with an overview of the range of hazardous waste situations along the U.S.-Mexico border, following with a discussion of domestic and bilateral regulatory trends. The implications of interdependence in this policy sphere for diplomacy and future progress are explored in the conclusion.

HAZARDOUS WASTE PROBLEMS ALONG THE U.S.-MEXICO BORDER

Both U.S. and Mexican communities adjoining the international boundary have experienced rapid urban and industrial growth in the last two decades, bringing with it a panoply of hazardous waste problems.

Although there is yet no comprehensive inventory of hazardous waste problems in the border region, the dimensions of the problem are suggested by one study that cited 9,000 identified hazardous waste sites in the nine U.S. and Mexican border states, 1,400 of them uncontrolled (Clarke, 1982: 13-14). In a survey of situations that already present binational problems, the U.S. Environmental Protection Agency (1984) points to the drainage of sewage and industrial wastes into transboundary rivers and streams, pesticide contamination, and problems related to the handling of hazardous substances and hydrocarbons along the international boundary.

Of greatest immediate concern are a range of Mexican sewage problems that threaten U.S. border communities. The failure of Mexican sewage systems and ad hoc dumping of industrial wastes into municipal collection systems frequently results in highly toxic sewage washing across the border. The principal "border sanitation problems" identified by the Environmental Protection Agency (EPA) and the International Boundary and Water Commission (IBWC) are located at San Diego-Tijuana and Calexico-Mexicali on the California-Baja California border, the twin communities of Nogales and Naco along the Arizona-Sonora border, and along the lower Rio Grande (U.S. Environmental Protection Agency, 1984).

Industrial waste and the handling of toxic industrial materials have also surfaced as problems along the border community. The contamination of the San Pedro River by copper tailings at Cananea, Sonora, adversely affected downstream agriculture and wildlife in Arizona in 1977-1978 and again in 1979. Industrial waste is part and parcel of most transboundary sewage problems, perhaps best seen at Calexico-Mexicali, where the New River has a reputation as one of the most contaminated rivers in the United States. The emission of toxic fumes from border industrial facilities has resulted in one well-documented case of mass lead poisoning in the city of Tijuana (Gross, 1983).

The fugitive export of industrial pollutants has also surfaced as a problem along the border. To cite one such case, a U.S. citizen was indicted by Mexican officials in 1981 for illegally dumping 160 drums of chemical waste, including 42 drums of PCBs, in the state of Zacatecas (Applegate and Bath, 1983: 233). More recently, in Febraury 1986, Mexican environmental officials discovered the illegal dumping of 10,000 gallons of heavy hydrocarbons and other toxic wastes at a rural community along the border near the Mexican city of Tecate, Baja California Norte, which is entirely dependent on groundwater for its water supply. In this case, several U.S. companies were identified as having sold the wastes to an unlicensed Tijuana recycling company found responsible for the incident (Briseno, 1986: B-1; McLaren and Romero, 1986: A-3). San Diego County officials believe such cases of illegal waste disposal are on the increase along the border (McLaren and Romero, 1986: A-3).

Finally, a range of pesticide hazards are found along the border. The

since 1978 that better the outlook
hazardous wastes along the border.
mplete and suffer shortfalls in
are the aforementioned differences
by the severe economic crisis in
e differences related to the costs,
ts, and the timing of abatement
ding to participate in binational
peen less forthcoming with actual
rs as *problemas cotidianas*, or day-
the other hand, has been reluctant
border communities and impose
compliance.

blems in binational regulation of
current dilemma. Presently, the
hest advanced in the area of water-
reinterpretation of language in the
h charges the IBWC to undertake
hay be mutually agreed upon by the
ntial attention to the solution of all
261 of the IBWC, concluded in
ng of that language to extend to all
oject to the conclusion of specific
ds in the case of each mutually
1'' along the boundary (Mumme,

C has sought specific solutions to
roblems. An agreement specifying a
New River at Mexicali-Calexico,
at agreement Mexico agreed to meet
lew River as it crossed the border in
channel sewage away from the New
Agency, 1984). Mexico, however,
or implementing the agreement due,
ic troubles.

ion problems have also been elusive.
Tijuana's municipal sewage system
drain from arroyos and streets into
ernational boundary into the United
as contaminated water supplies and
uth San Diego County, with severe
ually all of San Diego's beaches as far
ed for a period of eight months. By
ion was designated the most serious

widespread use of a number of highly toxic pesticides in Mexican agriculture has resulted in several U.S. embargoes on Mexican citrus and vegetable products destined for the winter vegetable market (Chimely, 1984: 5-A). The extent to which these chemicals pose dangers to consumers is difficult to ascertain since effective diagnostics are not available for all the pesticides currently in use (Applegate and Bath, 1983).

DEPENDENCY EFFECTS ON HAZARDOUS WASTE MANAGEMENT ALONG THE BORDER

Regulation of hazardous wastes along the border reflects the sharp economic differential between the two countries. This regulatory disparity may be treated as a "dependency effect," a product of differing national priorities arising from dissimilar levels of economic development, grounded in asymmetrical economic relations between the two countries. From this perspective, Mexico's dependency on the United States for trade and investment is a function of its comparative geographic and labor advantages harnessed to a strategy of rapid economic development. Mexico's comparative advantages in the U.S. market, however, are marginal compared to those of other developing nations. The external costs of environmental regulation further diminish its competitive edge. Coupled with a paucity of material, technical, and administrative resources, Mexico's economic dependency is a strong disincentive weighing against positive measures to regulate hazardous wastes.

Evidence for the dependency hypothesis and its effects on Mexican regulatory policy affecting hazardous wastes is seen in the case of the binational Border Industrialization Program, ongoing since 1965. Under this program U.S. firms receive special tariff advantages for locating in Mexican border communities. Over 600 U.S. companies employing almost a quarter million workers are involved in this program, which is part of a special Mexican policy promoting industrialization in border states (Williams, forthcoming). In addition to the tariff and labor advantages, part of the attractiveness of locating in Mexico is fewer regulations on the use of the factors of production. Export-oriented firms employing toxics in the production process have taken advantage of this situation. "Fugitive polluters" include several asbestos manufacturers and industries using carcinogeous substances like lindane, chlordane, polychlorinated biphenyls, trichlorethylene, hydrofluoric acid, and other chemicals. Disposal of such toxics is presently unregulated. They are commonly dumped on an ad hoc basis in municipal sewage collection systems, municipal landfills, or private property sites, with all the attendant health risks.

A brief review of environmental regulation in Mexico will amplify this point. Mexico's environmental legislation is constitutionally well advanced. Responsibility for regulation and enforcement is centralized at the national level. Under the 1982 Federal Environmental Protection Law and 1984 amendments, regulations are spelled out in spheres of air, water, marine, and soil contamination that affect hazardous wastes. Article 21 of the 1984 amendments prohibits the untreated discharge of contaminated wastewater; Article 34 prohibits the "unauthorized discharge, deposit, or infiltration of contamination into the soil" and charges the Secretaria de Dessarollo Urbano y Ecologia (SEDUE) to develop guidelines for hazardous waste disposal. Article 76 specifies sanctions for noncompliance (*Diario Official*, 1984: 30).

Evidence of enforcement is slight, however. The Mexican government has not yet issued implementing legislation—known in Mexico as a *reglamento*, or regulatory law—specifying standards and procedures in the area of soil contamination. In other spheres enforcement has been haphazard to nonexistent. In 1976 the government shut a silica mine in the state of Hidalgo after sixty workers were reported to have died of job-related pulmonary diseases (*Uno Mas Uno*, 1984: 22). Subsequently, in another regulatory action in 1981, the Mexican government closed down several factories in the states of Hidalgo, Mexico, and the Federal District for failing to reduce the pollutants they emitted (*Comercio Exterior*, 1981: 93). A canvass of all articles dealing with environmental subjects in Mexico's leading newspaper, *Excelsior*, for a period of twelve months (January–December 1984) revealed only twenty-five reports of enforcement activities ranging from investigations and warnings to fines (Table 13.2). Only eight instances of actual sanctions were reported.

Nor do Mexico's environmental administrators see themselves in a regulatory role. In an interview with the Mexico City daily *Uno Mas Uno* in May 1984, the undersecretary of ecology in SEDUE, Alicia Barcena, states, "we don't view ourselves discharging a regulatory function" (Weiser, 1984). Instead, as she went on to point out, SEDUE's priorities are those of identifying problem areas, developing an inventory of hazards, and attempting to develop low-cost planning solutions that avoid creating such hazards in future development, while working with the public and private sector to encourage voluntary compliance with environmental standards. Clearly, economic objectives take precedence over regulation. In June 1984 Barcena's department authorized re-opening the Hidalgo silica mine justifying that action on employment grounds despite protests that little corrective action had been taken (*Uno Mas Uno*, 1984: 22).

In sum, the regulation of environment hazards has not yet attained a high priority on the Mexican policy agenda and is still very much subordinate to national development priorities. At its present stage of policy development, however, one can safely say that Mexico has placed environmental policy on its national policy agenda and is gradually moving toward greater definition in law and administrative procedure of its environmental policy standards. Seen from a policy systemic perspective, however, it is not yet committed to the regulatory aspects of policy implementation.

bilateral agreements have been r for cooperative binational regula As yet, however, they remai implementation. Complicating pr in national policy priorities exag Mexico since 1982. Specifically, the apportionment of costs and projects. While Mexico has be solutions at the symbolic level, regulation, preferring to treat thes to-day problems. The United Stat to adopt the frequent suggestio economic sanctions to induce Me

A brief review of progress ar hazardous wastes is indicative binational regulatory framework related hazards. This is so due to 1944 U.S.-Mexico Water Treaty, "any sanitary measures or works two governments" and to "give p border sanitation problems." M September 1979, broadened the m classes of water pollution hazarc agreements on solutions and sta identified "border sanitation pr 1981).

Acting on this mandate, the several water-related hazardous wa solution to the contamination o Minute 264, was signed in 1980. B fixed water quality standards for t the short run and in the longer ter River (U.S. Environmental Prote has been unable to meet the sched in part, to its severe domestic eco

Agreements on other border san At Tijuana-San Diego, the failure regularly caused highly toxic sewag the Tijuana River as it crosses the States. Since 1980 regular spillage beaches in the estuarine region of economic consequences. In 1983, v north as Point Loma were quaran mid-1983, the Tijuana sewage situ

Table 13.2
Government Actions Reported in Excelsior, 1984*

Type of Government Action	Total Number
A. Education	7
B. Study	14
C. Regulatory action	105
a. fine	6
b. closure	2
c. sanction/threat	8
d. investigation	9
e. policy announcement	43
f. investment	23
g. other	14
D. Planning	6
E. Foreign Relations (U.S.A.)	17
F. Lack of Resources	6
G. Inter-agency affairs	5
H. Other	14
TOTAL ACTIONS	174

*Each article was coded as a discrete report, hence it is possible that a single action event was coded more than once.

Lax regulation, on the other hand, has both direct and indirect effects on U.S. border communities. As hazardous waste spills across the border, its management is contingent on bilateral regulatory cooperation. Such cooperation is difficult to achieve, however, illustrating the way dependence in the larger bilateral relationship is transformed into interdependence in this issue area.

INTERDEPENDENCE AND BINATIONAL REGULATION OF HAZARDOUS WASTES

Along the U.S.-Mexico border, the rapid growth of border communities has been accompanied by proliferating environmental hazards. Hazards with binational effects originate on both sides of the international frontier. However, greater public sensitivity to environmental problems coupled with higher regulatory standards and better domestic enforcement mean that most of the impetus for binational regulatory action emanates from the United States. Since the mid-1970s, the proliferation of transnational hazards originating in Mexico has intensified U.S. border communities' demands for abatement of these hazards. That, in turn, has led to intensified U.S. diplomacy aimed at ameliorating these conditions through unilateral (Mexican) or bilateral solutions.

These diplomatic initiatives have met with limited success. A number of bilateral agreements have been reached since 1978 that better the outlook for cooperative binational regulation of hazardous wastes along the border. As yet, however, they remain incomplete and suffer shortfalls in implementation. Complicating progress are the aforementioned differences in national policy priorities exaggerated by the severe economic crisis in Mexico since 1982. Specifically, there are differences related to the costs, the apportionment of costs and benefits, and the timing of abatement projects. While Mexico has been willing to participate in binational solutions at the symbolic level, it has been less forthcoming with actual regulation, preferring to treat these matters as *problemas cotidianas,* or day-to-day problems. The United States, on the other hand, has been reluctant to adopt the frequent suggestions of border communities and impose economic sanctions to induce Mexican compliance.

A brief review of progress and problems in binational regulation of hazardous wastes is indicative of the current dilemma. Presently, the binational regulatory framework is furthest advanced in the area of water-related hazards. This is so due to recent reinterpretation of language in the 1944 U.S.-Mexico Water Treaty, which charges the IBWC to undertake "any sanitary measures or works that may be mutually agreed upon by the two governments" and to "give preferential attention to the solution of all border sanitation problems." Minute 261 of the IBWC, concluded in September 1979, broadened the meaning of that language to extend to all classes of water pollution hazards subject to the conclusion of specific agreements on solutions and standards in the case of each mutually identified "border sanitation problem" along the boundary (Mumme, 1981).

Acting on this mandate, the IBWC has sought specific solutions to several water-related hazardous waste problems. An agreement specifying a solution to the contamination of the New River at Mexicali-Calexico, Minute 264, was signed in 1980. By that agreement Mexico agreed to meet fixed water quality standards for the New River as it crossed the border in the short run and in the longer term to channel sewage away from the New River (U.S. Environmental Protection Agency, 1984). Mexico, however, has been unable to meet the schedule for implementing the agreement due, in part, to its severe domestic economic troubles.

Agreements on other border sanitation problems have also been elusive. At Tijuana-San Diego, the failure of Tijuana's municipal sewage system regularly caused highly toxic sewage to drain from arroyos and streets into the Tijuana River as it crosses the international boundary into the United States. Since 1980 regular spillage has contaminated water supplies and beaches in the estuarine region of south San Diego County, with severe economic consequences. In 1983, virtually all of San Diego's beaches as far north as Point Loma were quarantined for a period of eight months. By mid-1983, the Tijuana sewage situation was designated the most serious border sanitation problem on the U.S.-Mexico agenda (U.S. Environmental Protection Agency, 1984).

U.S. border interests have sought to broaden the institutional scope of regulatory action along the border to address a large range of hazardous waste issues. While IBWC remains the principal institution responsible for seeking agreements on water-related hazards disputes, the U.S. Environmental Protection Agency has become an increasingly important player in the diplomatic game. In 1978, the EPA, together with the Undersecretariat for Environmental Improvement of Mexico's Secretariat of Health, signed a Memorandum of Understanding committing the two nations to "a cooperative effort to resolve environmental problems of mutual concern in border areas" (Memorandum of Understanding, 1978). The 1978 Memorandum was followed by the conclusion of a "Joint Marine Pollution Contingency Plan" in 1980 and efforts to obtain agreement on a contingency plan for handling hazardous materials spillage and contamination in the border zone (Hajost, 1984).

The limitations of these agreements led U.S. border states to press for inclusion of the environmental issue on the agenda of the second formal summit meeting between Presidents Reagan and De la Madrid in La Paz, Mexico, in August of 1983. The outcome of that meeting was a new, fully comprehensive executive agreement on "border environmental cooperation." The new agreement recognized the priority of "border sanitation problems" and other environmental hazards on the binational diplomatic agenda and formally committed the two nations to address these issues in a timely and cooperative manner. From the U.S. perspective, it firmly established the fact of Mexican responsibility for resolving its sewage problems by writing the "polluter-pays" principle into the agreement (U.S. Environmental Protection Agency, 1984: 4). The new agreement designated the EPA and SEDUE respectively as national coordinating agencies for the United States and Mexico and charged them to regularly consult and report hazards disputes. It thus reinforced existing bilateral commitments, comprehensively included all hazardous waste problems, reduced jurisdictional friction, and created additional diplomatic circuits for bringing these issues to executive attention in each country.

The border environmental cooperation agreement has already yielded positive results, though the diplomatic record is still blemished. In the case of the New River contamination it has yet to produce significant ameliorative action, although it has prodded Mexico to stronger verbal commitment to a solution. The issue was highlighted in the summer of 1983 when California state health officials reported "the situation quite serious," constituting an "imminent and substantial danger to the public health and welfare" (Clark, 1983). California State Water Quality Control Board tests identified pesticide levels "too high to be agriculturally derived" as well as high levels of other industrial wastes (*Albuquerque Journal*, 1983). The creation of a binational Water Quality Working Group pursuant to the 1983 agreement was followed in May 1984 by a meeting of technical experts from the two countries addressing border water pollution. Addressing the New River situation, Mexican officials agreed to take a number of corrective measures to reduce contamination, including rehabilitation of municipal sewage lagoons and expansion of the sewage collection system in Mexicali, issuance of cease and desist orders to industrial polluters, and relocation of a landfill near the river (U.S. Environmental Protection Agency, 1984; *Mexican News Synopsis,* 1984). Implementation has been halting, however, and little progress registered by late 1985 (Ybarra, 1985). The most recent annual meeting of the U.S. and Mexican National Coordinators of the 1983 agreement in July 1985 skirted this issue, committing to a further diagnosis of hazardous materials in New River water but issuing no progress report (Joint Communique, 1985).

Follow-up diplomacy in the case of the Tijuana sewage dispute finally produced a substantial set of agreements in April-July 1985 after protracted negotiations. The latest round of discussions began in the fall of 1983 with local San Diego efforts to construct an expensive ($730 million) joint international sewage-processing facility. The Reagan administration objected to both the price tag of the project and what it considered inadequate financial commitments by Mexico (Miller, 1984). Mexican officials, in turn, objected to both the direct and the indirect costs of the project. Meeting in March 1984 with U.S. officials under the aegis of the 1983 agreement, SEDUE officials announced that funds had been appropriated to repair the existing sewage collections system and a complete a new pumping plant-ocean outfall. However, they cautioned against expecting too much from Mexico, noting that Mexico was looking at border problems in a national context. Director of Ecology Barcena Ybarra affirmed that the Mexican project had "a plan with a budget" but observed, "every country has its capacity, its limits." As another Mexican official put it, "you talk about the problems of surfers in Imperial Beach. Go to the neighborhoods in Tijuana where they have no pavement, no water, or sewage system and tell them about the big problem of the surfers" (Miller, 1984).

Mexico's intention to proceed unilaterally with a solution was clarified in January 1985 when it approached the Inter-American Development Bank (IDB) for a $46.4 million loan to upgrade Tijuana's water distribution and sewage systems. The Mexican request generated heated opposition by local and state officials in California, who feared expansion of the water distribution system would further overburden the city's inadequate sewage facilities, exacerbating the spillage problem. Pressuring the Reagan administration, state officials were able to force postponement of the IDB decision. In response, Mexico proposed a series of binational meetings of the Water Quality Working Group to consider alternative plans for coping with the sewage problem (Richmond, 1985: A-11).

In a series of three meetings in February-March 1985 the framework for a solution was hammered out. In the first meeting, Mexican officials unveiled formal plans for a $91 million water and sewage project which included two new sewage treatment plants and upgrading and expansion of the collection network. The first plant, to be completed in 1986 with a capacity of 50 million gallons a day (mgd), would accommodate projected municipal demands through the year 2000, at a base cost of $5 million. Another plant would be added later to handle new growth on the city's mushrooming northeast side. U.S. delegates, in turn, insisted they receive formal assurances that the plants would meet U.S. industry standards and guarantee "100% reclamation." They also sought authorization and funding of a backup collection system in the United States, specific deadlines for project construction, and an agreement authorizing U.S. maintenance teams to perform emergency repairs should the Tijuana system fail (LaRue, 1985; *San Diego Tribune*, 1985).

Meeting subsequently in Mexico City, high-level delegations headed by Ambassador John Gavin for the United States and SEDUE's secretary, Marcello Javelly, for Mexico produced a tentative basis for a formal solution to the sewage problem. Mexico agreed to defer its request for a vote on the IDB loan until both countries were agreed on the design and technical standards to be met by the Tijuana system, while the United States accepted that Mexico was not obligated to comply with U.S. technical standards in constructing its plants, only to confer on transborder sewage flows. Further, Mexico agreed to:

1. seek an IDB loan to enclose the 5.6 miles sewage drainage canal to the proposed plant.
2. apply for an IDB grant to study environmental impacts of the plant.
3. participate in a joint emergency response team to deal with sewage emergencies.
4. take "immediate corrective action" without delay in the event of spillage.
5. delay expansion of water service until the sewage collectors were installed. (*San Diego Union*, 1985)

The final round of talks, in early March, produced a formal agreement on the IDB loan. By this agreement Mexico promised to build the 50 mgd sewage facility, complete an environmental study of its effects on the United States, and extend the system's collection network to include the rapidly growing Tijuana northeast. Disbursement of the loan was made contingent on mutually verified Mexican compliance with the terms of the agreement. It was, nonetheless, a compromise, with Mexico not conceding all the concessions indicated in the second round. Many of these specifics were left for subsequent IBWC negotiations on technical aspects of the plan's implementation, to be included in a final official annex to the 1983 border environment cooperation agreement. On this basis, the IDB approved the loan on March 6, 1985.

The negotiations at the IBWC level on particulars of implementation continued in March and April, producing an agreement, Minute 270, signed April 30, 1985 (IBWC, 1985). Mexico, while failing to cede all the performance guarantees demanded by U.S. negotiators, goes further than in any previous binational sanitation agreement to accommodate U.S. interests. Minute 270:

1. commits Mexico to construct and maintain the Tijuana sewage plant.
2. provides for the provision of standby equipment to be used in emergencies.
3. provides for integration of the Tijuana sewage system with any backup system that may be built in the United States (as contemplated by the city of San Diego).
4. sets timetables for the implementation of funding and construction.
5. establishes specific standards to be met by the Mexican project as agreed to by both countries.
6. provides for U.S. assistance at Mexico's request to help with emergency sewage situations.

Although noncompliance by Mexico does not directly invoke the sanction of withholding IDB funds, as would have been the case had U.S. diplomats achieved their optimum goal (the IDB agreement does not cover all of items 2, 3, and 6 and only partly covers items 4 and 5), the IBWC minute is a formal agreement with the status of an executive agreement in international law. It is, in sum, a remarkable agreement and a significant accomplishment implementing the commission's "border sanitation problems" mandate under the 1944 Water Treaty and Minute 261. It has been incorporated with the IDB agreement as the main documents consti- tuting an official settlement of the San Diego-Tijuana sewage dispute in Annex I of the supplementary annexes to the 1983 border environment co- operation agreement.[1]

The 1983 agreement spawned two more subsidiary agreements in 1985 and 1986 dealing with hazardous materials management along the border. Both of these agreements are the product of negotiations by the Hazardous Materials and Waste Management Working Group established by the 1983 agreement and charged with a mandate "to identify and address present and potential hazardous materials and waste management problems of mutual concern along the U.S.-Mexico border" (Joint Communique, 1985: 5). The first of these agreements, Annex II, known as the U.S.-Mexico Joint Inland Contingency Plan, was signed in July 1985. It establishes a mutual response program for hazardous materials spills and provides for the implementation of a pilot program in the Calexico-Mexicali region. The second of the two agreements, Annex III, was concluded in November 1986. It creates a border hotline on toxic materials, requiring each country to notify the other of hazardous materials shipments destined for that country at least forty-five days in advance and obligating each country to accept any toxic materials illegally shipped across the border. The agreement also makes private individuals and companies liable for civil and criminal damages to human health or the natural environment arising from such shipments (EPA, 1986; Stern, 1986). The Hazardous Materials Working Group further proposes to address the issue of agricultural chemicals, *maquila* industries' wastes, municipal and hazardous waste facility siting, and ocean incineration of toxic materials in forthcoming discussions (Joint Communique, 1985: 5-6).

In sum, the 1983 agreement on border environmental cooperation has significantly broadened the scope of binational cooperation and accelerated progress toward a comprehensive regulatory regime to manage hazardous materials along the border. Nevertheless, recent diplomatic achievements are only incipient motions toward this goal. An array of sanitation problems and hazards problems persist and will require specific solutions of a unilateral or bilateral nature in the future. It is worth considering the prospects for further cooperation in view of recent experience and existing constraints and priorities affecting diplomacy in this sphere.

DEPENDENCE AND INTERDEPENDENCE: IMPLICATIONS FOR BILATERAL COOPERATION IN REGULATING TRANSBOUNDARY HAZARDOUS WASTES

The preceding review of the progress and shortfalls in binational efforts at regulating transboundary hazardous wastes illustrates the real interdependence of both nations arising from the asymmetry of national development along the U.S.-Mexico border. This issue area manifests most of the political processes specified by Keohane and Nye's concept of complex interdependence. This interdependence, in turn, frames the possibilities for further binational cooperation in managing environment hazards along the border.

With respect to strategic national objectives, for instance, it is clear that solutions to hazardous waste problems along the border are often inversely related to policies which sustain the present asymmetries in border development. Reducing Mexican dependency is conducive to greater capacity and greater incentives to cooperate in managing the border environment. At present, however, the development differential creates alternative national priorities that weigh against cooperation as these problems are addressed at the bargaining table.

Similarly, the many binational interactions bonding Mexico with the United States limit each nation's respective capacity to alter the other's diplomatic agenda in this issue area. As suggested in our review of binational diplomacy in this area, the United States has been reluctant to employ serious economic sanctions in bargaining with Mexico. It recognizes that such sanctions are disproportionate to the problem at hand and likely to boomerang adversely in other issue areas within the bilateral relationship.

These dynamics are expressly evident in the case of the debate over issue linkage with respect to a settlement of the San Diego-Tijuana sewage problem. Spokesman for U.S. border interests have occasionally sought to link Mexican commitment to border hazards solutions to U.S. sanctions in other issue areas. This type of linkage, however, is unlikely within the bounds of complex interdependence.

The diplomatic limits of complex interdependence notwithstanding, however, several conditions for progress can be identified from our review of the diplomatic record above. First, while ham-fisted approaches to issue linkage are apt to be less successful in eliciting Mexican cooperation in managing border hazards, positive-sum linkages of highly similar issues may be successful in doing so. This is the case with the IDB's water and sewage loan to Tijuana. Here, no existing benefit was being denied to Mexico; instead, a potential benefit was held out as an incentive. And the benefit, financial support for an expanded water distribution system, was closely related to the need for improved sewage collection and processing.

Second, progress is apt to take the form of short-term solutions coupled with positive incentives for Mexican cooperation. Short-term solutions simply reflect Mexico's resource limits in contributing to expensive ameliorative works that may be seen domestically as responsive as much to foreign as to Mexican interests, carrying a political as well as economic liability.

On the other hand, some form of Mexican participation has been politically important in rationalizing U.S. federal appropriations for solutions to transborder environmental problems. Obtaining Mexican participation has been difficult, but where join international action is necessary there is an important precedent that provides an incentive. Under the 1944 Water Treaty, the two countries have agreed to apportion the costs of ameliorative works relative to the perceived national benefits, leaving the question of benefits in any given case to bilateral negotiation. The door is clearly left open to greater U.S. responsibility for shouldering the costs of projects that can be defined as "binational" in character. Given the difference in national priorities, it is inevitable that such measures would have more than limited effectiveness in this issue area. Federal statesmen at the level of the Department of State, the IBWC, and the EPA, as well as many local officials along the border, fear such sanctions would adversely affect other domestic interests while further alienating Mexico from cooperation in managing transboundary hazards. The risks of a more forceful U.S. diplomatic strategy, in short, are seen to exceed the benefits, an important indicator for Keohane and Nye that a true interdependence relationship exists.

Third, within this issue area a number of nontraditional, nonstate diplomatic actors play an important role in constructing solutions to transboundary hazards problems. At the international level, the IBWC has proven an active and important player in solutions to these problems, bringing its technical expertise and binational advocacy to bear on binational diplomacy. State and local interests on the U.S. side of the border have taken the lead in pressuring the federal government to pursue binational solutions to these problems. So active are they, in fact, that they are recognized as legitimate parties to diplomatic processes in designing solutions to this class of binational problems in the 1984 Environmental Cooperation Agreement. Once again, this is an important indicator of interdependence in Keohane and Nye's formulation.

What, then, does such interdependence imply for future progress in regulating binational hazardous wastes along the border?

Considering the differential in national regulatory priorities, and limitations on the use of stronger forms of leverage by the United States, progress is largely contingent on policy decisions in Mexico. In the long run, such progress depends on Mexican economic development. In the short run, however, bilateral diplomacy has made and may continue to make limited progress. The United States absorbs a proportionally greater share of the financial burden for hazards abatement than Mexico. While specific responsibility in each case is subject to bargaining and compromise, the United States is able to use its financial resources as a positive incentive when binational projects offer substantial benefits to Mexico.

Fourth, symbolic commitments are not without significance. The 1983 Border Environmental Cooperation agreement has stimulated continued diplomacy in this area, expanded the points of bilateral contact, raised the priority given the issues within the Mexican policy establishment, strengthened the coordination of domestic agency activities, and provided for greater participation of state and local interests in designing solutions to transborder environmental hazards problems. Such agreement in principle is an essential prerequisite for futher diplomatic progress.

In sum, beyond the level of symbolic cooperation, which is an important precondition for progress, interdependence dictates solutions that are not negatively linked to other issues, are short-term, and have positive incentives for Mexican cooperation. These patterns are seen in the diplomacy and solutions to other environmental problems in the past and are likely to continue in the future. It is doubtful that binational regulation along the border can optimally satisfy the interests of either country given current economic differentials. Within the constraints of dependence and interdependence, however, there are solid grounds for future progress.

REFERENCES

Albuquerque Journal, "Heavily Polluted River from Mexico Dangerous, California Official Says" (June 9, 1983), A-9.

Applegate, Howard G., and C. Richard Bath, "Hazardous and Toxic Substances in U.S.-Mexico Relations," *Texas Business Review* 57 (1983).

Briseno, Olga, "Mexico to Clear Illegal Toxic Wastes," *San Diego Union* (February 7, 1986), B-1.

Chimely, Eduardo, "Prohiben la Importacion a EU de Frutas y Verduras Mexicanas," *Excelsior* (September 3, 1984).

Clark, Cheryl, "New River Said Danger to Health," *San Diego Union* (June 8, 1983), A-1.

Clarke, Gail, "Environmental Problems along the U.S.-Mexico Borderlands: Summary Report," Paper prepared for the Border Atlas Project Meeting, November 30, 1982, San Diego, California, pp. 13-14.

Comercio Exterior, "Ecology and the Environment: Companies Closed," 27 (March 1981).

Diario Official, Decreto por el que se Reforman, Adicionan y Derogan diversas disposiciones de la Ley Federal de Proteccion al Ambiente (February 27, 1984).

Gross, Greg, "Did Lead Poisoning Kill Mother of Eight?" *San Diego Union* (January 20, 1983).

Hajost, Scott A. "U.S.-Mexico Environmental Cooperation: Agreement between the United States of America and the United Mexican States on Cooperation for the Protection and Improvement of the Environment in the Border Area," *Environmental Law* (Spring 1984), 1-3.

International Boundary and Water Commission (IBWC), Recommendations for the First Stage Treatment and Disposal Facilities for the Solution of the Border Sanitation Problem at San Diego, California-Tijuana, Baja California. Minute 270. Ciudad Juarez, Chihuahua, April 30, 1985.

Joint Communique, Report on Second Annual Meeting of the National Coordinators to Purse Implementation of the Border Environmental Cooperation Agreement Signed by President Reagan and President de la Madrid at La Paz, Baja California Sur, on August 14, 1983. Issued July 18, 1985, in San Diego, California.

Keohane, Robert O., and Joseph S. Nye, *Power and Interdependence* (Boston: Little, Brown, 1977).

LaRue, Steve, "Mexico Bares Plan to End Sewage Woes," *San Diego Tribune* (February 5, 1985), A-1.

Memorandum of Understanding between the Subsecretariat for Environmental Improvement of Mexico and the Environmental Protection Agency of the United States for Cooperation on Environmental Programs and Transboundary Problems, Mexico City, June 6, 1978.

Mexican News Synopsis, "Contamination of the New River in Mexicali, Baja California and Calexico, U.S.A." (October 29, 1984), 2.

McLaren, John, and Fernando Romero, "New Rules Due Soon on Toxic Wastes," *San Diego Tribune* (February 13, 1986), A-3.

Miller, Marjorie, "S.D. Plan for Sewage Plant a 'Dead Issue,'" *Los Angeles Times* (March 10, 1984).

Mumme, Stephen P., "The Background and Significance of Minute 261 of the International Boundary and Water Commission," *California Western International Law Journal* 11 (Spring 1981): 223-235.

Ojeda, Mario, "The Future of Relations between Mexico and the United States," in Clark W. Reynolds and Carlos Tello, eds., *U.S.-Mexico Relations: Economic and Social Aspects* (Stanford: Stanford University Press, 1983), 315-330.

Richmond, Michael, "Sewer-Loan Request for Tijuana on Hold," *San Diego Diego Tribune* (January 17, 1985), A-11.

San Diego Tribune, "Binational Border Sewage Plant" (February 11, 1985), B-6.

San Diego Union, "Sewage: Mexico Meeting Ends with No Final Solution" (February 15, 1985), A-1.

Stern, Marcus, "U.S., Mexico Sign Accord on Toxic Waste Shipments," *San Diego Union* (November 13, 1986), A-3.

Uno Mas Uno, "Autorizan la reapertura de una fabrica contaminante" (June 4, 1984).

U.S. Environmental Protection Agency, Update on status of U.S.-Mexico border Environmental Problems. In house summary report made available to the author by Mr. Walter J. Hunt, Western Hemisphere Environmental Programs Manager, August 16, 1984.

U.S. Environmental Protection Agency, "Annex III to the Agreement between the United States of America and the United Mexican States on Cooperation for the Protection and Improvement of the Border Area. Agreement of Cooperation between the United States of America and the United Mexican States Regarding the Transboundary Shipments of Hazardous Wastes and Hazardous Substances." Signed in Washington, DC, November 12, 1986.

Weiser, Teresa, "Se necesita una solucion integral al problema de la contaminacion del DF," *Uno Mas Uno* (May 28, 1984).

Williams, Edward J., "The Maquiladora Program at Midpoint: Progress, Problems, and Prospects," in Stanley R. Ross, ed., *Views across the Border*, 2nd ed. (Albuquerque: University of New Mexico Press, forthcoming).

Ybarra, M. R., Letter to the author from the Secretary of the IBWC, U.S. Section, September 26, 1985.

Selected Bibliography

BOOKS

Brown, Michael, *Laying Waste: The Poisoning of America by Toxic Chemicals* (New York: Pantheon, 1980).

Doniger, David D., *Law and Policy of Toxic Substances* (Baltimore, MD: Johns Hopkins, 1979).

Epstein, Samuel S., Lester O. Brown, and Carl Pope, *Hazardous Waste in America* (San Francisco: Sierra Club, 1982).

Gibbs, Lois Marie, *Love Canal: My Story* (Albany, NY: SUNY Press, 1982).

Greenberg, Michael R., and Richard F. Anderson, *Hazardous Waste Sites: The Credibility Gap* (New Brunswick, NJ: Center for Urban Policy Research, 1984).

Harthill, Michalann, ed., *Hazardous Waste Management: In Whose Backyard?* (Boulder, CO: Westview Press, 1984).

Lehman, John, ed., *Hazardous Waste Disposal* (New York: Plenum Press, 1983).

Lester, James P., and Ann O'Bowman, eds., *The Politics of Hazardous Waste Management* (Durham, NC: Duke University Press, 1983).

Levine, Adeline G., *Love Canal: Science, Politics, and People* (Lexington, MA: Lexington Books, 1982).

Morell, David L., and Christopher Magorian, *Siting Hazardous Waste Facilities: Local Opposition and the Myth of Preemption* (Cambridge, MA: Ballinger, 1982).

Nader, Ralph, Ronald Brownstein, and John Richard, eds., *Who's Poisoning America: Corporate Polluters and Their Victims in the Chemical Age* (San Francisco: Sierra Club, 1981).

O'Hare, Michael, Lawrence Bacow, and Debra Sanderson, *Facility Siting* (New York: Van Nostrand, 1983).

Piasecki, Bruce, ed., *Beyond Dumping* (Westport, CT: Greenwood Press, 1984).

Vogel, David, *National Styles of Regulation; Environmental Policy in Great Britain and the United States* (Ithaca, NY: Cornell University Press, 1986).

Whiteside, Thomas, *The Pendulum and the Toxic Cloud* (New Haven, CT: Yale University Press, 1979).

BOOK CHAPTERS AND JOURNAL ARTICLES

Andrews, Richard N. L., and Terrence K. Pierson, "Local Control or State Override? Experiences and Lessons to Date" *Policy Studies Journal* (September 1985).

Applegate, Howard, and Richard Bath, "Hazardous and Toxic Substances in U.S.-Mexico Relations," *Texas Business Review* (September-October 1983).

Arnott, Robert, "Waste Management in Northern Europe," *Waste Management and Research*, no. 4 (1985).

Barke, Richard, "Policy Learning and the Evolution of Federal Hazardous Waste Policy," *Policy Studies Journal* (September 1985).

Bowman, Ann O'M., "Intergovernmental and Intersectoral Tensions in Environmental Policy Implementation; The Case of Hazardous Waste," *Policy Studies Review* (November 1984).

_____, "Hazardous Waste Management: An Emerging Policy Area within An Emerging Federalism," *Publius* (Winter 1985).

_____. "Hazardous Waste Cleanup and Superfund Implementation in the Southeast," *Policy Studies Journal* (September 1985).

_____, "Explaining State Response to the Hazardous Waste Problem," *Hazardous Waste* (Fall 1984).

_____, and James Lester, "Hazardous Waste Management: State Government Activity or Passivity?" *State and Local Government Review* (Winter 1985).

Carnes, Sam A., "Confronting Complexity and Uncertainty: Implementation of Hazardous Waste Management Policy," in Dean E. Mann, ed., *Environmental Policy Implementation* (Lexington, MA: Lexington Books, 1982).

Cohen, Steven, "Defusing the Toxic Time Bomb: Federal Hazardous Waste Programs," in Norman Vig and Michael Kraft, eds., *Environmental Policy in the 1980s: Reagan's New Agenda* (Washington, DC: CQ Press, 1984).

_____, and Marc Tipermas, "Superfund: Preimplementation Planning and Bureaucratic Politics," in James Lester and Ann Bowman, eds., *The Politics of Hazardous Waste Management* (Durham, NC: Duke University Press, 1983).

Davis, Charles E., "Substance and Procedure in Hazardous Waste Facility Siting," *Journal of Environmental Systems,* no. 1 (1984-1985).

_____, "Implementing the Resource Conservation and Recovery Act of 1976," *Public Administration Quarterly* (Summer 1985).

_____, "Perceptions of Hazardous Waste Policy Issues among Public and Private Sector Administrators," *Western Political Quarterly* (September 1985).

_____, "Public Involvement in Hazardous Waste Facility Siting Decisions," *Polity* (Winter 1986).

_____, and Joe Hagan, "Exporting Hazardous Waste: Issues and Policy Implications," *International Journal of Public Administration*, no. 4 (1986).

Elliot, Michael, "Improving Community Acceptance of Hazardous Waste Facilities through Alternative Systems for Mitigating and Managing Risk," *Hazardous Waste* (Fall 1984).

Getz, Malcolm, and Benjamin Walter, "Environmental Policy and Competitive Structure: Implications of the Hazardous Waste Management Program," *Policy Studies Journal*, vol. 9 (Winter 1980).

Goldfarb, William, "The Hazards of Our Hazardous Waste Policy," *Natural Resources Journal*, vol. 19 (1979).

Grunbaum, Werner, "Developing a Uniform Federal Common Law for Hazardous Waste Liability," *Policy Studies Journal* (September 1985).

Hadden, Susan G., Joan Veillette, and Thomas Brandt, "State Roles in Siting Hazardous Waste Disposal Facilities: From State Preemption to Local Veto," in Lester and Bowman, eds., *The Politics of Hazardous Waste Management* (Durham, NC: Duke University Press, 1983).

Jorling, T. C., "Hazardous Substances in the Environment," *Ecology Law Quarterly*, vol. 9 (1981).

Kamieniecki, Sheldon, Robert O'Brien, and Michael Clarke, "Environmental Policy and Aspects of Intergovernmental Relations," in David Morgan and Edwin Benton, eds., *Intergovernmental Relations and Public Policy* (Westport, CT: Greenwood Press, 1986).

Kraft, Michael, and Ruth Kraut, "The Impact of Citizen Participation on Hazardous Waste Policy Implementation; The Case of Clermont County, Ohio," *Policy Studies Journal* (September 1985).

Kramer, Kenneth W., "Institutional Fragmentation and Hazardous Waste Policy: The Case of Texas," in Lester and Bowman, eds., *The Politics of Hazardous Waste Management* (Durham, NC: Duke University Press, 1983).

Landy, Marc, "Ticking Time Bombs!!! EPA and the Formulation of Superfund," in Helen Ingram and Kenneth Godwin, eds., *Public Policy and the National Environment* (Greenwich, CT: JAI Press, 1985).

Lester, James P., "Hazardous Waste and Policy Implementation: The Subnational Role," *Hazardous Waste* (Fall 1985).

———, "New Federalism and Environmental Policy," *Publius* (Winter 1986).

———, James Franke, Ann O'M. Bowman, and Kenneth Kramer, "Hazardous Wastes, Politics, and Public Policy: A Comparative State Analysis," *Western Political Quarterly* (June 1983).

———, and Ann O'M. Bowman, "Subnational Hazardous Waste Policy Implementation: A Test of the Sabatier-Mazmanian Model," Paper delivered at the 1986 Annual Meeting of the American Political Science Association, Washington, DC.

———, and Michael S. Hamilton, "Intergovernmental Relations and Ocean Policy in the 1980s: The Politics of Policy Change," in Maynard Silva, ed., *National Ocean Policy in the 1980s* (Boulder, CO: Westview Press, 1986).

Lieber, Harvey, "Federalism and Hazardous Waste Policy," in Lester and Bowman, eds., *The Politics of Hazardous Waste Management* (Durham, NC: Duke University Press, 1983).

Mangun, William, "A Comparative Analysis of Hazardous Waste Policy Formulation Efforts among West European Countries," *Policy Studies Journal* (September 1985).

Matheny, Albert, and Bruce Williams, "Knowledge vs. NIMBY: Assessing Florida's Strategy for Siting Hazardous Waste Disposal Facilities," *Policy Studies Journal* (September 1985).

Mitchell, Robert, and Richard Carson, "Property Rights, Protest, and the Siting of Hazardous Waste Facilities," *American Economic Review* (May 1986).

Morell, David L., "Technological Policies and Hazardous Waste Politics in California," in Lester and Bowman, eds., *The Politics of Hazardous Waste Management* (Durham, NC: Duke University Press, 1983).

Mumme, Stephen, "Dependency and Interdependence in Hazardous Waste Management along the U.S.-Mexico Border." *Policy Studies Journal* (September 1985).

O'Brien, Robert, Michael Clarke, and Sheldon Kamieniecki, "Open and Closed Systems of Decision-Making: The Case of Toxic Waste Management," *Public Administration Review* (July-August 1984).

O'Hare, Michael, "Not on My Block You Don't: Facility Siting and the Importance of Compensation," *Public Policy* (Fall 1977).

Portney, Kent, "Allaying the NIMBY Syndrome: The Potential for Compensation in Hazardous Waste Treatment Facility Siting," *Hazardous Waste* (Fall 1984).

_____, "The Potential of the Theory of Compensation of Mitigating Public Opposition to Hazardous Waste Treatment Facility Siting: Some Evidence from Five Massachusetts Communities," *Policy Studies Journal* (September 1985).

Powell, John Duncan, "Assault on a Precious Commodity: The Local Struggle to Protect Groundwater," *Policy Studies Journal* (September 1985).

Riley, Richard, "Toxic Substances, Hazardous Wastes, and Public Policy: Problems in Implementation," in Lester and Bowman, eds., *The Politics of Hazardous Waste Management* (Durham, NC: Duke University Press, 1983).

Ristoratore, Mario, "Siting Toxic Waste Disposal Facilities in Canada and the United States: Problems and Prospects," *Policy Studies Journal* (September 1985).

Rosenbaum, Walter, "The Politics of Public Participation in Hazardous Waste Management," in Lester and Bowman, eds., *The Politics of Hazardous Waste Management* (Durham, NC: Duke University Press, 1983).

Rowland, C. K., and Roger Marz, "Gresham's Law: The Regulatory Analogy," *Policy Studies Review* (November 1981).

Schnapf, David, "State Hazardous Waste Programs under the Federal Resource Conservation and Recovery Act," *Environmental Law* (1982).

Seferovich, Patrick, "United States Export of Banned Products: Legal and Moral Implications," *Denver Journal of International Law and Policy* (1981).

Senkan, Selim M., and Nancy W. Stauffer, "What to Do with Hazardous Waste," *Technology Review,* vol. 84 (November-December 1981).

Sheehan, Michael, "Economism, Democracy, and Hazardous Wastes: Some Policy Considerations," in Sheldon Kamieniecki, Robert O'Brien, and Michael Clarke, eds., *Controversies in Environmental Policy* (Albany, NY: SUNY Press, 1986).

Shue, Henry, "Exporting Hazards," *Ethics* (July 1981).

Tofner-Clausen, John, "Danish Hazardous Waste System," in John Lehman, ed., *Hazardous Waste Disposal* (New York: Plenum Press, 1983).

Walter, Benjamin, and Malcolm Getz, "Social and Economic Effects of Toxic Waste Disposal," in Sheldon Kamieniecki, Robert O'Brien, and Michael Clarke, eds., *Controversies in Environmental Policy* (Albany, NY: SUNY Press, 1986).

Wells, Donald, "Site Control of Hazardous Waste Facilities," *Policy Studies Review* (May 1982).

Williams, Bruce A., and Albert R. Matheny, "Hazardous Waste Policy in Florida: Is Regulation Possible?" in Lester and Bowman, eds., *The Politics of Hazardous Waste Management* (Durham, NC: Duke University Press, 1983).

———, "Testing Theories of Social Regulation: Hazardous Waste Regulation in the American States," *Journal of Politics* (May 1984).

Wolbeck, Bernd, "Political Dimensions and Implications of Hazardous Waste Disposal," in John Lehman, ed., *Hazardous Waste Disposal* (New York: Plenum Press, 1983).

Worthley, John A., and Richard Torkelson, "Managing the Toxic Waste Problem: Lessons from the Love Canal," *Administration and Society*, vol. 13 (1981).

Worthley, John, and Richard Torkelson, "Intergovernmental and Public-Private Sector Relations in Hazardous Waste Management: The New York Example," in Lester and Bowman, eds., *The Politics of Hazardous Waste Management* (Durham, NC: Duke University Press, 1983).

Wurth-Hough, Sandra, "Chemical Contamination and Governmental Policy-making: The North Carolina Experience," *State and Local Governmental Review* (May 1982).

PUBLISHED REPORTS

Commission for Economic Development, State of California, *Poisoning Prosperity: The Impact of Toxics on California's Economy* (Sacramento, CA: Commission for Economic Development, 1985).

Conservation Foundation, *State of the Environment: 1984* (Washington, DC: Conservation Foundation, 1984).

Council of State Governments, *Waste Management in the States* (Lexington, KY: Council of State Governments, 1982).

Governor's Hazardous Waste Policy Advisory Council, *Hazardous Waste: A Management Perspective* (Tallahassee, FL: Institute of Science and Public Affairs, Florida State University, 1981).

ICF Incorporated, *Analysis of Community Involvement in Hazardous Waste Site Problems: A Report to the Office of Emergency and Remedial Response* (Washington, DC: U.S. Environmental Protection Agency, July 1981).

Kamlet, Kenneth S., *Toxic Substances Programs in U.S. States and Territories: How Well Do They Work?* (Washington, DC: National Wildlife Federation, 1980).

Minnesota Waste Management Board, *Charting a Course: Public Participation in the Siting of Hazardous Waste Facilities* (Crystal, MN: Waste Management Board, 1981).

National Conference of State Legislatures, *Hazardous Waste Management: A Survey of State Legislation*, 1982 (Denver, CO: NCSL, 1982).

Office of Technology Assessment, *Technologies and Management Strategies for Hazardous Waste Control* (Washington, DC: OTA, 1983).

_____, *Serious Reduction of Hazardous Waste* (Washington: DC: OTA, 1986).

Organization for Economic Cooperation and Development, *Economic Aspects of International Chemicals Control* (Paris: OECD, 1983).

Paparian, Michael, Patricia Wells, and Peter Fearey, *Integrated Hazardous Waste Systems in the Federal Republic of Germany and Denmark* (Sacramento: California Foundation on the Environment and the Economy, 1984).

Index

Contributors

RICHARD N. L. ANDREWS is a professor of environmental sciences and engineering and director of the Institute for Environmental Studies at the University of North Carolina in Chapel Hill. He also holds joint appointments in ecology, city and regional planning, and health policy and administration. His research interests focus on the relationships among environmental conditions, public values, and forms of governance; recent publications include research reports on state and local approaches to hazardous waste management and book chapters on the politics and economics of environmental regulation.

RICHARD BARKE is an assistant professor of political science at Georgia Tech University. His interests include regulation, policy analysis, public bureaucracy, and science and technology policy. Articles on these subjects have appeared in *Public Choice* and *Journal of Behavioral Economics,* and he is author of *Science, Technology, and Public Policy* (1986).

ANN O'M. BOWMAN is an associate professor in the Department of Government and International Studies at the University of South Carolina. Her areas of research interest include environmental policy and state and local government. Her book *The Resurgence of the States* was published in 1986.

CHARLES E. DAVIS is an associate professor of political science at Colorado State University. Teaching and research interests lie in the areas of environmental policy and public personnel management. He has recently authored or co-authored articles appearing in *Polity*, *Western Political*

Quarterly, Environmental Law, Policy Studies Journal, Policy Studies Review, and other scholarly journals.

DAVID B. GOETZE is an assistant professor of political science at Utah State University. He holds a Ph.D. in political science from Indiana University and an M.S. in the same discipline from the University of Kansas. His research interests include environmental policy and natural resource management from a social choice perspective. His work has appeared in *Public Choice* and other journals.

WERNER F. GRUNBAUM is a professor of political science at the University of Missouri-St. Louis. He is the author of a monograph, *Judicial Policymaking: The Supreme Court and Environmental Quality*. His articles have appeared in *Byte Magazine, Publius, Journal of Politics, Public Opinion Quarterly, Western Political Quarterly, Southwestern Social Science Quarterly, Houston Law Review,* and *Washington University Law Quarterly*.

MICHAEL E. KRAFT is a professor of political science and public administration at the University of Wisconsin-Green Bay. During the 1984-1985 academic year he was a visiting professor in the Environmental Studies Program at Oberlin College. His latest book, co-edited with Normal J. Vig, is *Environmental Policy in the 1980s: Reagan's New Agenda* (1984).

RUTH KRAUT is a recent graduate of the Environmental Studies Program at Oberlin College. She is currently the editor of *Ecology Reports*, the newsletter of the Ecology Center of Ann Arbor, Michigan.

S. C. LEE is a graduate student at the University of Kansas.

JAMES P. LESTER is an associate professor of political science and former coordinator of graduate studies in political science at Colorado State University. During 1987-1988, he will be a visiting scholar at the University of Kentucky. His teaching and research interests are in the areas of science and technology policy, environmental policy, and public policy analysis. He has recently authored or co-authored articles appearing in *Western Political Quarterly, Polity, Publius, Policy Studies Review, Policy Studies Journal, Simulation and Games,* and other scholarly journals. He is also co-editor of *The Politics of Hazardous Waste Management* (1983).

WILLIAM R. MANGUN has a doctorate in political science from Indiana University and was formerly the project manager for policy analysis and national surveys for the U.S. Fish and Wildlife Service in Washington, DC. He now teaches at Indiana State University. He is the author of *The Public*

Administration of Environmental Policy and co-author of *Nonconsumptive Use of Wildlife in the United States* and has published articles on air and water pollution control, wildlife policy, and comparative environmental policy in such journals as *Environmental Management, Public Administration Review, Environmental Conservation, Journal of Environmental Systems,* and *Leisure Sciences.*

ALBERT R. MATHENY is an associate professor of political science at the University of Florida and has published in the areas of regulatory politics, administrative law, science policy, and criminal justice. He is currently writing a book about regulatory politics and hazardous waste with Professor Williams and is conducting research on law and social change in America.

STEPHEN P. MUMME is an associate professor of political science at Colorado State University. His research focuses on U.S.-Mexican environmental affairs and comparative environmental policy in Latin America. Published articles and reviews appear in *Western Political Quarterly, Publius, Social Science Journal, Journal of Inter-American Economic Affairs,* and other publications.

KENT E. PORTNEY is an associate professor of political science and director of the Citizen Survey Program, Tufts University. He currently directs the Graduate Program in Public Policy and Citizen Participation. He has published research on environmental policy, tax policy, and distributional impact research. He is the author of the book *Approaching Public Policy Analysis* (1986).

JOHN D. POWELL is an associate professor and chairman of the Political Science Department, Tufts University. He is actively involved in the Tufts Center for Environmental Management and in local and state governmental efforts to deal with toxic contamination of groundwater.

C. K. ROWLAND is an associate professor of political science and director of graduate studies at the University of Kansas. He is co-author of *Politics and Policy Making in the Federal District Courts* and has published articles in the *Journal of Politics, American Journal of Political Science,* and other scholarly journals. He is currently working on applications of catastrophe theory to regulatory policy.

BRUCE A. WILLIAMS is an associate professor of political science at the University of Kentucky and has published in the areas of organization theory, regulatory politics, administrative law, science policy, and urban politics. He is currently writing a book about regulatory politics and hazardous waste with Professor Matheny and is conducting research on community politics in Florida.

RAE ZIMMERMAN is an associate professor and director of the Urban Planning Program in the Graduate School of Public Administration at New York University. She has conducted extensive research in the area of risk assessment related to technology-intensive issues.